RED LETTERS

FRESH REFLECTIONS ON THE WORDS OF JESUS

WILLIAM J. PETERSEN
AND
RANDY PETERSEN

Revell
Grand Rapids, Michigan

Published by Fleming H. Revell
a division of Baker Publishing Group
P.O. Box 6287, Grand Rapids, MI 49516-6287

Printed in the United States of America

Library of Congress Cataloging-in-Publication Data
Petersen, William J.
    Red letters : fresh reflections on the words of Jesus / William J.
Petersen and Randy Petersen.
        p.   cm.
    ISBN 0-8007-5923-0 (pbk.)
    1. Jesus Christ—Words—Meditations. 2. Devotional calendars.
I. Petersen, Randy. II. Title.
BT306.P45 2005
242′.5—dc22   2004030606

CONTENTS

PREFACE

Jesus used many different methods of speaking. Of course he was known for his stories, the parables, which drew spiritual lessons from everyday activities. A man on a journey, a shepherd with his flock, a woman sweeping a floor—each of these characters took on new meaning as Jesus taught.

He also used a device that modern communicators might call the "sound bite," capturing great wisdom in a few well-chosen words. "Those who are healthy don't need a physician," he said. "Only the sick do." And in these dozen words he summed up his ministry.

On other occasions, Jesus taught with Beatitudes, pronouncing God's blessing—and sometimes the corresponding "woe." He challenged people with questions, especially when opponents were questioning him, and he drew comical word pictures. (A man with a plank in his eye doing eye surgery on someone else—that's a comedy sketch waiting to happen.)

Jesus could quote Scripture with the best of the scribes, and sometimes he offered commentary. He also employed descriptive metaphors—"I am . . . the Way . . . the Bread from heaven . . . the Light of the World . . . the Door . . . the Good Shepherd." And here's where he differed from the other rabbis of his time. Ultimately, he was teaching about himself.

This book celebrates the teachings of Jesus in all their variations. Learning from him, and learning about him, we can't help but grow in our faith. Spend a year with this book, digging into the Scriptures we cover, and you'll feel like you've gained a new Friend, a new Teacher, perhaps a new Lord.

HOW TO USE THIS BOOK

Devotional books tend to offer a page of inspiring commentary for each day of the year. We're doing something a bit different. The words of Jesus deserve a deeper treatment, a thorough exploration, a courageous application. That takes more than a page.

We also suspect that many Christians aren't doing the *daily* devotional anymore. Sure, it's still a great idea to start or end each day in Scripture, but people have crazy schedules. This book is designed for people who want to go at their own pace. There are fifty-two chapters or sections, one for each week of the year, if you choose to follow that pattern. Included are meditations for the eight days of Passion Week, Palm Sunday through Easter. These are found at the end of the book.

Each section has a seven-day guide, Every Day with Jesus, for those who want to use this book as a daily devotional. But if you're just coming to it two or three times a week, that will work too. We also hope that some might use this book as a weekly family devotional.

The seven-day guide is our suggestion for going through one chapter of the book in one week, but feel free to adapt it to your schedule and study preferences. Use the suggestions and think about the questions even if you're not following it as a seven-day guide. We often suggest a topic for prayer on Saturday. This doesn't mean, of course, that Saturday is the only day for prayer. In fact you might use the Saturday prayer suggestion as a guide for prayer throughout the week. We have placed Sunday at the end with the idea that this can be a day of celebration and praise of the Savior whose words you have meditated on as you've worked your way through the chapter.

As you glance at the following pages, you'll see lots of additional tidbits of information, called such things as In the Mirror, Checkout Counter, and Quote to Note. We're not trying to distract you. It's just that you never know what fact might challenge or what insight might change someone's life. Since Jesus used so many different forms of communication, it only makes sense for us to use different forms as we explore his teaching. Grab what you like and skim over the rest.

Ultimately our goal is to help you connect with the wonderful words of Jesus. You don't need to lock into any schedule. Just come when you can and hear what he says.

USING *RED LETTERS* WITH A SMALL GROUP

This book can be useful as a small-group study guide. Your group can work through the Bible passages, using the background and analysis given here as a starting point. In addition, the extra features—In the Mirror, Greek Peek, Cross Ref, and others—should give your group lots to talk about. Pay special attention to the Every Day with Jesus section. While this is designed to help individuals use this book for daily devotions, the questions will provide some good fodder for group discussion as well.

If your group meets every week, you can get through this book in a year. Most groups, however, have shorter stints. So here are some ideas for breaking down the material in *Red Letters*.

- Take nine weeks to study the Sermon on the Mount, using chapters 6–14 of this book.
- Take seven weeks to look into Christ's parables and miracles (using chapters 17, 22, 30, 32, 34, 36, 38).
- Do a thematic study on how to be a stronger disciple (using chapters 2, 25, 26, 27, 28, 36).

  If you are leading a seekers group, consider selections from John's Gospel (using *Red Letters* chapters 4, 5, 16, 18, 20, 33, 34, 35, 38, 40).

- The eight chapters for Passion Week at the end are intended for daily use from Palm Sunday through Easter. But these could also be used once a week in your small group as a two-month Lenten study.

We've tried to be creative in presenting Jesus' teaching in a fresh and informative way. We challenge you to be creative as well, as you share these crucial truths with your group.

Many thanks to Ardythe Petersen, who serves not only as Bill's wife and Randy's mother but also as our research director.

1
GONE FISHING

PART 1

● "Come, follow me . . ."

Mark 1:17

They were just minding their own business. Literally. Their business was fishing, a common trade on the Sea of Galilee. But these two pairs of brothers—Andrew and Peter, James and John—were about to face a moment of decision, a moment that would change their lives forever.

They hailed from the town of Bethsaida, which means "House of Fish" (just one of many indications of how important fishing was in this region). The historian Josephus, who governed this territory a generation later, counted 338 fishing boats plying their trade in Galilee. Such boats typically held six to ten crewmembers. That adds up to two or three thousand fishermen working on this sizable lake.

For James and John, fishing was a family business. They were working with their father, Zebedee, who apparently owned the boat and hired extra fishermen to help out. Seaside, they were straightening out their nets, probably removing debris and searching for tears. Andrew and Peter were already in the water, preparing to cast a net from their boat, when the rabbi

Monday: Read part 1 of this chapter. What times in your early life prepared you to respond to Jesus' call?

Tuesday: Read part 2 of this chapter. How can you participate in Jesus' new fishing business?

Wednesday: Read part 3 of this chapter. What does following Jesus look like in your life?

Thursday: Read Mark 1:16–20. Remember the time you began to follow Jesus. How have things changed?

Friday: Read Mark 10:17–22. Are there things in your life that keep you from following Jesus fully?

Saturday: Read Luke 9:23–25. How can you take up your cross daily?

Sunday: Read John 1:35–42. Worship God as the One who leads you.

came along with his radical request and a strange promise.

"Follow me," he said, "and I will make you fishers of men."

This was not the first time they had seen this rabbi. According to John's Gospel, Andrew had already been supporting the ministry of John the Baptizer, as he called Jews to a new repentance. Then Jesus appeared and the Baptizer announced to his followers, *This is the Lamb of God, the One who will take away the world's sin* (see John 1:29).

So the decision to follow Jesus wasn't totally impulsive. These fishermen knew something about who Jesus was. Still, he was calling them to leave their fishing business and enter a whole new life. It's one thing to know who Jesus is and quite another to commit your life to him.

PART 2

● ". . . and I will make you fishers of men."

Mark 1:17

As he wooed these new disciples, what did Jesus have to offer? What kind of benefits package, job security, perks? He was asking them to leave their livelihood to walk beside him. As an itinerant preacher, Jesus had no steady home. He relied on the kindness of strangers. *Foxes have dens and birds have nests*, he once said, *but I have nowhere to lay my head* (see Matt. 8:20).

To all appearances, following Jesus did not seem like a good career move. Fishing was hard work but solid business. James and John would have been in line to inherit Dad's business, perhaps hire a few more men, buy a few boats. Nothing wrong with any of that, but here was the Messiah calling them to leave their nets and follow.

He said it would be a whole new kind of fishing business. Fishers of men? What a concept!

IN THE MIRROR

Note the sense of urgency in the whole scene. Is there any sense of urgency about your life, your calling? If you opened your front door and Jesus was standing there saying to you, "Come, follow me," how would you respond?

PART 3

● "Follow me."

Mark 2:14; Mark 10:21; Matthew 8:22; John 1:43

Throughout his ministry, Jesus kept asking people to follow him. Matthew was sitting at a roadside tollbooth when Jesus said, "Follow me." Jesus said the same thing to Philip. He gathered twelve special disciples, who followed him everywhere, but Scripture speaks of many others who followed as well.

What did it mean to follow Jesus? Of course there's the literal sense. When Jesus up and moved to, say, Jerusalem, his entourage walked with him. He led the way geographically, and they followed in his footsteps. But following Jesus also meant learning from him—that's what *disciple* means, "learner." In many situations learning can be a passive thing. (Maybe you still wonder what high school algebra has done for you.) You can learn facts and never do anything with them. Not so with Jesus' teaching. To hear Jesus' words and not put them into practice was like building a house on sand. Jesus required an active response, not just saying, "Lord, Lord," but doing what he said.

Follow me, Jesus said, and one man wanted to bury his father first. *Let the dead bury the dead*, Jesus replied—which might sound harsh until you realize that the father may not have been dead yet (see Matt. 8:21–22). The reluctant disciple wanted to wait

11

DARE TO COMPARE

Though Jesus was trained as a carpenter, both the beginning and the ending of his earthly ministry involved fishing (see John 21:1–14).

for more favorable social circumstances, as many do today. "After I get married and have kids . . . when I find a good church . . . when I get a better job . . . *then* I'll do whatever you want, Lord." Jesus calls us *now* to live at a higher level, to follow his footsteps out of the deadly day-by-day and into a life that overflows.

Follow me, Jesus said to a young aristocrat looking for a better life. *Oh, but first sell everything you have and give the money to the poor.* Possessed by his possessions, the man couldn't do it (see Matt. 19:16–22).

Later Jesus talked about the need for a follower to "take up his cross and follow me." Once again, Jesus was calling his disciples to a new plane of operation. The Lamb of God knew he was headed toward a sacrificial death. His disciples might have to follow him there. In fact tradition tells us that Andrew and Peter and James and Matthew and Philip all died for their faith in Jesus. Reportedly, Peter died on a cross.

In one of the Gospels, Jesus asks the would-be follower to "take up his cross *daily*," and that word brings it into our world. As we sacrifice ourselves day after day, loving those around us with selfless courage and commitment, we are placing our feet in his footprints.

QUOTE TO NOTE

The disciple is one who has come with his ignorance, superstition and sin, to find learning, truth and forgiveness from the Savior.

V. Raymond Edman

2
IN THE DESERT

● "It is written: 'Man does not live on bread alone, but on every word that comes from the mouth of God.'"

Matthew 4:4

Crags and canyons mark the Judean desert where Jesus faced his temptation. A thousand years earlier David hid out in these caves, chased by a crazy king. Jesus wasn't chased; he was "led" or "sent" by the Spirit. This was his time of testing.

First, Jesus fasted for forty days. If you see any similarity between Jesus' forty days in the desert and the forty years the Israelites wandered through similar terrain, you're right on target. The connections between Jesus' temptation and the wilderness wanderings are just beginning.

Fasting was a regular practice in Israel at the time of Jesus. Religious leaders observed a fast one or two days a week. Some of them used these fasts to show everyone how holy they were (Matt. 6:16), but that doesn't mean all fasting is bogus. Throughout the Bible, we find extended fasts occurring in times of repentance or in efforts to draw closer to God.

The whole point of a fast, it seems, is to get one's priorities straight. Food is very, very important to us. Without food, we die.

13

Monday: Read part 1 of this chapter. In what areas are you most vulnerable to temptation? What Bible verses can help?

Tuesday: Read part 2 of this chapter. In what ways do you demand that God conform to your expectations?

Wednesday: Read part 3 of this chapter. What other "gods" are you tempted to worship?

Thursday: Check out the verses that Jesus quoted—Deuteronomy 8:3; 6:16; 6:13. Why did he use these?

Friday: Read Hebrews 4:15–16. What significance does Jesus' temptation have for us?

Saturday: Consider a skip-a-meal fast today. Instead of eating food, chew on Scripture.

Sunday: Worship God as the One who sustains you against temptation.

But fasting indicates that there's something more important than food. It puts our relationship with God ahead of this basic human need. Not that there's anything wrong with eating—but God comes first.

Ever been on a diet? After three or four days of self-deprivation, you get to a point where everything reminds you of food. Your toaster resembles a chocolate cake. Every hubcap is a pizza. Well, you can imagine how Jesus must have felt after nearly six weeks. And that's when the tempter showed up and pointed to some loaf-sized rocks. "If you are the Son of God," he said, "tell these stones to become bread" (Matt. 4:3).

At his baptism a short time earlier, a voice from heaven had declared Jesus the beloved Son of God (3:17). *Is that so, Jesus?* you can almost hear the devil chuckling. *Then prove yourself!*

So here's Jesus, challenged to prove his own divine authority by making rocks edible. But he refused, quoting from Deuteronomy. The original verse was about manna, actually, and the surrounding verses were about wandering in the wilderness. The parallels to Jesus' situation are striking. "Remember how the LORD your God led you [as Jesus was led] all the way in the desert these forty years [Jesus was forty days in the desert], to humble you and to test you [as Jesus was being tested] in order to know what was in your heart, whether or not you would keep his commands. He humbled you, causing you to hunger [as Jesus was hungering] and then feeding you with manna . . . to teach you that *man does not live on bread alone but on every word that comes from the mouth of the LORD*" (Deut. 8:2–3, emphasis added).

14

The tempter was saying: *If you're the Son of God, you shouldn't have to experience hunger.*

Jesus was essentially responding: *Because I'm the Son of God, I'll go through anything my Father wants; my relationship with him is more important than food.* And note that Jesus is doing exactly what he's saying. He is relying on God's words to give him strength against temptation.

> **GREEK PEEK**
>
> The Greek word translated "It is written" is the perfect passive tense of *write*, so it could also be translated "It has been written and still stands written." God's Word doesn't go out of date.

PART 2

● "It is also written: 'Do not put the Lord your God to the test.'"

Matthew 4:7

The second temptation takes Jesus to a new location, the pinnacle of the temple in Jerusalem. Here the devil quotes Scripture back to Jesus. *Throw yourself down from this spot, because God promises that angels will catch you, right?*

It's not clear exactly where the temple's "pinnacle" was. The temple was erected on a man-made plateau atop Jerusalem's main mountain. In several spots a person could walk on a wall and look down a hundred feet or more. To jump from any of these places without a bungee cord would mean death or extreme disability—if it weren't for those angels.

The tempter quotes a portion of Psalm 91, "He will command his angels concerning you to guard you in all your ways; they will lift you up in their hands, so that you will not strike your foot against a stone" (v. 11). The psalm goes on to say, "You will tread upon the lion and the cobra; you will trample the great lion and the serpent." You can't blame the tempter for leaving out that trampling part. The day of the devil's greatest victory, when as a serpent he induced the sin of Adam and Eve, God cursed the serpent by saying, "I will put enmity between you and the woman, and between your offspring and hers; he will crush your head, and you will strike his heel" (Gen. 3:15). A second Eve would emerge, who would obediently bear a Child, who would crush the head of the tempter. And this Serpent Trampler was now standing before the serpent himself.

While Psalm 91 applies to every believer, it would have a special application to the Messiah. How could God let his own Son suffer harm? Once again, the devil uses the preface, "If you are the Son of God." *Prove your identity, Jesus.* If this occurred in a crowded temple, then a swan dive from the pinnacle with a soft landing would make a big splash—so to speak. Everyone would know that Jesus was someone special.

Jesus didn't fall for it. His response was once again from Deuteronomy. At first it seems as if Jesus is chiding the devil for tempting him, but that's not it. Jesus would be testing God the Father by jumping.

But what's wrong with testing God?

The text that Jesus quotes comes within a passage that exhorts the people to honor and obey God. "Do not test the LORD your God *as you did at Massah*" (Deut. 6:16, emphasis added). Massah (which means "testing") was the desert campsite where the Israelites demanded water. They were complaining that Moses had led them out of Egypt only to let them die of thirst. "Is the Lord among us or not?" they murmured.

That kind of testing is spiritual blackmail. *Do this, or else we won't believe in you.* It tries to force God to do what we want rather than submitting ourselves to what he wants. We decide how God should behave, and then we punish him if he doesn't come through for us.

Force God to protect you, Jesus! But Jesus knew that there would be better ways to prove himself. At another time of temptation, Jesus obediently prayed, "Not my will, but yours be done." Then he went forth to be crucified. That would be the way to prove himself as the Son of God.

PART 3

● "Away from me, Satan! For it is written: 'Worship the Lord your God, and serve him only.'"

Matthew 4:10

The third temptation took Jesus up to a "high mountain." If the tempter met Jesus in the Judean desert, perhaps they crossed the Jordan and climbed Mount Nebo, where Moses had looked down on the Promised Land before his death. In any case, the devil promised Jesus "all the kingdoms of the world" in exchange for his worship. The devil is good at offering things that aren't his. But the Bible does recognize the power that Satan holds over the earth. It was just a matter of time before Jesus conquered the devil at the cross, but now the devil was offering Jesus an easy way to avoid all that suffering.

This temptation sounds something like the tempter's first salvo to Eve: "You will not surely die" (Gen. 3:4). *You don't have to die, Jesus. Just bow to me now and look what you can win!*

> ## CLUES TO USE
>
> Both James 4:7 and 1 Peter 5:8–9 tell us to resist the devil. But how? Jesus used one weapon, which is the same weapon we have: "the sword of the Spirit, which is the word of God" (Eph. 6:17).

> ## IN THE MIRROR
>
> What area in your life is most vulnerable to Satan's attack? Do you have an "It is written" in mind to fight this attack? How can you do a better job of living "on every word that comes from the mouth of God"?

At this, Jesus dismissed the tempter, calling him (for the first time) by his proper name, Satan. He had finally gone too far. And for the third time Jesus quoted Deuteronomy. In a world awash with other deities, this was God's first commandment. No other gods. God made it clear: It's not me and Baal. Not me and Osiris. *Just me.*

If God had to share human allegiance with anyone else, he wouldn't be God. And what good would all the kingdoms of the world be, if the King were no longer in charge?

The responses of Jesus provide a picture of the Christian life. First, we draw our nourishment from the Lord. Communication with him is more important than food. Second, we submit our wills to God, trusting him to help us but refusing to force our will onto him. Finally, we reserve our fullest devotion for him. He is the one we worship and serve. No promise of wealth or power will sway us from our wholehearted worship of him.

3

MARKET FORCES

● "Dear woman, why do you involve me?" Jesus replied. "My time has not yet come."

John 2:4

Imagine a teenager lounging on the couch when his mother asks him to clean his room. If he responds with these words of Jesus, surely he gets grounded, or worse.

Strange, then, that Jesus sounds like such a slacker just before working his first miracle. In fact this is among the first quotations of Jesus that John gives us. You might think he'd be eager to show Jesus as a wise sage or righteous rabbi. Instead, this sounds like sass. Shouldn't he show a little more respect to his mother? Is it just a problem with translation, or is there more to this scene? Both.

Let's set the situation. Jesus has just called his first disciples, and he's partying with them at a wedding reception not far from where he grew up. In those days, wedding festivals lasted for days, and the bridegroom was responsible for providing massive amounts of food and wine. At this party, however, they have run out of wine. Mary approaches Jesus and mentions this simple fact. Throughout human history, mothers have assigned

18

household chores merely by pointing out needs. Mary says, "They have no more wine." She means, *Why don't you do something about that?*

What did she expect him to do? He had not yet worked any miracles. Did she know he had wonder-working power? This story certainly implies that.

Jesus offers this strange response. Admittedly, the translation is difficult. The form of address— "Dear woman" (in Greek it's just "Woman")—is not as rude as it sounds, but it is not at all tender. And the rest of the sentence—"Why do you involve me?"—is a colloquial phrase that's hard

Monday: Read part 1 of this chapter. In your imagination, go to the wedding in Cana. Imagine you are standing next to Mary. What does she see when she looks at her son?

Tuesday: Read part 2 of this chapter. Do you think some people are using the church as a market today?

Wednesday: Read part 3 of this chapter. In what way is Jesus your Temple?

Thursday: Reflect on this: The Bible uses marriage as a picture of the relationship between Christ and the church. Is it significant that Jesus chose a wedding for his first miracle?

Friday: If Mary could ask Jesus to provide more wine for a wedding reception, for what sorts of things can we ask the Lord?

Saturday: Do you ever get angry? Jesus did. What makes some anger good and other anger bad? Talk to Jesus about this now.

Sunday: Praise the Lord as you read Psalm 95. Notice, in verses 10–11, what makes God angry.

to nail down. Literally, Jesus said, "What to me and to you?"

It sounds harsh, and uncharacteristic of Jesus. Why wouldn't he want to help out? Jesus explains himself by saying, "My time has not yet come." What time is that?

John's Gospel is especially concerned with timing. Jesus teaches in the temple and stirs up opposition, but he doesn't get arrested because "his time had not yet come" (7:30; 8:20). But as he approaches the final week of his ministry, he says, "The hour has come for the Son of Man to be glorified" (12:23). And John begins his description of the Last Supper by saying, "Jesus knew that the time had come for him to leave this world and go to the Father" (13:1).

At the time of the wedding, Jesus knew what was ahead of him. Up until then, he had been waiting, growing, preparing.

After thirty years lying low in Nazareth, he had just begun to emerge—getting baptized, gathering disciples, teaching publicly. But working miracles? That would certainly signal a new era, not only in Jesus' life but in the history of Israel.

The prophet Amos had predicted, "The time is surely coming, says the LORD, when . . . the mountains shall drip sweet wine, and all the hills shall flow with it. I will restore the fortunes of my people Israel, and . . . they shall plant vineyards and drink their wine" (Amos 9:13–14 NRSV).

Did Mary remember that prophecy from Amos when she turned to the servants and said, "Do whatever he tells you"? We don't know. All that Scripture tells us is that Jesus got up and told them to fill several vats with water, which he would turn into wine.

Did Mary push Jesus into his first miracle? No, the text shows Jesus as an independent agent. But he was a good son, honoring both his earthly mother and his heavenly Father. Perhaps God used Mary to tell Jesus it was time to get started.

PART 2

● "Get these out of here! How dare you turn my Father's house into a market!"

John 2:16

Along with thousands of other Jews, Jesus journeyed to Jerusalem on a Passover pilgrimage. But when he got there, he didn't like what he found. Animals were braying, caged pigeons were squawking, and coins were clinking as the sacrifice sellers did their business in the temple courts. To some extent, such business was necessary. Pilgrims from far away had to buy their sacrifices locally, and such purchases were transacted in sacred temple shekels, not the tainted Roman currency (hence the need for money changers). We have some indications that such business was previously conducted on the Mount of Olives.

Now, possibly through some political shenanigans, the merchandising had moved into the temple courts. This got Jesus mad.

> **CROSS REF**
>
> In John 2:4 Jesus talks about his "time." Other passages refer to divine timing too:
>
> John 7:6, 8
> John 12:23
> John 17:1
> Matt 26:18, 45
> Mark 14:41

He probably tore a leash from one of the animals and used it as a whip, driving the animals away and turning the tables, sending coins every which way, and shouting, "How dare you turn my Father's house into a market!"

My Father's house. Flash back eighteen years or so. As a boy, Jesus stood in this same temple court, exchanging opinions with the local rabbis. When his parents worried about his whereabouts, he said, "Didn't you know I had to be in my Father's house?" (Luke 2:49). Maybe some of those same rabbis were still in the temple as the adult Jesus came back to clean house.

Here toward the start of his public ministry, Jesus is serving notice that he has a special connection to this place. People worship his Father here, and anything that hinders that worship has to go. The temple must not become a market; it must remain the place where people go to meet God.

What's wrong with markets? Nothing. You don't need to feel guilty about shopping at the neighborhood Wal-Mart. But markets have their own mentality: Everything has its price; you get what you pay for. And when that mentality merges with religion, it goes against Jesus' message of grace. Over the next few years, Jesus would throw open the gates of God's kingdom to all sorts of sinners—folks who couldn't pay for God's blessings and didn't have to.

PART 3

● "Destroy this temple, and I will raise it again in three days."

John 2:19

So Jesus gets angry and vandalizes the temple mart. How do you think people reacted? Nowadays he'd get arrested or

21

at least sued. Even then, such a major disturbance would have brought some Roman soldiers to the scene. But the response of the people is more curious than vindictive. Perhaps they knew he was right.

Prophets of the past had criticized various temple abuses, so there was precedent. "See, I will send my messenger," wrote Malachi, "who will prepare the way before me. Then suddenly the Lord you are seeking will come to his temple. . . . He will purify the Levites and refine them like gold and silver. . . . And the offerings of Judah and Jerusalem will be acceptable to the LORD, as in days gone by, as in former years" (Mal. 3:1–4). Could Jesus be a messenger from God? The people asked him for a sign, some miracle that would prove his authority as a prophet of God. This was his answer.

Destroy this temple. . . . Add this to your collection of Jesus' clever responses to impertinent requests. The temple had been under construction for forty-six years, and it still wasn't finished. How could Jesus rebuild it in half a week? Well, that would be a miracle, wouldn't it? So Jesus offers them a genuine sign, but they'd have to destroy the temple to see it, and that would never happen. Of course the statement has a secondary meaning, one that his hearers wouldn't get until years later. The temple he spoke about was his own body. They would destroy it, and in three days he'd be up and around again.

Screenwriters have a dictum: If there's a gun on the mantel in the first scene, you can bet it will be fired before the last scene. For Jesus, this saying is the gun on the mantel. You might say it's the weapon that killed him. When he stood trial for blasphemy, two false witnesses came forward with a twisted version, claiming that he had vowed to destroy the temple (Mark 14:58).

A powerful theological truth resides in this double meaning: Jesus is the new Temple. Think about it. The temple was the place of sacrifice, where people showed their repentance and received forgiveness. Jesus became the ultimate sacrifice; his blood brings forgiveness to repentant sinners. The temple was the holy place where people met God. Jesus, the holy Lamb of God, called himself "the Way" and "the Gate." Through him, believers would step into a worshipful relationship with his Father.

A generation later, the Roman army would destroy the Jerusalem temple. The sacrificial system of Judaism would essentially become obsolete. But the sacrifice of Jesus remains in effect, and the power of the risen Lord continues to energize his followers.

QUOTE TO NOTE

Whenever Jesus comes into life, there comes a new quality which is like turning water into wine. Without Jesus life is dull, and stale, and flat; when Jesus comes into life, life becomes vivid and sparkling and exciting.

William Barclay

4
SURPRISE BY NIGHT

● "I tell you the truth, no one can see the kingdom of God unless he is born again."

John 3:3

"It was a dark and stormy night." So begins the mystery novel that the beagle Snoopy keeps trying to write. Somehow he never gets beyond that first sentence.

It's not a bad start, though. Night seems intermeshed with mystery and surprise. And so it was late one evening in first-century Jerusalem when a distinguished Jewish leader, one of the esteemed Pharisees, cautiously made his way up a narrow street for a secret meeting with a renegade rabbi. Scripture gives us few details of the circumstances of this hush-hush rendezvous, but perhaps we can apply a novelist's imagination to it.

Was there a full moon that night? Yes, since it was Passover. In fact the Galilean Rabbi had come to Jerusalem to celebrate the feast. This would mean more people milling about the moonlit streets. Perhaps the Pharisee pulled his cloak over his face, not only because of the chill night air but also to avoid recognition. If people found out about this meeting, they might get the wrong idea.

Where did the Rabbi and the Pharisee meet? Far from the temple, certainly. Too many eyes and ears there. Probably a house in the residential quarter. Many homes had outside stairs that led to the roof. Rooftops served as guest rooms in Judea; they also served as studies for rabbis and scholars, who would spend nighttime hours meditating and praying there. So we might imagine that Nicodemus, this distinguished Pharisee and member of the ruling Sanhedrin, gave one last cautious look before climbing up to meet the miracle worker from Galilee.

Monday: Read part 1. In what ways are you like Nicodemus? Do you know other people like him?

Tuesday: Read part 2. What does "born again" mean to you? What does it mean to your next-door neighbors?

Wednesday: Read part 3. Consider the double meaning of "lifted up." We lift Jesus up by exalting him, but Jesus was talking about the cross. In both ways, he draws people to himself.

Thursday: Do the "Dare to Compare" study in this chapter.

Friday: If someone came to you one night asking what Jesus was all about, what would you say?

Saturday: If you have any doubts about your relationship with Jesus, pray about it right now. If you have loved ones or acquaintances who don't have such a relationship, pray for them now.

Sunday: Read Psalm 16:7–11. Let your heart soar in thanksgiving to the Lord for his salvation.

Jesus had been teaching openly each day. People flocked to him for healing. From time to time, he even had public conversations with Pharisees, but Nicodemus wanted more than that. He needed an extended, private conversation with him. The miracles that Jesus had performed had caught his attention, but he was not going to check up on the miracles. Instead, he wanted to probe Jesus' orthodoxy, as well as his credentials as a rabbi. He had no desire for a public debate; he just needed to know what Jesus was all about.

No doubt Nicodemus rehearsed his opening line on the way there. Most of Jesus' followers were simple Galileans, and Jesus excelled in speaking their common language. Perhaps Nicodemus thought that Jesus would enjoy a good theological discussion on a deeper level.

So Nicodemus began: "Rabbi, we know you are a teacher who has come from God. For no one could perform the miraculous signs you are doing if God were not with him." The intellectual meeting of the minds had begun.

But before Nicodemus could launch the first point on his outline, Jesus surprised him with these mysterious words: "No one can see the kingdom of God unless he is born again."

What? Scrap the outline. Forget the theological exchange. For all his highfalutin education, Nicodemus was thoroughly confused.

PART 2

● "You must be born again."

John 3:7

In modern times "born again" has become a cliché. For a while there, the phrase was everywhere, from bumper stickers to end zone banners. Then Madison Avenue caught the craze, and it seemed that anything and everything was "born again," from cornflakes to cognac.

Is this what Jesus had in mind when he used the term in his midnight meeting with a Pharisee? Nicodemus was no dummy. No doubt he knew about the mystery religions of Greece that talked about rebirth; he knew about John the Baptist who had gained a huge following in Judea by preaching repentance; and of course he knew the process that proselytes to Judaism went through to begin life all over again as a Jew. But what did Jesus mean?

Nicodemus asked a seemingly stupid question: "How can a man be born when he is old? He can't reenter his mother's womb, can he?"

Jesus repeated the phrase and strengthened it: "You must be born again." Nicodemus could relate to the word *must*. There were hundreds of Old Testament rules and regulations that as an orthodox Jew he *must* follow. Piled on top of that, the codified scribal law, the *Mishnah*, elaborated further, adding even more to his "must" list. So Nicodemus was encumbered with

26

"musts." Heaping another "must" onto the pile wasn't going to throw him. But he still didn't know what Jesus was talking about.

Only three of Nicodemus's statements are recorded in John 3, and two of them begin with the little word *how*. That's what Nicodemus wanted to know: *How can I be born again?*

> **DARE TO COMPARE**
>
> Other Gospel accounts show seekers interacting with Jesus. Compare Nicodemus with the rich young man in Mark 10:17–22 and the scribe in Mark 12:28–34.

Jesus gave two answers. To the first *how*, Jesus' answer was the Holy Spirit. Entrance to God's kingdom would require water-birth and Spirit-birth. Christians have often struggled with the meaning of the word *water* in this verse. Does it refer to John's baptism of repentance, Christian baptism, or the Word of God? (Paul mentions "the washing with water through the word" in Ephesians 5:26.) But Jesus' emphasis here was not on water; it was on the Spirit. He went on to compare spiritual rebirth to the blowing of the wind.

If this meeting took place on a rooftop, the wind analogy makes sense. But note also that the word for Spirit in Hebrew is the same as the word for wind. (That's also true in Greek.) Jesus acknowledged the mysterious nature of the Spirit's work by referring to the mystery of the wind. Why does the wind blow this way today and that way tomorrow? We feel the effects of the wind, but we don't know where it starts or finishes. In the same way, spiritual rebirth defies explanation. We feel its effects, but we must acknowledge that the mechanics of it are beyond our understanding—and something we can't manipulate. Being born again is not a fad nor a confirmation class nor a recitation of the Apostles' Creed. It is a work of the Holy Spirit.

At the dawn of creation in Genesis 1, the Holy Spirit got the creative process moving, and now Jesus was saying that the Holy Spirit had to accomplish this new creation.

Is this regeneration always instantaneous? It might not be immediately obvious. A baby does not recognize its own personhood right away, and similarly the light may dawn gradually on some new babes in Christ. But make no mistake about it, there is a "before" and an "after." Sometimes the instant change is

CROSS REF

How does Jesus compare to the serpent lifted up in the wilderness? See Numbers 21:6–7 and Romans 6:23. Also take a look at Numbers 21:8 along with Romans 8:3 and Galatians 3:13.

quite dramatic, like the before and after photos of a man who has lost two hundred pounds on a fad diet, but not always.

What would have happened if Nicodemus had responded to Christ's invitation that gusty evening? What if he had become born again? How would that have changed his life? He was already one of the Pharisees, recognized as the most righteous people in the land. If Nicodemus had been born again that night, he would have lost his baggage, those loads of "must" that had been encumbering him. He would have found an inner joy and peace that he had never known before. And even if the outward changes weren't dramatic, Nicodemus would have known the difference.

PART 3

● "The Son of Man must be lifted up, that everyone who believes in him may have eternal life."

John 3:14–15

So Nicodemus asks the *how* question again. This time Jesus answers, "Believe."

Jesus refers to the Old Testament story in Numbers 21, where the Israelites were smitten by a plague of snakes. When Moses prayed for a miracle drug, God told him to put a bronze snake on a pole and lift it up in the middle of the camp. Whoever would look at that snake would live. It seems downright silly. No doubt some laughed at it . . . and died.

No doubt Jesus' words seemed downright silly to Nicodemus at the time. Jesus was implying that he would, sometime in the future, be lifted up on a pole (whatever that could mean) and that everyone who looked at him on the pole and believed in him would have eternal life. How ridiculous! Apart from the absurdity of the pole, it was ludicrous to think that people could find eternal life just by believing. That was way too simple for a legalist like Nicodemus.

And even today some people argue that Jesus must have meant something different. Surely he taught that those who wanted to enter the kingdom of God would have to follow the Ten Commandments, the Golden Rule, or the entire Sermon on the Mount. We'd like to think that eternal life requires a little effort on our part, a few workouts at a spiritual gym or something.

But no, that's not what Jesus said.

Nicodemus, you can't go on as you're living, he was saying. *You've got to face up to the fact that you can never become good enough to get into God's kingdom on your own. Even though you're a leading Pharisee, you've got to confess that you are a helpless sinner. And then, just as the ailing Israelites did the ridiculous thing and looked up at the bronze serpent, so you must look in faith to me when I am "lifted up."*

It's interesting that, even this early in his ministry, Jesus already realized he was living in the shadow of the cross.

What did Nicodemus take away from that conversation with Jesus? We can't be sure, but he comes back into John's Gospel two more times. In John 7:50–51, he tells his peers of the Sanhedrin not to be too hasty in their condemnation of Jesus. Then in John 19:38–39, after the crucifixion, he appears again to assist with Christ's burial.

You have to wonder whether Jesus' mysterious statement on that Jerusalem rooftop finally made sense to Nicodemus. He had seen Jesus lifted up on a pole, and he knew he must believe in him.

QUOTE TO NOTE

The new birth will establish its presence by producing a new sensitivity to spiritual things, a new direction of life, and an increasing ability to obey God.

Millard J. Erickson

5

PERPETUAL SPRING

When you think about happy times, you may think about a wedding or the birth of a baby or a family vacation by a bubbly mountain stream.

Interesting, isn't it, that when the apostle John began telling about Christ's ministry, he wrote of a wedding, of the new birth, and about streams of living water. The new life that Jesus offered was a life of joy.

The key people in these three stories—Mary (John 2), Nicodemus (John 3), and the Samaritan woman (John 4)—were totally different from each other. Nicodemus, for instance, wouldn't be caught dead within fifty feet of the Samaritan woman. Yet in one respect, all three were alike. When they met Jesus, each one had a problem.

Jesus is both a problem solver and a joy dispenser. And he's been that for two thousand years, no matter who the person is, no matter what kind of past the person has had. And make no mistake about it, the woman of Samaria had a past.

The story goes like this.

Jesus and his disciples were heading north from Jerusalem to their home turf in Galilee, about eighty miles away. That's a long walk even when you're used to walking. There were two ways to go, the fast way and the proper way. The proper way was to take a detour across the Jordan River and add an extra day to the trip. The fast way wasn't kosher. Why? Because you had to cut through the province of Samaria. Let's just say there was no love lost between Jews and Samaritans.

Proper Jews considered the Samaritans heretics and half-breeds, worse than Gentiles. Samaritans responded with prejudice of their own. If the Samaritans saw Jews heading south from Galilee toward Jerusalem, they assumed the travelers were planning to worship in the Jerusalem temple, so they made things difficult. In this case, however, Jesus and his disciples were northbound, so the danger might have been somewhat less.

It was noon. Jesus and his disciples must have been walking five or six hours already. As the disciples went into the small town of Sychar for some food, Jesus rested at Jacob's well, which even today is Samaria's main tourist attraction. Onto the scene came a woman, a Samaritan woman.

Two problems: She was a Samaritan and she was a woman. A strict Jewish rabbi wouldn't speak in public to a woman—even his wife or daughter. Some devout Pharisees even closed their eyes when they saw a woman on the street. They kept walking with their eyes closed, earning the nickname "the bruised and bleeding Pharisees" because they bumped into so many walls.

But Jesus had no qualms about breaking down prejudices, whether they were between Jews and Samaritans or between

Monday: Read part 1 and check out the "W's" for further background.

Tuesday: Read part 2. How well does Jesus know you?

Wednesday: Read part 3. What does it mean to worship in "spirit and truth"?

Thursday: Read part 4. Are there "Samaritans" in your life, people you try to avoid? What would happen if they met Jesus?

Friday: What can you learn about living water from the following passages: Revelation 7:17; 21:6; Isaiah 44:3; Psalm 42:1; and Jeremiah 2:13?

Saturday: Review this whole chapter. Pray that the living water will flow through you to others.

Sunday: Praise God this day by reading Isaiah 12 (note verse 3 especially).

men and women, for that matter. He started by asking a favor
from this woman, and he was even willing to drink from her
Samaritan bucket. Good thing Nicodemus wasn't along!

The woman was amazed—maybe even shocked—that this
Jew would even speak to her. She told him so.

Then, just as suddenly as he had told Nicodemus that he had
to be born again, Jesus launched his preemptive strike on the
woman by saying that he could give her living water—not just
well water, but sparkling, bubbly, living water.

● **"If you knew the gift of God and who it is that asks you for
a drink, you would have asked him and he would have
given you living water."**

John 4:10

You have to wonder what was going through her mind. Was
he crazy? Was he overcome by the heat? Or was he a con artist?
Maybe he was making a pass at her.

The Samaritans accepted only the first five books of the Old
Testament; the Psalms and the Prophets were off-limits to them.
In the Psalms, David speaks of drinking from the river of delights:
"For with you is the fountain of life" (Ps. 36:9). Isaiah writes, "With joy you will draw water from the wells of salvation" (Isa. 12:3), and Jeremiah acknowledges God as "the spring of living water" (Jer. 2:13).

But the Samaritan woman was baffled by the concept of living water. So she drew him out. *I know this area better than you do, stranger,* she said in effect. *I know where all the wells are, and this one, dug by patriarch Jacob, is the best. Do you think you're better than Jacob?*

"Well, yes," Jesus answered. Jacob's well quenches thirst temporarily, but Jesus was offering satisfaction for a longer term.

W'S

Where: *Samaria* was a part of Palestine between Judea and Galilee. It was part of the area once inhabited by the Northern Kingdom of Israel but was conquered by Assyria in 722 BC and thoroughly resettled. The resulting influx of Gentiles and the intermarriage created a new culture that was part Jewish but dangerously different. *Mount Gerizim*, once the scene of a dedication service led by Joshua, was now the site of a rival temple for the Samaritans' unique brand of worship. *Jacob's well*, fed by an underground spring, was not just a water source but a symbol of the Samaritans' connection with the Jews.

PART 2

● "Whoever drinks the water I give him will never thirst. Indeed, the water I give him will become in him a spring of water welling up to eternal life."

John 4:14

She didn't know what to make of this man. For that matter, most people today don't know what to make of him. If you were standing on a street corner drinking your bottled Perrier, what would you think of a stranger saying something like that to you?

"Sir, give me this water," she said. Scholars wonder about her tone of voice. Was she skeptical or eager? Probably she was dubious—like a housewife with a vacuum cleaner salesman at the door. "It sounds too good to be true, but if it checks out, it's a deal I shouldn't refuse."

Then Jesus changed the subject. At least it seems that way. If he was playing salesman, he had been about to close the deal. Instead, he made a seemingly impertinent request: *Bring your husband.* And that question got to the core of her need.

Flustered, she answered, *I'm not married.*

True, Jesus said, *you're not married, but you have been married five times, and the man you're currently living with is not your husband.*

Now another piece of the puzzle falls into place for us. We know that most women in that desert culture would go to the town well early in the morning, before the day got too hot. Why was this woman there at noon? We can only surmise that the other townswomen shunned her, and now we know why. She was a loose woman, perhaps a home wrecker. Her lifestyle was immoral. So we can guess that this woman had gotten into the habit of going to Jacob's well at noon to draw her water in peace, free from the judging taunts and glares of her neighbors.

Add this to the barriers Jesus was smashing here. Not only was she a despised Samaritan with whom no devout Jew would converse, and not only was she a woman at whom no devout rabbi would choose to look, she was an *immoral* woman, shunned by her village. Certainly this is a third strike against her. How could we expect a Messiah to have any contact with her?

33

But none of these barriers stopped Jesus. He saw that she had a problem and was unfulfilled and unhappy in life. Marriage had been a colossal disappointment, again and again and again. Maybe men were using her. What sort of opinion did she have of herself, of her own value? And now, although she needed a man in her life, she may have feared another marriage because she had been burned so many times.

Here at the well she was meeting an unusual man who seemed to know her better than she knew herself. Maybe he was some kind of prophet.

So she put up another barrier—religion. Samaritans had different worship rituals than those of the Jews, she said. Who's right? Who's wrong? Is it all right to pray on this Samaritan mountain, or will God only hear prayers launched from the Jerusalem temple?

Jesus knocked this barrier down too. Although he confirmed that the Jews were following a more complete revelation than the Samaritans, he went on to say that the location of worship isn't as important as the attitude involved. The internals are more important than the externals. "True worshipers," Jesus said, "will worship the Father in spirit and in truth."

PART 3

● "God is spirit, and his worshipers must worship in spirit and in truth."

John 4:24

It was beyond her. In effect, the woman said, *I'm just a simple Samaritan girl; I don't understand deep theology. When the Messiah comes, maybe he can explain it.*

Jesus answered simply, "I who speak to you am he." She was an unlikely candidate for a divine revelation, but Jesus identified himself to her as the Messiah. What divine grace! But then, what divine grace he shows to us when he brings us salvation. He knows us inside and out, all our flaws and foibles, and still he reveals his greatness to us.

DARE TO COMPARE

Compare the conversations that Jesus had with Nicodemus in John 3 and with the Samaritan woman in John 4. What are the similarities and differences?

Off ran the Samaritan woman. Still bewildered, she left her water jar at Jesus' feet and went to tell the townspeople of her discovery. Frankly, she didn't have much spiritual understanding. She was no great expounder of Scripture. She didn't have to be. Like the healed blind man of John 9 who simply said the "one thing" he knew—"I was blind but now I see"—this woman shared what little she knew about Jesus. "He told me everything I ever did." Then she asked, "Could this be the Christ?" The townspeople went to see for themselves and, because of her testimony, "many of the Samaritans from that town believed" (v. 39).

PART 4

● "Open your eyes and look at the fields! They are ripe for harvest."

John 4:35

No doubt, the disciples didn't know what Jesus was talking about. Most of them were fishermen, not farmers. And they were still learning about discipleship. This lesson had to do with opening their eyes. They had seen a woman who was so low-class she had to draw water in the heat of the day. In their terminology, she was a fish that ought to be thrown back into the lake—not worth their time or effort. But Jesus had seen her as a needy soul and a potential missionary. They saw a dangerous mob headed in their direction. Jesus saw an excited group of men and women who needed to learn about him.

It's surprising that Jesus and the disciples stayed two more days in Samaria. After meeting Jesus, the townspeople told the woman, "We no longer believe just because of what you said; now we have heard for ourselves, and we know that this man really is the Savior of the world" (v. 42). Notice the progression of information here. The woman saw Jesus first as a mystery man, then as a prophet, and then she told the others he was possibly the Messiah. But after two days with Jesus, the towns-folk claimed him not only as a prophet, not only as the Messiah, but as their Savior.

YOU LUCKY DOG!

PART 1

"Blessed are the poor in spirit, for theirs is the kingdom of heaven. Blessed are those who mourn, for they will be comforted. Blessed are the meek, for they will inherit the earth."

Matthew 5:3–5

People play lotteries every day, hoping to be lucky enough to win big money. Once in a while, jackpots soar into the megamillions, and players line up at newsstands and convenience stores to take their chances. They're dreaming of all the things they would do with that sudden fortune. If they could just guess the lucky number, surely their troubles would be over.

Big jackpots are big news, but occasionally the press will do a follow-up story years later. How are those lucky winners doing? Amazingly, the stories are often quite dismal. The influx of money has certainly changed the lives of the winners, but not in a good way. There are divorces and other broken relationships, swindles and bad investments, lost trust and compounded fears. The big win has caused major losses.

Who are the real winners then? You might say that the luckiest people are those who *don't* get the millions, because they have the opportunity to enjoy their relationships and life's simple pleasures.

Monday: Read part 1 of this chapter. Think about the meaning of the words *poor*, *mourn*, and *meek*.

Tuesday: Read part 2 of this chapter. This was a revolutionary way of thinking, and it still is today. What would it mean for your life, your church, or your workplace if everyone showed these qualities?

Wednesday: Read part 3 of this chapter. Think about the blessings offered to those who show these qualities.

Thursday: Read Psalm 24:3–5 about purity of heart and continue through the rest of the psalm to find out about seeking and praising God.

Friday: The Beatitudes give us God's values. Review them all today (Matt. 5:3–10) and pray to understand them better.

Saturday: How do you think these values compared to the values of the Pharisees? How do they compare to the values of your world today?

Sunday: Worship God today as the one who blesses us as we humbly seek him.

Jesus said that long ago, as he sat on a mountaintop in Galilee and instructed his followers. His pronouncements turned common knowledge upside down. Most people, then and now, would say, "Blessed are the winners, the self-confident, the go-getters, the upbeat." But Jesus had a different take on who the fortunate folks are.

The word *blessed* really means "lucky." In Greek, and in the Hebrew form it's based on, this isn't necessarily a religious concept. "These are the people who really have it good," Jesus was saying. And who was he talking about?

The poor in spirit. You might think it's important to be spiritually rich. Aren't we supposed to nurture our spiritual lives, growing strong and robust in our relationships with God? Well, sort of. But the more we grow, the more we know we *need* to grow. Once you start saying, "I'm spiritually strong," you're missing the point. The poor in spirit are humble, knowing how needy they are, recognizing that they must thoroughly depend on God.

Those who mourn. Jesus might be talking about all who suffer losses in their lives—this is the same word used for Jacob mourning when he thought his favorite son, Joseph, had died—but Jesus might also be referring to sorrow for sin. Those who are poor in spirit, recognizing their failures, mourn over their inability to please God consistently.

The meek. This word was used for a tamed animal. The meek person doesn't go wild and fight for his own rights. The Greeks prized this quality. Aristotle placed it at the perfect midpoint between unbridled anger and comatose calm. But you may have noticed that in our world meekness doesn't make things happen. People flock after the loud and boisterous leaders, the passionate and untamed voices. They mistake meekness for weakness.

W'S

Who: Jesus was teaching his disciples at the beginning (Matt. 5:1), but crowds responded to him at the end (7:28). So it's possible he said these things on several occasions to different groups.
Where: On a hillside in Galilee
When: Early in his ministry
What: This Sermon on the Mount is recognized as a masterpiece by Christians and non-Christians alike. It's a theme statement of Jesus' whole teaching ministry.

Let's stop there in our catalog of fortunate folks and see what we've got. The dependent, the depressed, the doormats. Does Jesus really know what he's saying? Keep listening to him and you'll hear him say that "the last shall be first" and "whoever wants to lead should be a servant." So far, these beatitudes fit right into his topsy-turvy view of life. But now it's time to open the curtain and see what these lucky contestants have won.

The poor in spirit win . . . *the kingdom of heaven.* The kingdom was Jesus' major teaching theme—both a place and an idea, a future hope and a present reality, marked by grace and judgment and many surprises. Simply put, God's kingdom is wherever God rules as king. And that makes sense of this blessing. The spiritually poor know they must depend on God totally, so they trust in him and seek to obey him, honoring him as their only king.

This first beatitude, then, encapsulates much of Jesus' teaching, especially in his face-offs with the Pharisees. Don't let the spiritually proud people tell you that they own God's kingdom! It belongs to you humble souls, because you are trusting in God.

Those who mourn . . . *will be comforted.* The passive verb implies that God himself will do the comforting. You might be wondering why God allows good people to suffer, and there's no easy answer. But this principle brings a nugget of wisdom to the question. God knows what it's like to suffer, and you can know him in a new way when you come to him for comfort.

The meek . . . *will inherit the earth*. Inheritance is a future blessing held in store for those who faithfully wait. That's what the meek do. They faithfully wait while fools rush in to gather the spoils of this present world. The future world will be ruled by God's principles, and so the meek will finally get their chance to take charge.

PART 2

"Blessed are those who hunger and thirst for righteousness, for they will be filled. Blessed are the merciful, for they will be shown mercy. Blessed are the pure in heart, for they will see God."

Matthew 5:6–8

There are two ways to live: the way of mercy and the way of keeping score. Jesus and his disciples lived in a world dominated by scorekeepers. The Pharisees were proud to total up their righteousness and quick to criticize others for their lack of it. But Jesus said they were not the most blessed people in their society. *You who are parched and famished, you are the lucky ones.*

We hunger and thirst for what we don't have. The psalmist saw himself as a deer panting with thirst, craving a relationship with God (Psalm 42). That's what Jesus is talking about here—not the satisfaction of a good deed well done but the gut-level longing for the ability to do what pleases God.

In these Beatitudes and throughout his ministry, Jesus presented a new spiritual economy. The scorekeepers had set up their rigid system of actions and consequences, but Jesus offered the way of mercy.

Of course, being dependent on God's mercy, we show that same mercy to others. It makes no sense to start keeping score with those around us when God has smashed the scoreboard.

But don't miss the point by totaling up your acts of mercy. We don't earn mercy by showing mercy. That would be a contradiction. We live in the way of mercy. We forgive our debtors because God has forgiven our debts.

We might encounter the same contradiction with "the pure in heart." Many believers try to scour their thoughts and motives to earn the blessing listed here, but that's scorekeeping. "Who may ascend the hill of the LORD?" the psalmist wondered. "Who

> **IN THE MIRROR**
>
> Should you start to do good deeds so you will be "blessed," or is this passage blessing you for the character you already have?

may stand in his holy place? He who has clean hands and a pure heart" (24:3–4). The Pharisees of Jesus' day specialized in clean hands, but they had neglected their hearts. "Everything they do is done for men to see," Jesus charged (Matt. 23:5). They went through the motions of pleasing God, but they were just padding their own spiritual résumés.

Those who truly seek God when they approach the gates of God's presence will get what they came for. Without ulterior motives fogging up the works, they will "see God."

PART 3

● "Blessed are the peacemakers, for they will be called sons of God. Blessed are those who are persecuted because of righteousness, for theirs is the kingdom of heaven."

Matthew 5:9–10

A few years ago, the Israelis and Palestinians carved out one of their tentative peace agreements, and days later there was an interesting item in the newspaper. Palestinian kids were throwing rocks at Israeli soldiers, shouting, "We don't want peace!" The soldiers hollered right back, "We don't want peace either!"

What a snapshot of our world! As Isaiah moaned, "The way of peace they do not know" (Isa. 59:8). But the biblical concept of peace involves more than international cease-fires. The Hebrew word is *shalom*, which means well-being, satisfaction, cooperation, it's all good. The ancient Israelite greeting was not "How ya doin'?" but "Is there *shalom* with you?"

So then, who are the peace*makers*? Those who bring *shalom*. Those who work for the well-being of those around them. Remember that Jesus was speaking primarily to his disciples. This was the task he would assign to them: preaching the good news of God's kingdom, the gospel of peace. This message would certainly change society, but the greatest *shalom* was with God. God sends us out as peacemakers, telling others that he wants to end his war with them. As we carry out this assignment, we act not only as God's emissaries but as his own sons and daughters, bearing his image, following in his peace-loving footsteps.

It's a difficult task, to be sure. Peace is pricey, and sometimes it costs us our very lives. But the final promise is just like the first: "theirs is the kingdom of heaven." While the poor in spirit live out God's kingdom on earth, trusting God and seeking his will, the persecuted find their blessing in the heavenly kingdom. That is why they are truly fortunate.

Looking over all the Beatitudes, it is tempting to see them as a new kind of law, Jesus' new rendition of the Ten Commandments. We could easily put all of these on our "To Do" list: "Work at being poorer in spirit, more mournful, meeker," and so on. But the tone of Jesus' sermon is much different. He's not handing out homework; he's offering congratulations. *Don't let those religious folks slam the door of God's kingdom on you,* Jesus is saying. *The blessings of God's kingdom come to you who are humble, mournful, meek, passionate, merciful, motivated, peace-seeking, and misunderstood. You might think these qualities put you in the doghouse, but cheer up! You've just won the lottery.*

QUOTE TO NOTE

This dual love for God and others is like the positive and negative poles of a battery—unless both connections are made, we have no power.

Billy Graham

7
LIGHT AND TASTY

PART 1

● "You are the salt of the earth."

Matthew 5:13

Perhaps, in your struggle against high blood pressure, you have sampled some low-salt foods. If so, you know the problem. Sorry to say, they ought to call these "low-taste" foods. Take out the salt, and the meal becomes bland.

That's part of what Jesus had in mind as he called his disciples "the salt of the earth." They would lend zest and flavor to the world around them. All too often, we Christians have done just the opposite. In our attempts to promote disciplined living and self-control, we have squeezed the enjoyment out of life.

Jesus came so that we might live life abundantly, "to the full" (John 10:10). We should be actively sharing the joy of Jesus and thus making life tasty for all who come in contact with us.

But salt had another purpose in ancient times. It was a preservative. In the days before Frigidaires, meat was salted to prevent spoilage. Was Jesus saying that his followers would preserve the earth in some way? Does our joy make the world a better place? Do our acts of mercy and selfless charity influence those around us? Would our society be even more violent, despairing,

Monday: Read part 1 of this chapter. In what ways do you make life "tastier" for those around you?

Tuesday: Read part 2. How has Christ brought light to your life?

Wednesday: Read part 3. How do you bring Christ's light to the people in your life?

Thursday: Christians might become proud of being the light. Meditate on 2 Corinthians 4:5–7. Make this very personal in your thoughts.

Friday: A few years ago the lights went out in several states. New York and other cities were in darkness. How do people react to the absence of light—physically and spiritually?

Saturday: Today take to Jesus your thoughts about salt and light. Ask him to show you how to apply them in your daily life.

Sunday: Praise the Lord with the reading of Psalm 27 and remember he is our light!

and self-destructive if it weren't for Christians? Maybe our Christlike attitude can help to save the world from itself.

No one eats a meal and says, "Wow! That's good salt!" Salt generally doesn't call attention to itself. It merely enhances the flavor of whatever dish it happens to be residing in. That might be the key to our "saltiness" as well. Remember that this teaching follows the Beatitudes, where Jesus shocked everyone by blessing not the most openly religious members of society but the poor in spirit, the meek, the strugglers, and so on. God's true children would enhance and preserve the world not by sounding trumpets and enforcing laws but by showing mercy and hungering for the righteousness they lacked.

Don't get too frazzled by Jesus' reference to salt that has lost its saltiness. This is probably just one of Jesus' absurdities, like a plank in the eye. If salt isn't salty, it isn't salt! The chemical properties of sodium chloride make it salty. It doesn't have to work at being salty—that's what it is! So the message to Jesus' disciples, then and now, is simply this: Be who you are, and let your natural flavor bring zest to the world.

PART 2

● "You are the light of the world. A city on a hill cannot be hidden. Neither do people light a lamp and put it under a bowl. Instead they put it on its stand, and it gives light to everyone in the house."

Matthew 5:14–15

Jerusalem in Jesus' day must have been an awesome sight. Unpopular King Herod had tried to curry favor with the people by rebuilding the temple in glorious fashion. He was still unpopular, but the building project was impressive. No doubt all of Jesus' hearers had made the trek to the Holy City for one festival or another. They knew the joy of rounding the bend and seeing that city set on a hill, its limestone pillars gleaming in the sun. At night, the effect would have been stunning too, especially during the festivals when the tall lampposts were blazing in the temple courtyard.

> ## CLUES TO USE
>
> In Hebrew thinking, wisdom was sometimes seen as salt. This might be why Paul tells the Colossians to let their speech be seasoned with salt (Col. 4:6)—he means wisdom. Anyway, the word Jesus uses for salt losing its saltiness is literally "to become foolish," reflecting this double meaning.

> ## CROSS REF
>
> See John 5:35, referring to John the Baptist. What kind of light did he give? Also check Proverbs 20:27 to see what else light can do.

The Hebrew Scriptures talked about Jerusalem as a light to the world. All nations would be drawn to the light of God emanating from his chosen city. "See, darkness covers the earth and thick darkness is over the peoples," the prophet said, "but the LORD rises upon you and his glory appears over you. Nations will come to your light, and kings to the brightness of your dawn" (Isa. 60:2–3).

On one occasion, Jesus had stood near those temple lampposts and proclaimed, "I am the light of the world" (John 8:12), but now he was saying, You *are that light, you my followers. You will light up the world.*

And that's pretty much what happened. From the time the tongues of fire lit upon the disciples at Pentecost (more light!), they were involved in setting the world ablaze with the message of Jesus. Later, as Paul explained his missionary calling, he borrowed language from Isaiah: "I have made you a light for the Gentiles, that you may bring salvation to the ends of the earth" (Acts 13:47; see Isa. 49:6).

45

PART 3

● "In the same way, let your light shine before men, that they may see your good deeds and praise your Father in heaven."

Matthew 5:16

An actor, appearing in a brilliant new comedy, fidgeted nervously backstage during intermission. "They're not laughing enough," he complained to the director, "but I'm punching up every line as much as I can. Why aren't they laughing? This is good material. What am I doing wrong?"

"You're working too hard," the director wisely responded. "Relax. Let the lines come out naturally."

Sometimes Christians try too hard. We want to blaze brightly with the light of Christ so everyone around us will come to faith. But sometimes when we work so hard, it starts to be all about us. The truth is we can't *make* people believe, no matter how brilliantly we speak about Christ, but we can let them see how brilliant Christ is. As we let his light shine *through* us, people may be drawn to that light.

IN THE MIRROR

Carl Jung said, "As far as we can discern, the sole purpose of human existence is to kindle a light in the darkness of mere being." How would you adjust that statement to describe your life?

The gospel of grace gives us an interesting problem. The Bible makes it clear that we are saved by God's generosity, not through our own works. We recognize that even as God's Spirit is transforming us, we will struggle to live righteously. But as soon as we start focusing on our own good works, we become like the Pharisees: proud, complacent, and self-righteous.

Yet the Spirit does transform us. The light of Christ floods our lives and is seen in actions that please God. This is the light that Jesus wants shining from us. People will see the good things we do and praise God for them.

There's a lovely comment early in the book of Acts, as the civic leaders saw Jesus' disciples preaching powerfully in public. They knew these guys were just uneducated fishermen. What qualifications did they have to teach in the temple? The leaders "were astonished and they took note that these men had been with Jesus" (Acts 4:13).

That's how it should be with us too. As we bring flavor and enlightenment to the world around us, we should never grab any glory for ourselves. Whatever we do, whoever we are, it's a result of our being with Jesus.

QUOTE TO NOTE

Light cannot hide. It is by very nature a showoff. Light tells all. It is the bright braggart—wild and uncontainable—knowing no secrets. . . . You are light! When you are filled with my [Christ's] being, you become that brilliance that helps the world locate its value system.

Calvin Miller

WHISPERS OF LOVE

● "You have heard that it was said . . . 'Do not murder' . . . 'Do not commit adultery . . .'"

Matthew 5:21, 27

As a child, you may have played "Whisper Down the Lane," or some variation. Somebody at one end of a line whispers something to the next person, who whispers it to the next person, and so on. Through the series of rehearings and retellings, the message usually changes substantially. "My mom went to the store for bread" becomes "A monster lives under my bed." It's less comical when the same thing happens in real life. You discreetly ask a friend to pray for your sore throat, and eighteen phone calls later the whole neighborhood thinks you're dying of malaria.

Clearly, a message can lose something in transmission, and that's the problem Jesus was tackling. People had heard things about the behavior that God wanted, but did they really get the message?

Jesus had started this sermon with some stunning reversals. God's blessings would be lavished not on the pious but on the poor in spirit, not on those who were filled to the brim with their own religious actions but on those who were hungry for God's righteousness. He was handing God's kingdom to the ordinary folks in the crowd and obviously dissing the religious leaders. Those leaders were students of the Scriptures, experts in the law, so you might expect Jesus to dismiss the law entirely. Instead, he cautioned, "Do not think that I have come to abolish the Law or the Prophets; I have not come to abolish them but to fulfill them" (v. 17).

The word *fulfill* is really to *fill*, like pouring liquid into an empty cup. It's as if Moses had set the table and now Jesus was dishing out the food. The law of God is good and great, paving inroads into the mind of our Creator. But Jesus was now sharing the very heart of God, filling up those legal structures with new meaning and new challenges.

Most of Jesus' examples come directly from Old Testament Scripture, some from the Ten Commandments. They had "heard it said" that it was wrong to murder, because God had said it on Mount Sinai. So there's nothing wrong with the statements here. Murder and adultery are definitely wrong. The problem was in how the people dealt with these commands. Oh, they obeyed them, but then they felt as if they had accomplished the sum total of God's desires. According to Jesus, that obedience should be just the beginning.

Monday: Read part 1 of this chapter. Do you think it is possible to obey the Ten Commandments completely? Why or why not?

Tuesday: Read part 2 of this chapter. Is it possible to obey the stricter version of the commandments that Jesus offers here? Why or why not?

Wednesday: Read part 3. How would you react if a known prostitute or someone else whose lifestyle you oppose came to worship in your church? How would your church respond?

Thursday: Read part 4. In what ways can your faith become more mature?

Friday: Read John 15:13 and think about how Jesus treated us as friends instead of enemies. Thank him for that.

Saturday: Pray about your own attitudes toward others. Ask the Lord to help you be less judging and more loving. Pray also for your church, that they may view everyone who enters as a gift from God, a fellow sinner who needs love too.

Sunday: Honor Jesus as the "perfecter" of your faith (Heb. 12:2).

PART 2

● "But I say to you . . ."

   Matthew 5:22, 28, 32, 34, 39, 44 NRSV

It is tempting to see Jesus' statements as a new law. And Matthew sets it up that way. We see Jesus on a mountain, like Moses, quoting some of Moses' commandments and making his own adjustments. *Don't be satisfied with abstaining from murder,* we might say as we apply this new law. *Jesus says we will be truly holy only when we conquer road rage.* But as we live by that even stricter law, we can begin to feel just as self-righteous as the leaders of Jesus' day. No, we're not just dealing with a new law here. We're dealing with a whole new way to follow God.

> **CHECKOUT COUNTER**
>
> Check out Romans 5:6–8 to see how God loves his enemies.

A little boy once accompanied his father to the gas station. When the attendant came by, the boy said, "I'll do it, Dad." He handed a baseball card to the man and said, "Fill 'er up with riggiter." Yes, this boy had "heard it said" that you could get a tank of gas by producing a card and saying those words, but he didn't understand the true economy of that transaction. It's not the act of handing out a card that pays for the gas but the credit in the account that the card represents.

Jesus was saying the same sort of thing in Matthew 5, and it's a theme picked up in the rest of the New Testament. The commandments are great, but they're child's play. To live a complete life that delights your Creator, you need to establish a credit account with him. You need a heart so committed that your love for him challenges and neutralizes the everyday temptations to anger and lust.

Isn't it hard to do what Jesus asks? Isn't it almost impossible to keep from hating the person with a full shopping cart in the "10 items or less" lane? Isn't it crazy to think we can avoid lustful thoughts in our sex-mad society? Maybe so. And the poor in spirit will acknowledge that it's a constant struggle.

PART 3

● "You have heard that it was said, 'You shall love your neighbor and hate your enemy.' But I say to you, Love your enemies and pray for those who persecute you, so that you may be children of your Father in heaven; for he makes his sun rise on the evil and on the good, and sends rain on the righteous and on the unrighteous."

Matthew 5:43–45 NRSV

Six times Jesus quotes Scripture and then adds his own demands. Some of the quotations come from the Ten Commandments, others from lesser-known parts of the law. This sixth one is the only one to include nonbiblical material, and in the process it gives us a good picture of the problem.

"Love your neighbor" is right out of Deuteronomy. No problem there. But the law doesn't say anything explicitly about hating your enemies. However, scholars have found writings from the strict Essene sect, in Jesus' time, that use this sort of "us-them" language. And we only have to look at the Pharisees' frequent complaints about the people Jesus was hanging out with to see that enemy hating was common among the most religious folks.

In fact it was their nit-picking approach to the law that brought them to that point. They agreed that they were to love their neighbor, but who was their neighbor? That's exactly the question that prompted Jesus' story of the good Samaritan, and it was a common debate topic among the rabbis. The Pharisees were very good at drawing lines around God's laws and defining precisely what should and should not be done. If I define my neighbors as only A, B, and C, then I'm free to hate X, Y, and Z.

Not so, says Jesus, using a great comparison and a brilliant piece of logic. First, he says that God loves his enemies as well as his friends. This idea might have seemed troubling to some of Jesus' hearers, who assumed that God showered his blessings only on his own faithful followers. Yet Jesus presented evidence that everyone knew from nature. When it rained, didn't all the farms get watered, whether they belonged to the righteous or

51

the unrighteous? Both devout Jews and idolatrous Gentiles benefited from the sunshine, didn't they?

Jesus' next question sums up his whole sermon: If you love only those who love you, what's so special about that? All people love their friends. So that's no great thing. What will truly set you apart as a Godlike person? Loving your enemies.

Nowadays all sorts of churches consider themselves friendly. They celebrate their warm Christian fellowship. Some even put up signs: "The Friendly Church." That's all well and good, but according to Jesus, that's nothing special. The real challenge is to love those outside the circle, the people whose lifestyle you disagree with, the people whose opinions rankle you, even the people who consider themselves enemies of the Christian faith. How are we going to love them?

PART 4

● "Be perfect, therefore, as your heavenly Father is perfect."

Matthew 5:48

The word for perfection really has to do with completion or maturity. Jesus is challenging us to grow up, to move beyond the letter of the law and into its spirit. He wants us to get beyond the rules and start making mature decisions based on the wholeness of our relationship with the Father. This doesn't nullify the rules, but it opens up a whole new realm of thought. Murder is wrong, and it will always be wrong, because it emanates from a heart of hatred. We find completion not in avoiding murder but by dealing with the hate in our heart. Love is good, and it will always be good, but loving only our friends is kid stuff. Mature love turns enemies into neighbors.

When we define *perfection* here as maturity, it casts a new light on this teaching. There is a growing process that must be followed. We grow as we follow Jesus. We are moving toward the maturity of the Father, but it takes time.

When a child is behaving immaturely, we may say, "Grow up!" or "Act your age!" In the same way Jesus is chiding his hearers to stop reviewing the ABCs all the time and start moving forward into the deep poetry of God's heart!

QUOTE TO NOTE

Virtually always for Jesus, "love" was not a noun but a verb. It was compassion in action. . . . For Jesus, love was not merely a lofty ideal but a lifestyle.

F. Lagard Smith

3
THE GOLDEN YARDSTICK

You don't usually find nice people going around killing other people, and you don't usually find nice people robbing banks. It's just not the thing to do. So if you're a nice person, you probably aren't tempted to murder your boss or crack the safe of the First National. At least not seriously tempted. If society in general frowns on certain practices, we tend to avoid them whether or not there are biblical reasons to do so.

But some of Christ's teachings are not as easy to practice, and the reason is that, according to many nice people, some of his teachings are not realistic. For instance, if someone takes your coat, give him your shirt too. Does that make sense? Pretty soon your closet will be bare. If someone punches you in the jaw, turn your face so he can fatten your lip on the other side. Oh, come on now!

Maybe teachings like that resonate with a bunch of monks living in a monastery, but to men and women working in the real dog-eat-dog world, raising ordinary kids who struggle with self-esteem, and living with neighbors who take advantage of you at every turn, they just don't make sense. Get real, Jesus!

Scholars call the last two-thirds of Luke 6 the Sermon on the Plain. It's similar to the Sermon on the Mount in Mat-

54

thew 5–7, and yet there are differences. No doubt Jesus repeated some of his teachings to his disciples at different times to make sure they sank in. Like us, the disciples didn't always catch on right away.

And who were these disciples? Were they monks in a monastery? Senior citizens playing shuffleboard on a Caribbean cruise? Hardly. Most of them were rugged fishermen, two of whom were nicknamed "Sons of Thunder," and a third (Peter) seemed pretty quick with a sword (at least when Jesus was arrested). Another had been a tax collector, squeezing money out of people who didn't want to pay. Another was a Zealot, one of the terrorists of that time.

Can you imagine the raised eyebrows and the side-glances the disciples gave one another when Jesus said:

● "Love your enemies, do good to those who hate you, bless those who curse you, pray for those who mistreat you."

Luke 6:27–28

Loving your neighbor as yourself is hard enough, but Jesus told his rough and tough disciples, "Love your enemies." Of the four Greek words for love, Jesus here used the word *agape*, which refers to a love that extends to the unworthy, love that cannot be earned. *Agape* goes beyond "nice." It's a kind of love that only the Holy Spirit can produce.

Monday: Read part 1 of this chapter. Pray for an "enemy" right now.

Tuesday: Read part 2. Think of the last time you retaliated. How would things have gone differently if you had forgiven the offense?

Wednesday: Read part 3. What difference do you think it makes to have the Golden Rule phrased positively ("Do" instead of "Don't do")?

Thursday: Read part 4. By looking at you, how would your neighbors describe Jesus?

Friday: Compare and contrast the attitude toward enemies in Psalm 58 with that of Jesus. How do you account for the difference?

Saturday: Think about your acquaintances and list those you need to love even though they may be unlovable. Pray for more love to give.

Sunday: Read 1 Corinthians 13. Praise God for his wonderful love for us!

Doing good to those who hate you is not easy either. If you think the other person is evil, don't you want to sabotage his efforts? Why would you want to offer to mow his lawn for him?

Blessing others? The only time most of us bless others is when we say *gesundheit!* The Greek word, from which we get *eulogy*, means "to speak well about" or "to invoke a benediction upon." Can you imagine doing that to someone who has just sworn a blue streak at you? But isn't that what Jesus is saying?

And pray for those who mistreat you. That sounds easier. Yet Jesus isn't saying that you should pray that God will riddle their path with potholes. He is saying that your prayer for them should be positive.

PART 2

In case that isn't enough, Jesus went on to make it all very specific:

● "If someone strikes you on one cheek, turn to him the other also."

Luke 6:29

Bible scholars don't agree on how this should be translated. Some say it's a slap on the cheek; others say it's a punch in the jaw. In either case, it's offensive, painful, and possibly injurious. Is Jesus asking us to put up with that? Should we make ourselves vulnerable to those who might hurt us?

Yes, that seems to be exactly what he's saying. It goes against common sense, but that's the point. This is the way of *agape* love, a lifestyle in which you put other people ahead of your own honor or ease. When you truly love someone, you will give him your shirt even if he has just taken your coat. Love "goes the extra mile." That phrase, from Matthew's version of this teaching, probably refers to the practice of Roman soldiers forcing Jews to carry their supplies for them. A Godlike love doesn't just bear the offense, it responds with extra kindness. As Paul put it, "Overcome evil with good" (Rom. 12:21).

Now Jesus is not talking about whether or not you should give your teenage son money for new sneakers after he has squandered his allowance for the third month in a row. There's a time for tough love, and sometimes, out of love, you have to say a firm *no*.

Nor is he talking about whether or not to call the police when a burglar invades your home, or whether a wife should report a husband's abuse. Sometimes the most loving thing to do, for the offender and for society, is to try to end the offending behavior.

But the question is: How should we respond when people humiliate us, when they cause us grief, when they take advantage of us? Jesus wants us to respond not with vengeance but with love. *But that lousy cheek-striker doesn't deserve to be shown love!* you might protest. Exactly. That's what *agape* is all about.

W'S

Who: Jesus was teaching "a large crowd of his disciples," that is, not only the Twelve but a larger group of followers and curiosity seekers.

When: This is still rather early in Jesus' ministry, but he has become quite famous by now.

Where: Luke puts this sermon "on a level place." Matthew had Jesus preaching on a mountain. The two sermons are similar but not identical. It's likely that Jesus preached the same general message on several different occasions.

What: This Sermon on the Plain has some Beatitudes (along with "woe" statements) and other teaching on loving enemies and not judging.

CROSS REF

Did Jesus "turn the other cheek"? See John 18:19–23.

It's how God operates, and with the Holy Spirit living within us, we are to live in the same way. In *The Message*, Eugene Peterson paraphrases Ephesians 2:3–5 to read: "It's a wonder God didn't lose his temper and do away with the whole lot of us. Instead, immense in mercy and with an incredible love, he embraced us. He took our sin-dead lives and made us alive in Christ."

That's the pattern. If God so loved us, who made life miserable for him, we ought to be able to love those who are making life miserable for us.

PART 3

● "Do to others as you would have them do to you."

Luke 6:31

Jesus was positively positive.

Take the Golden Rule, for example. Other religions had similar expressions. Confucius, who seems to have had something to say about everything, said, "Never do to others what you would not like them to do to you." Buddhism taught, "Hurt not others in ways that you yourself would find hurtful." Hinduism said, "Do nothing unto others which would cause you pain if done to you." In Judaism, the Talmud declared, "What is hateful to you, do not to your fellow men."

See the difference?

The others start with the negative: "Never do," "Hurt not," "Do nothing." Jesus is positively positive: "Do." Or to use another very Christian word: "Love."

Right living, according to Jesus, is based on proactive love, not on reactive avoidance of evil. "We love," wrote the apostle John, "because he first loved us" (1 John 4:19). Because of God's proactive love, we know the secret of living out the Golden Rule. God so proactively loved the world that he gave his only Son. Even though the world rejected him, Jesus Christ laid down his life to save us.

When John said, "Let us not love with words or tongue but with actions and in truth" (3:18), he was beautifully defining this proactive love. Maybe John had in mind the Golden Rule when he wrote, "If anyone has material possessions and sees his brother in need but has no pity on him, how can the love of God be in him?" (v. 17). It's not enough to avoid doing harm to others. That's certainly a nice way to live, but it's not the proactive *agape* love Jesus was promoting. He had a more positive approach in mind.

PART 4

Toyohiko Kagawa was an illegitimate Japanese child, half-starved and beaten by his parents. His stepmother despised him;

he knew nothing of love. As a teenager, he was diagnosed with tuberculosis. A doctor said he had less than a year to live. Forced to live in a small fisherman's shack, he was isolated from the world. Afraid of catching the disease, his friends refused to visit him. But then a missionary came to see him. "Dr. Myers was not afraid," Kagawa later wrote. "He came and slept with me in that cottage for four days."

> **IN THE MIRROR**
>
> As you look over the last year of your life, how have other people hurt you? What specific things could you do to return good for the evil you have received?

When Kagawa asked the missionary, "Aren't you afraid of me?" the missionary responded, "Although your disease is contagious, love is more contagious."

Kagawa got over his TB, but the missionary's contagious love infected him. "I decided then," he wrote, "that I must love the people of the slums of Tokyo the way the missionary loved me."

So he went to live in a six-by-six-foot hut in the slums. He swept chimneys to earn money and shared his rice with the needy. When young hoodlums came, demolished his hut, and knocked out four of his front teeth, Kagawa responded with love. He began Sunday schools, then orphanages, farmers' cooperatives, settlement houses, and churches. He was imprisoned several

> **CHECKOUT COUNTER**
>
> Check out Paul's teaching on retaliation (or the lack thereof) in Romans 12:17–21.

times because of his opposition to the Japanese warlords, but still he continued. Beaten by drunks and spat on by prostitutes, Kagawa became a social activist working to help the people who were abusing him.

"He put religion in his shoes," said one observer. A Japanese skeptic finally admitted, "This Jesus that he is always talking about must be something like Kagawa."

And that's a yardstick we can apply to our own lives.

10

SHOW BUSINESS

● "Be careful not to do your 'acts of righteousness' before men,
to be seen by them. If you do, you will have no reward
from your Father in heaven."

Matthew 6:1

On TV the other day there was an interview with a man who
said he was working undercover with the CIA. Gazing openly at
the camera, he told a fascinating cloak-and-dagger story of his
ongoing exploits in spying for the government, double-crossing
drug lords and foreign agents. But despite all the intrigue of his
tale, it was still hard to believe. Why? Well, because secret agents
are *secret*. Sure, it's great to bask in the glory of being a master spy,
but once you blow your cover, you can't be a spy anymore.

Good deeds are something like that.

Jesus urged his followers to be careful about their motives.
A few minutes earlier, he had told them to let their light shine
before others so people would see their good works and glorify
God. Glory to God is the key. When you start doing good deeds to
attract attention to your own goodness, you have a problem.

The problem is this. You can get people's praise, but then that's all you get. You won't also get God's rewards. You can't have it both ways. If your motive is personal image building, public relations, fame, or fortune, you might achieve that. But like the loud-mouth CIA operative, you build your personal reputation at the cost of your true calling. If your "good deed" is really just a marketing ploy, then it's really not a good deed, is it?

Monday: Read part 1 of this chapter. How do you set a good example without calling attention to yourself?

Tuesday: Read part 2. Why do you give what you give?

Wednesday: Read part 3. Jesus talked about a prayer closet. Do you have a private time and place for prayer?

Thursday: Finish the chapter. How important is it to be considered "religious"?

Friday: Review the entire chapter. How can you do good deeds and yet remain humble about them?

Saturday: In your prayer today, put aside any of your familiar ways of praying. Just bow before the Father and let him show you how he likes to hear from you.

Sunday: Read Psalm 25:8–10. Humility pleases the Lord. Praise the Lord as the one who lifts up the humble.

The Jewish leaders of Jesus' day promoted three kinds of good deeds: donations to the poor, prayer, and fasting. Here in Matthew 6 Jesus deals with each of them in turn. Jesus had just been calling his followers to live a complete, mature lifestyle, with a righteousness that "surpasses that of the Pharisees and the teachers of the law" (5:20). Now he shows them how.

PART 2

- "So when you give to the needy, do not announce it with trumpets, as the hypocrites do in the synagogues and on the streets, to be honored by men. I tell you the truth, they have received their reward in full. But when you give to the needy, do not let your left hand know what your right hand is doing, so that your giving may be in secret. Then your Father, who sees what is done in secret, will reward you."

Matthew 6:2–4

You may know people who don't just *arrive* at places—they *make entrances*. Every statement is a pronouncement, every move a flourish. Apparently some of the religious leaders of Jesus' day were practicing their faith like that. There were alms boxes in the temple where people made their donations while the crowds milled about. The synagogues also had collection boxes, and there were beggars on the streets. If you wanted, you could make a big deal of your charity. The fanfare Jesus mentions is probably a figure of speech. Most likely the givers had no real trumpets, but they did everything possible to draw attention to themselves.

Perhaps these people thought they were setting a good example for others. Maybe they figured they were doing society a favor by inspiring others to be just as generous as they were. But Jesus sees through all of that and recognizes that they really enjoy the acclaim of their audience. And for the first time, Jesus uses a word that aptly describes these showmen: *hypocrites*. This term has acquired a moral meaning, probably because of Jesus. Now we see hypocrites as those who pretend to be righteous while hiding their own faults, all the while judging others for doing the same things that they do secretly. But in Jesus' time the term had a very specific meaning: *actors*.

Since the days of Alexander the Great, three centuries earlier, the culture of Greece had swept through the Mediterranean world, and Greek drama had come with it. Like most major cities of that region, Jerusalem had a theater where, presumably, actors wearing masks presented classic Greek dramas and comedies. No doubt you've seen this theater symbol, the smiling mask and the frowning mask. These masks often had built-in megaphones—sort of mini-trumpets—so the actors' voices could be heard.

Devout Jews would have resented the encroachment of Greek culture into Jerusalem, so the religious leaders (and probably Jesus) would have avoided this bastion of Gentile entertainment. But the language of the theater crept into the local culture, and it applied perfectly to these showy donors.

They're just playacting, Jesus said. It's like they're wearing masks, displaying a righteousness they don't really have. It's an act. They just want your applause.

And if that's all the reward they want, they can have it. Just don't think they're getting any treasures in heaven. Jesus uses a business term—*paid in full*—to talk about the rewards of these hypocrites. If it's all about applause, then the transaction is complete. But *you*, says Jesus, turning to his disciples, to his listeners, and to us, *you* still have rewards coming. When you give quietly, secretly, out of a true desire to help the needy, you are opening an account that will have eternal payback.

PART 3

● "And when you pray, do not be like the hypocrites, for they love to pray standing in the synagogues and on the street corners to be seen by men. I tell you the truth, they have received their reward in full. But when you pray, go into your room, close the door and pray to your Father, who is unseen. Then your Father, who sees what is done in secret, will reward you.

Matthew 6:5–6

Prayers were said at various times of day, and the most religious Jews had certain prayers prescribed for different times—sunup, noon, sundown, and so on. Standing was the usual posture for prayer, sometimes with arms outstretched or raised. Jesus was probably implying that these leaders intentionally stood around in public places near prayer time so they would have a good-sized audience

By contrast, Jesus said that his followers should go into a private room and pray alone. The Greek word means an "inner room" with no windows, perhaps a storeroom. Many Christians speak of a "prayer closet," taken from the King James Version of this verse. Of course Jesus is using metaphors—you don't have to kneel under the coat hangers. But he is defining prayer as a private exchange with God not for public display.

Note that the Father is "unseen," just like you, if you're shut away in your closet. There, away from observation, you can have a real heart-to-heart.

CROSS REF

Other instruction on giving:
Luke 21:2–4
2 Corinthians 9:6–15

Having critiqued the prayer styles of the Jewish leaders, Jesus turned to the Gentiles and found their "babbling" just as inappropriate. Is it wrong to pray a lot? No. But it's wrong to think you can force God's hand by praying a lot or by saying the right words at the right times. God will not be manipulated like that. He is not a machine on which you need to push the right buttons. He is your Father and he wants to meet your needs. Prayer is not a magic formula. It's an opening of your heart to the Lord who loves you.

PART 4

● "When you fast, do not look somber as the hypocrites do, for they disfigure their faces to show men they are fasting. I tell you the truth, they have received their reward in full. But when you fast, put oil on your head and wash your face, so that it will not be obvious to men that you are fasting, but only to your Father, who is unseen; and your Father, who sees what is done in secret, will reward you."

Matthew 6:16–18

TOUGH QUESTION

If God "knows what you need before you ask him," why pray at all? First, prayer is more than just making requests. Take time to praise, thank, commit, and listen. But elsewhere we are explicitly told to bring God our requests (Phil. 4:6). God wants us to turn to him and trust him. Our requests reflect our faith in him to meet our needs. So talk with him about your needs; just don't try to manipulate him with the words you use or the way you pray.

Jesus occasionally used puns that are hard to translate. Here's one. In verse 16, *disfigure* and *show* are forms of the same word. And remember that he's talking about the *faces* of *masked* actors (hypocrites)! We might translate it like this: "These somber mask-wearers put on *unsightly* faces so the *sight* of their faces will make it clear that they're fasting."

Devout Jews fasted twice a week. Originally, fasting was a sign of repentance, mourning for one's own sin or the sin of the nation. But it had become something very different: a badge of pride. The Pharisees were mourning the nation's sins, but they saw themselves as leading the way toward righteousness. So their fasting was a way of telling everyone else, "*We're* repenting for *your* sin."

Jesus calls for a secret fast. Wash your face and do your hair and try to look happy and well fed. God is the only one who needs to know you're fasting, and he does.

Many Christians don't fast these days, but they may do other religious things to demonstrate how faithful they are. Jesus is telling us, "If it's attention you want, if you want applause for being a great Christian, then that's what you'll get. That and nothing else. But if you want a deeper relationship with God, if you want to please your heavenly Father with the way you live, if you want to do things that will make him smile from one end of eternity to the other, then you need to go undercover. Don't be so obvious about your actions. Enter the secret service.

QUOTE TO NOTE

Christian prayers are measured by weight, and not by length.

Charles Haddon Spurgeon

11

DEAR DAD

PART 1

In the middle of his Sermon on the Mount, Jesus offered a simple pattern for communicating with our Creator. Many Christians recite this "Lord's Prayer" today, in private or as part of public worship services. Sometimes it becomes habitual, a routine utterance of syllables that have lost their meaning. This is sadly ironic, especially when *in the previous verse*, Jesus charged us to avoid the "babbling" of those who "think they will be heard because of their many words." We need to keep digging into the deep meaning of this rich prayer.

● "Our Father in heaven, hallowed be your name."

Matthew 6:9

When people get married, they often face an awkward problem: what to call the in-laws? "Mr. and Mrs." is way too formal. Some go by first names, but that can seem weird. Sometimes they all just have to talk about it: "You're in the family now. You can call us Mom and Dad."

In Jesus' day, the idea of God as Father was rather new. You find the idea in a few Old Testament verses, but it was not a common way of addressing God. Even David, that "man after God's own heart," didn't call him Father. You would expect Jesus, as God's Son, to call him Father, but here he invites his followers to do the same. *You're in the family now. My Father is your Father. Call him Dad.*

Names are important, especially in Scripture. Look at Peter ("the Rock") or Barnabas ("the Encourager") or a number of other Bible folks whose names had special meaning. In God's case, his name was especially precious. He had commanded his people to avoid using his name "in vain," and so faithful Jews found all sorts of ways around saying his name or even writing it. One way was to praise "the Name."

So when we say, "Hallowed be your name," we're saying, "*You*, Lord, are holy."

But what is holiness? For humans, it means being set apart for God's work or following God's commands or being like God, but what does it mean for *God* to be holy? In a way it's a tautology: God is Godlike. That might seem very obvious, but it's important for us to remember. He is God, and there is no other God. He is God, and we're not. It makes perfect sense to start a prayer by acknowledging that God is, in fact, God.

Monday: Read part 1 of this chapter. When you pray, would you ever address God as "Dear Dad"?

Tuesday: Read part 2. Learn more about the kingdom of God from Isaiah 35.

Wednesday: Read part 3. What daily needs could you bring before the Lord?

Thursday: Read part 4. What are some grievances you carry against someone else? Read Colossians 3:13.

Friday: Read part 5. Think about the areas of life where you are most tempted.

Saturday: Do the exercise at the end of the chapter, adding your own words as you pray the Lord's Prayer.

Sunday: Read Psalm 145:14–16 and praise God as your Provider.

CLUES TO USE

When addressing his Father in prayer, Jesus sometimes used the Aramaic word *Abba*. It was a child's endearment, a playful extension of the basic word for father, *Ab*. The most accurate translation would be something like "Daddy." In Galatians 4:6 Paul invites us to use the same term as we pray.

PART 2

● "Your kingdom come, your will be done on earth as it is in heaven."

Matthew 6:10

The kingdom of God was Jesus' favorite subject, and yet, despite all his teaching, it's still hard for us to define. It's as huge as the heavens and as tiny as a mustard seed. It's coming someday in the future, at a time we don't know, and yet it's "near," and even "within you." It's a place of joy and judgment, full of surprises. Some Bible experts talk about the kingdom as "already and not yet." It has already gained a foothold on earth in the work of Jesus, but it has not yet arrived in its heavenly fullness.

> **GREEK PEEK**
>
> The word *hallowed* isn't used much nowadays. But the Greek word in the original text wasn't common either. It's the verb form of the adjective *holy*. To get a more modern-sounding equivalent, we might coin the term *holified*. May God's name be holified!

So when we pray, "Your kingdom come," we are trying to pull some of the future into the present. We look forward to an existence without sickness and sorrow, so we pray for healing *now*. We look forward to a time when lions will lie down with lambs, and so we pray for peace *now*. God may have different timing in mind, or different details, but we can't go wrong when we pray for the sort of thing God has already promised.

The simplest definition of God's kingdom sounds very obvious, but it opens up this prayer for us: *The kingdom of God is wherever God reigns as King.* And so, in a very real way, we can answer this prayer ourselves. When we pray for God's kingdom to come, we are acknowledging that he is King in our hearts. When we pray for his will to be done, we are saying that we want what he wants and are committing ourselves to do his will in our lives.

PART 3

● "Give us today our daily bread."

Matthew 6:11

In these days of savings accounts and 401(k)s, many Christians don't have to trust God so much for daily bread. They already know where tomorrow's bread is coming from, or at least how they'll pay for it. But of course many of us do go through tough times financially, when we're not sure where we'll find the money for the next bill. These times are emotionally difficult, but Jesus says they can be good for us spiritually. "Blessed are you who are poor," Jesus said (Luke 6:20), with the idea that the poor have the opportunity to trust God for their daily needs.

> **CROSS REF**
>
> In Exodus 16 we see the wandering Israelites receiving their daily bread, manna from heaven. By the way, the Hebrew word *manna* means "What is it?" Well, if you woke up and saw bread covering the ground, what would you call it?

Of course we have a variety of daily needs besides food. We can also ask God for daily safety, daily companionship, or daily sanity. James cautioned us against assuming that our lives will go according to our own plans. "Why, you do not even know what will happen tomorrow" (James 4:14). Faithful followers of Jesus receive each day, each moment, as a gift from the Father.

PART 4

● "Forgive us our debts, as we also have forgiven our debtors."

Matthew 6:12

If Jesus' favorite subject was the kingdom of God, what was his second favorite? Money. Seriously. Jesus spoke about money more than anything else except the kingdom. You might not expect that from a poor, traveling preacher, but he knew his listeners, and he used the stuff of their lives to communicate his truth.

Debts is a business term, obviously. More than once, Jesus referred to our spiritual standing with the Father in economic language. In fact this line of the Lord's Prayer neatly encapsulates a parable Jesus told about a servant who was forgiven a huge debt but then demanded payment of a small debt from someone else (18:23–35). "You wicked servant," said the master,

DARE TO
COMPARE

In Luke's version, this prayer uses the word *sins* or *trespasses* instead of *debts*. It's not surprising that Matthew, the old tax collector, would prefer the business word. Even today, some churches say, "Forgive us our debts," in the Lord's Prayer while others say, "Forgive us our trespasses."

"I canceled all that debt of yours because you begged me to. Shouldn't you have had mercy on your fellow servant just as I had on you?" (vv. 32–33).

Imagine your credit card company erasing your balance. Or what if the bank burned your mortgage? Maybe it's your college debts that get forgiven. In any case, you are free and clear! That's the kind of forgiveness we seek from the Father. Our sins have run up huge moral debts, but he offers to wipe the slate clean, to remove our transgressions "as far as the east is from the west" (Ps. 103:12). Hallelujah!

But then there's that matter of forgiving our own debtors. Is Jesus saying that we won't be forgiven if we don't forgive others? It sure seems like that (and Matthew 6:14–15 spells it out even more clearly), but our willingness to forgive is not some way of "earning" God's forgiveness. It's a package deal: If you truly seek forgiveness, if repentance is melting your heart, then, as a matter of course, you will offer the same forgiveness to those who have wronged you. Forgiven people forgive others.

PART 5

- "And lead us not into temptation, but deliver us from the evil one."

Matthew 6:13

We all go through times of temptation and testing. God doesn't promise that our path will never lead through temptation, and that's why we need deliverance. In his temptation in the wilderness, Jesus was "delivered" as he used God's Word, God's wisdom, and God's own nourishment to resist the clever jabs of the evil one. And because he fought temptation and won, we can rely on his power to do the same. "God is faithful," we are assured. "He will not let you be tempted beyond what you can bear. But when you are tempted, he will also provide a way out so that you can stand up under it" (1 Cor. 10:13).

James distinguishes between "testing" (which builds our character) and "tempting" (which leads us into sin). Temptation arises from our own evil desires, he says, not from God (James 1:13–15). So we can't say, "I prayed that he wouldn't lead me into temptation, and he did anyway, so my sin is his fault." No, even when we are tempted, he provides a way out. It's up to us to take it.

As with other parts of the Lord's Prayer, we are called to participate in the answer. We let God's will be done in our own lives, and we forgive as we are forgiven. Here we must rely on the strength God offers to avoid and resist temptation. The gambling addict who prays this prayer shouldn't hang around Las Vegas.

As you take one more look at the Lord's Prayer, try using it as a fill-in-the-blank template.

"Our Father in heaven, hallowed be your name." [Fill in other divine qualities you want to praise him for.]

"Your kingdom come, your will be done on earth as it is in heaven." [Fill in specific prayer requests for healing, peace, witness, and so on and listen for God's guidance. How might he want you to accomplish his will?]

"Give us today our daily bread." [Fill in specific needs you have today and in the immediate future.]

"Forgive us our debts, as we also have forgiven our debtors." [Fill in your confession of specific sins and promise to forgive specific people who have hurt you.]

"And lead us not into temptation, but deliver us from the evil one." [Fill in specific struggles that you face spiritually.]

12
ALL THESE THINGS

Darcy never cared much about football. But then a friend talked her into joining the office football pool just for laughs. She'd pay a dollar each week and pick certain teams to win. At first, she just chose the team names that sounded stronger—the Bears would surely defeat the Dolphins—but then she started studying up on the game. Soon she found herself glued to the TV every Sunday afternoon, watching not only the game on the screen but also the scores from around the league. A year earlier she didn't know a TD from a DVD, but now she had money riding on these games, and so she cared deeply.

You could say her treasure was invested in the office football pool, and so that's where her heart was too. Jesus talked about that sort of thing in his Sermon on the Mount, making a number of pithy comments about money and possessions. He wasn't scolding people for having too much. That probably wasn't an issue for his hearers, who were mostly working-class folks from Galilee. But Jesus zeroed in on the main issue—not what they had but what they *wanted*. He challenged their value system.

● "Do not store up for yourselves treasures on earth, where moth and rust destroy, and where thieves break in and steal. But store up for yourselves treasures in heaven, where moth and rust do not destroy, and where thieves do not break in and steal. For where your treasure is, there your heart will be also."

Matthew 6:19–21

Jesus once told a very strange parable about a dishonest business manager (Luke 16:1–8). It seems this man got a pink slip from his employer for "wasting possessions," but apparently he had a few days after that to wrap things up at the office. Shrewdly, he devised a plan to help him get his next job.

One by one, he met with his employer's debtors and reduced their indebtedness. Why? Because he hoped that later one of them would hire him.

Now here's the strange part. When the employer learned what this business manager was doing, he commended him "because he had acted shrewdly."

It's really quite an accurate picture of our earthly existence. Look at it this way. Our boss is the world itself. Our job is just living on this earth. But we've been given notice; we won't be here forever. At some point in the future, we will have to leave this world. Whatever time we have left in our lives, we're just wrapping things up. So wouldn't it make sense to use our earthly resources—whatever authority, ability, or fortune we now have—to invest in our future?

Monday: Read part 1 of this chapter. In what ways are you storing up treasures in heaven?

Tuesday: Read part 2. So why not try to live the life described in this part of the lesson? Give it a try for even a day or two.

Wednesday: Read part 3. Spend time reviewing the Mary and Martha story (Luke 10:38–42). Which are you, a Mary or a Martha?

Thursday: Read part 4. How could you spend your mental energy if you stopped worrying?

Friday: Make plans to talk with your family (or a friend) this weekend about God and money.

Saturday: When you pray today, ask God for help in fulfilling the Scriptures in Matthew 6 that you have just studied.

Sunday: Read Psalm 34:1–10 and praise God as the One who satisfies.

GREEK PEEK

The word for *rust* in Matthew 6:19 really means "eating." Translators assume that one's earthly treasure gets eaten away by rust.

How do we do that? By storing our treasures in heaven. And what does that mean? Well, in Luke's account of a similar teaching, Jesus spells it out: "Sell your possessions and give to the poor." In that way, he says, you will "provide . . . a treasure in heaven that will not be exhausted, where no thief comes near and no moth destroys" (12:33).

Jesus told another story of a rich man who tore down his barns and built bigger ones (12:16–20). That man was foolish, Jesus said, because one day all his wealth would be worthless. You can't take it with you. The question is, How can we use our current resources to invest in eternity?

PART 2

- "No one can serve two masters. Either he will hate the one and love the other, or he will be devoted to the one and despise the other. You cannot serve both God and Money."

Matthew 6:24

The managing editor was racing to get the publication finished by the deadline, and she was going a little crazy. Whenever she finished working on an article, she emailed it to her senior editor and the company president. Both of them would suggest changes, but they didn't always agree. Finally, she sent a desperate message to both of her bosses: "I can't do this anymore. When one of you makes a change, the other one changes it back. I can't keep you both happy! You two figure out who I'm supposed to listen to and tell me, please!!!"

It doesn't take a business expert to know that you can't have two bosses. Jesus said as much. In fact Jesus' statement is much stronger than our editorial office scenario. He was literally saying, "No one can *be a slave of* two masters."

Yet we still keep trying to have it both ways. Money is our master in many areas of life.

Recently, reality TV shows have asked the question, "What will people do for money?" The answer seems to be, "Just about anything." We might laugh at such reckless greed on TV, but we routinely serve money in our own lives. How many Christian parents spend so much time earning money that they hardly ever see their kids? How many of us take jobs or choose careers merely because the money's good? How many get caught up in the race to acquire the latest techno-gadgets, the nicest car, or the bigger house?

We have learned to rationalize quite well. "Don't you see? I'm providing *for* my family, which is why I don't have time to see them." "I earn more so I can give more to the church." Or "Doesn't God want his children to be successful?" But those are smoke screens for the plain reality that we are enslaved to money and the things money can buy.

What's the answer? A new way of seeing, says Jesus. Some people see the world around them and look for opportunities to get ahead, to make more money, to take advantage of others. But what happens when our single-minded focus is on loving others, meeting needs, and honoring God? That clear vision fills our lives with light.

So what would happen if you lived like that for a month, a week, even a day? Why not give it a try?

PART 3

● "Therefore I tell you, do not worry about your life, what you will eat or drink; or about your body, what you will wear. Is not life more important than food, and the body more important than clothes? Look at the birds of the air; they do not sow or reap or store away in barns, and yet your heavenly Father feeds them. Are you not much more valuable than they? Who of you by worrying can add a single hour to his life?"

Matthew 6:25–27

Jesus taught his disciples to pray, "Give us today our daily bread." Now he's asking them to believe that God will do just that. Here again, he's talking about a state of mind, a single-eyed focus on God and his priorities. Don't let your mind race around with anxiety over the basic provisions of life. It won't do you any good.

CROSS REF

Philippians 4:6—"Don't worry about anything; instead, pray about everything" (NLT).

We see a picture of this in Jesus' visit to the home of Mary and Martha. While Mary kept her focus on Jesus, listening as he taught, Martha bustled about the kitchen, fussing with the provisions for Jesus and his disciples (Luke 10:38–42). When she asked Jesus to send her sister in to help, he calmed her down. "Martha, Martha, you are worried and upset about many things." *Worry*—the same word that we see in the Sermon on the Mount. No doubt Jesus was grateful when Martha finally served the food, but he used this incident to teach something important. Martha was distracted by all the preparations that had to be made, while Mary was focused on Jesus. It was Mary, he said, who made the better choice.

In the same way, we can easily be distracted by the everyday stuff of life—job, family, home, bills. Aren't these things important? To a degree, yes, but there's something far more important—our trust in God.

PART 4

● "But seek first his kingdom and his righteousness, and all these things will be given to you as well."

Matthew 6:33

What if you took all the mental energy you spend worrying, and you used that energy to devise new ways to advance God's kingdom on earth? How would that change your life? Think about it. Jesus had just mentioned how the "Gentiles"—he meant those who didn't know God—spent a lot of effort "seeking" the best food and clothing. But God's own children should seek something else: his kingdom and his righteousness.

Let's say you're watching *Wheel of Fortune* some evening, and a screaming contestant wins a new car. As she is handed the keys, she says, "It has to have a cup holder! Does this car have a cup holder?"

"Yes, of course it has a cup holder," the host responds. "Just take the car, and the cup holder will be given to you as well."

Who worries about a cup holder when they've just won a new car? And why worry about basic provisions when God promises a kind of life beyond anything we could ever imagine?

QUOTE TO NOTE

To break the habit of worry, you must develop the habit of prayer.

Charles Stanley

13

PEARLS

● "Do not judge, or you too will be judged."

Matthew 7:1

Andy was maybe seven or eight years old. His kid sister, Kathy, was four. The family had always prayed before meals, and the children had learned three very basic rules of prayer: Bow your head; close your eyes; fold your hands. But one day, after the lunchtime prayer, Andy accused his sister: "Kathy wasn't closing her eyes when we prayed!"

No doubt he was expecting that Kathy would get some sort of discipline or scolding for her misbehavior. But Mom wisely turned to Andy and asked, "How do you know?"

So at that tender age, Andy learned the lesson that Jesus was teaching at the beginning of Matthew 7. Like those ancient Pharisees, Andy was quick to judge someone else for failing to observe a certain code of conduct. But how could he know her eyes were open unless his were too? Judged by the same standard, he was just as guilty. His judgment came right back at him.

Nowadays Matthew 7:1 might be the best-known Bible verse among non-Christians. You hear it launched on TV talk shows whenever anyone dares to call any behavior immoral. "Do not judge, lest you be judged!" announces the accused offender with a so-there attitude. "Doesn't your Bible say you shouldn't judge?" The inference is that no one has a right to call anything right or wrong because we all do bad things. Like so many dangerous ideas, that interpretation is half right.

It's true that we all do bad things. Even though we may be innocent of a particular sin, there are certainly other sins with which we struggle. You might attack someone else for sexual immorality, but your own greed or hatred is no less sinful, biblically speaking. As Jesus said when men picked up stones to throw at an adulteress, "Let anyone among you who is without sin be the first to throw a stone at her" (John 8:7 NRSV). None of us meets that standard.

Monday: Read part 1 of this chapter. Think back a few weeks and search for times when you have been judgmental.

Tuesday: Read part 2. What are your "pearls" in your opinion? What "dogs" or "pigs" should you watch out for?

Wednesday: Read part 3. What free thing are you trying to pay for?

Thursday: Have you ever asked God for something you have not received? What do you think went wrong?

Friday: Is there any difference between asking, seeking, and knocking, or are they three words for the same idea?

Saturday: In your prayer today, ask God to supply all your need, according to his riches in Christ Jesus (Phil. 4:19).

Sunday: Read Hebrews 13:15–16. Praise God today with your words and your deeds.

FUN STUFF

Don't miss the comedy sketch in Matthew 7:3–5. Jesus must have had the crowd in stitches as he told the one about the guy with a plank in his eye trying to do eye surgery on his friend.

Jesus says that we will all be judged by the same measuring stick we use to judge others. Dish it out, and you'll have to take it too.

So do we have any right to identify sin when we see it? Does "Do not judge" mean we give up all sense of right and wrong?

No way. We are called to seek God's kingdom and his righteousness above all else. We hunger and thirst for righteousness. We long to live in the wholeness of a right relationship with God, and we want others to know the joy of abundant life as well. We mourn the damage that sin does in people's lives. So when we

GREEK PEEK

The word *judge* is used to express a variety of meanings: determine, call into question, damn, conclude, avenge, condemn, decree, esteem, go to law, think, conclude.

see bad behavior messing up our world, we have a right to say so, but we must bathe our attitude in humility. We are passionate about pleasing God, yet we are mourners not scolders, mercy-givers not judges. For as soon as we accuse others, we know we are indicting ourselves as well.

Jesus said to Nicodemus, "God did not send his Son into the world to condemn the world, but to save the world through him" (John 3:17). As we follow our Master, it's not our job to condemn the world but to participate in its saving.

PART 2

● "Do not give dogs what is sacred; do not throw your pearls to pigs. If you do, they may trample them under their feet, and then turn and tear you to pieces."

Matthew 7:6

Jesus excelled at word pictures. He used the stuff of life—fields and flocks and coins and creatures—to make his points about God's kingdom. Here's a picture that's very vivid. Pearls are tossed to wild boars, which fail to appreciate their value and instead attack the tosser. It's a clear, dramatic image—but what on earth does it mean?

Some have suggested that Jesus was warning his followers not to share his teaching with the Gentiles. But this wouldn't fit with the rest of Jesus' teaching, especially in Matthew's Gospel, which has a strong theme of outreach to the Gentiles.

Is it possible that Jesus was correcting a possible misunderstanding from his "Do not judge" teaching? In case someone thought he might be removing all standards of behavior, he might have been saying, *No, there are wicked "dogs" and "pigs" who can still do damage by ignoring righteousness and promoting sin. Be merciful, but also be discerning. Don't judge, but don't get torn to pieces either.*

Or is Jesus advising us to avoid the path of temptation? Notice that ever since the Lord's Prayer, Jesus has been offering commentary on that prayer, phrase by phrase. "Do not judge" echoes the need to forgive our debtors. Could this pearls-to-pigs verse have anything to do with "Lead us not into temptation"? Look out for those evil "dogs" and "pigs" who will trample on your special relationship with God. We should still be salt and light in this world, but we must be careful to take care of the gem of faith within us.

PART 3

● "Ask and it will be given to you; seek and you will find; knock and the door will be opened to you."

Matthew 7:7

Here we find the heart of Jesus' message of grace. In this marvelous sermon, Jesus has surprised us and challenged us. He took God's kingdom out of the hands of the high and mighty and placed it squarely in the embrace of the humble and struggling. He announced that God's righteousness is not a matter of keeping rules but of seeking his heart. He taught us to pray in humble faith, committing ourselves to his kingdom and his will, trusting in his daily provision, and extending mercy to others because we know we need much mercy ourselves. And in our day-to-day struggles, we rely on his protection from overwhelming temptation and his powerful deliverance from the grip of evil.

And how do we get this protection, this power, this righteousness, this daily bread? We ask for it.

It's hard to ask. Most guys will drive ten miles the wrong way before they stop to ask for directions. We learn to be self-sufficient. That's a sign of strength, of adulthood. We don't want to rely on the kindness of others. It embarrasses us to bum a few bucks from a friend or have someone else pick up the tab at dinner. We want to pay our way.

When you ask for help, it means you've come to the end of your own power. You cannot succeed on your own, and

CROSS REF

Some other verses about asking:
John 15:16
1 John 5:14–15

so you reach out to someone stronger, someone richer, someone who's able to provide what you need. It is a humbling thing, to ask.

And that's exactly where God wants us.

In the following verses, Jesus compares God to a human father whose child asks for fish and bread. Does the father provide a snake or a rock instead? No! Parents provide for their children, because children can't provide for themselves. And if human fathers do that, our heavenly Father will do that even more, making sure we have what we need. We just have to ask.

The story is told of an actress in the touring company of a famous play. The troupe was coming through a town where an old college friend of hers lived, so the actress invited her friend to the show. The friend never came, but she called as the troupe was leaving town.

"I tried to get a ticket," the friend explained, "but it was nearly sold out, and the only tickets they had left were way up front and very expensive. I was trying to work some overtime so I could afford a ticket, but I still couldn't. Sorry."

The actress replied, "There was a complimentary ticket waiting for you, right down front. It was totally free. All you had to do was ask."

People keep trying to work hard to pay for tickets to God's kingdom. But Jesus says it's free. All you have to do is ask.

14

ROCK SOLID

Years ago a clever TV commercial was pushing the services of a Wall Street brokerage firm. It showed a group of business people having lunch at a busy restaurant. Amid the chatter and glass clinking, we heard one man ask something about investments. "Well, my broker is E. F. Hutton," said another, "and E. F. Hutton says . . ."

Suddenly, silence. The busy restaurant came to a halt. You could hear a toothpick drop. All the other diners were leaning, craning to hear what the broker was saying about the market. The tag line: *When E. F. Hutton talks, people listen.*

That's sort of the effect Jesus had in the Sermon on the Mount. Matthew says, "The crowds were amazed at his teaching, because he taught as one who had authority" (7:28–29). Other teachers might cite the teaching of previous rabbis or name-drop some of their personal credentials, but Jesus was announcing a new way to understand God and his kingdom. He had no need for the approval of other teachers, and he felt no compulsion to prove himself to the crowd. He simply spoke the truth.

As he finished this marvelous address, he showed that he realized his message might be hard to accept.

● "Enter through the narrow gate. For wide is the gate and broad is the road that leads to destruction, and many enter

Monday: Read part 1 of this chapter. Why do you think the gate in Matthew 7:14 is small and narrow? Does it seem scary to walk this lonely road? Are you really alone?

Tuesday: Read part 2. What are we supposed to watch out for?

Wednesday: Read part 3. Who is like the wise builder who builds on rock? Why isn't it good enough just to hear Jesus' words?

Thursday: Do you see the fruit of the Spirit (Gal. 5:22–23) in your life? How can you produce more of it?

Friday: How many songs or Bible verses can you think of having to do with Jesus as "the rock"? Why is this such a popular theme?

Saturday: As you pray today, ask for help in traveling that narrow road and for wisdom to discern false prophets.

Sunday: Exalt the Lord as you read David's song of praise in 2 Samuel 22:47–51.

through it. But small is the gate and narrow the road that leads to life, and only a few find it."

Matthew 7:13–14

The few. The proud. The Marines.

As long as we're talking about TV commercials, there's one that counted on the appeal of the narrow gate. Not everyone can be a Marine, but *maybe* you can be good enough.

The narrow-gate idea is woven through Scripture. The Old Testament speaks of God preserving a remnant of the Jewish people. And in that tradition, Jesus describes the eight-lane expressway headed to destruction. He urges his followers to take the first exit and find the narrow footpath that leads to life. That may not be easy, but it's worth it.

At first glance, it might seem that Jesus is referring to the wantonly sinful behavior of the masses. When the world is going to hell in a handbasket, you must be disciplined enough to follow God's rules. The few. The proud. The righteous.

But think about what Jesus has been saying for two and a half chapters. *Blessed are the poor in spirit. Don't put your religion on display. Forgive as you are forgiven. Do not judge.* He certainly wasn't telling people to be more religious. The religious folks embodied everything he was opposing. He was calling people into a radically honest, humble, struggling relationship with the Father. Self-avowed sinners who trusted in his grace would populate God's kingdom.

In Jesus' day, a city gate wasn't just a passageway. It was a meeting place. It was the public hall where business was conducted. It was where the E. F. Huttons of that time gathered. A big city like Jerusalem would have wide gates, and that area would be bustling with commerce.

For many people, then and now, religion is a business, and that doesn't necessarily have anything to do with money. We're talking about transactions of good deeds for divine blessings, holy activity exchanged for good reputations. That sounds great, but it's not the way Jesus operated. God's economy runs by grace. He gives; we receive. We ask; he provides. We have no currency to pay with, and he blesses us anyway. That's hard for a lot of people to grasp, but it's the entry point to the kingdom.

PART 2

● "Watch out for false prophets. They come to you in sheep's clothing, but inwardly they are ferocious wolves. By their fruit you will recognize them."

Matthew 7:15–16

We sometimes think prophecy is just about prediction. Not necessarily. *Sometimes* God has things to say about the future; but often he's just talking about now. A prophet is anyone who delivers God's messages. A *false* prophet, obviously, is one who claims to bring a message from God but is actually just making it up.

The Old Testament is full of pronouncements against false prophets. Jeremiah complained: "Do not listen to what the prophets are prophesying to you; they fill you with false hopes. They speak visions from their own minds, not from the mouth of the LORD. . . . Which of them has stood in the council of the LORD to see or to hear his word?" (Jer. 23:16, 18).

The New Testament also picks up these cautions. Paul warned about future times

IN THE MIRROR

Robert Frost wrote about "two roads" that "diverged in a yellow wood." He "took the one less traveled by and that has made all the difference." Have you made such a choice in your life? What difference has it made?

when people would reject sound doctrine. "Instead, to suit their own desires, they will gather around them a great number of teachers to say what their itching ears want to hear" (2 Tim. 4:3). Just take a whiff of the smorgasbord of spiritual teaching available today and you'll realize that Paul's prediction has come true.

Is that what Jesus is talking about? Perhaps in part. But he seems to be referring to some who appear to be Christians—they try to fit in with the flock—and yet they're actually "ferocious," wanting to destroy the flock's faith. That's a pretty fair description of the false teachers who plagued Paul as he carried the gospel around the Mediterranean. It's not enough to trust in Jesus, they said; you must also follow the Jewish law. This was damaging to people's faith and divisive in many churches. So the first false prophets the church had to deal with were, like the "hypocrites" of Matthew 6, legalists. They were pushing their form of adherence to the law while denying the power of simple trust.

"By their fruit you will recognize them," says Jesus. On one occasion John the Baptist challenged the religious leaders to "produce fruit in keeping with repentance" (Matt. 3:8). It wasn't enough to show up at the river and watch the baptisms. They needed to demonstrate actions and attitudes that showed they were serious.

Paul had something to say about fruit too. Take a look at the "fruit of the Spirit" in Galatians 5:22–23: love, joy, peace, and so on. These are *attitudes* that are reflected in behavior. That's the sort of fruit Jesus wanted his disciples to seek.

PART 3

● "Therefore everyone who hears these words of mine and puts them into practice is like a wise man who built his house on the rock. The rain came down, the streams rose, and the winds blew and beat against that house; yet it did not fall, because it had its foundation on the rock."

Matthew 7:24–25

It was a beautiful house in a nice section of the city. The owners had saved all their lives to buy it and took great care of it once they moved in. But then the ground gave way. To the owners' horror, the house was built on a sinkhole. After one especially torrential downpour, the

> **CROSS REF**
>
> Read more about firm foundations:
> 1 Corinthians 3:11–14
> James 1:22–25

house simply caved in. The TV reporters swarmed to show the damage and to interview the owners, who were still in shock.

It's important to have a firm foundation, and Jesus used this same image—the house crashing down—to teach his followers to base their lives on his words.

Perhaps you know people whose lives seem groundless. They don't believe in anything. They have no root values. They flit here and there, influenced by public opinion. James said such a person is "like a wave of the sea, blown and tossed by the wind" (James 1:6).

Others have a foundation for their lives, but the foundation isn't solid. Maybe they're trusting in money to support them. Or maybe they think life is all about having a good time. These are foundations of sand. When trouble comes, these lives will crumble into sinkholes.

But the words of Jesus provide a rock-solid foundation for our lives. We can anchor ourselves on his teaching. Questions will arise that puzzle us, but we can seek answers from the Master. Problems will occur that shake our faith, but we can rest on Jesus' assurance that God loves us and provides for us.

QUOTE TO NOTE

Christians are not permitted to be judges, only fruit inspectors.

Calvin Miller

15

THE OUTCAST OF NAZARETH

Towns and cities develop reputations, sometimes justified, sometimes not. Chicago, for instance, got a reputation partly because of gangster Al Capone and the bootlegging of the Prohibition era, and the city has been trying to live that down ever since. Other cities have developed other reputations. Las Vegas, San Francisco, Paris, New Orleans, Nashville, and Milwaukee all have auras associated with their names.

The hometown of Jesus was Nazareth in the province of Galilee—and Nazareth had an aura about it. In fact the whole region of Galilee had a reputation. Isaiah called it "Galilee of the Gentiles" because of all the foreigners who settled there (Isa. 9:1). Only about two hundred years before Jesus' birth was it recolonized by Jews. Galileans spoke with an accent and were generally looked down on by the "true" Jews of the southern province of Judea.

But Galileans themselves looked down on Nazareth. Another Galilean, Nathanael, was invited to become a follower of Jesus, but when he heard where Jesus was from, he exclaimed, "Nazareth! Can anything good come from there?" (John 1:46).

Why was Nazareth so despised? No one knows for sure. Set in a basin surrounded on three sides by hills, the town was considered isolated and aloof. Nearby ran three major trade routes, giving it access to the major cities. Yet Nazareth was considered a Podunk town. It wasn't mentioned in the Old Testament because it didn't exist then, and the Jewish historian Josephus, who wrote shortly after the time of Christ, didn't mention it either. No doubt we wouldn't be aware of Nazareth, except for the fact that Jesus grew up there.

Then the hometown boy became famous as a preacher, teacher, and healer in the bustling town of Capernaum, twenty miles northeast. The people of Nazareth had heard that he had even done miracles. Now he was returning to Nazareth as a visiting rabbi. Naturally, he was invited to teach in the synagogue.

As was the custom, Jesus stood to read the text. Usually the synagogue followed a schedule of 155 defined lessons to complete the reading of the Torah in three years. After the reading in the Old Testament law, there was a reading from the prophets. On this Sabbath day in Nazareth, the scroll of Isaiah was handed to Jesus, and he read the assigned text:

Monday: Read the "W's" and then Luke 4:14–30. Imagine yourself inside that scene.

Tuesday: Read part 1 of this chapter.

Wednesday: Read part 2. What is Jesus telling these people?

Thursday: Read part 3. Are you stuck with certain images of Jesus? Do you need a fresh look?

Friday: What do you think the poor, the captives, the blind, and the downtrodden have in common? Read Luke 6:20–22 and 14:12–14.

Saturday: Do you consider yourself spiritually needy? You can settle that with Jesus right now. Talk to him. Ask him to guide you in your next steps to belief and enrichment.

Sunday: Read John 4:23–24 and worship the Lord today in spirit and truth.

W'S

Where: Jesus was speaking in his hometown synagogue.

When: The beginning of his public ministry.

What: His reading of Isaiah 61 became a mission statement. By announcing its fulfillment, he was subtly claiming to be the Messiah.

Who: These were people he had grown up with, making it that much harder for them to accept him.

● "The Spirit of the Lord is on me, because he has anointed me to preach good news to the poor."

Luke 4:18

89

DARE TO COMPARE

Compare Luke 4:18 with Luke 1:51–53. How does the mission Jesus claimed line up with Mary's prophetic song?

CHECKOUT COUNTER

When John the Baptist had questions about who Jesus really was, how did Jesus answer him? Check it out in Luke 7:22.

After Jesus had read the entire passage from Isaiah 61, he gave the scroll back to the synagogue attendant and sat down to give his commentary on the passage. "The eyes of everyone in the synagogue were fastened on him," one version says. Another says, "Everyone's eyes were riveted on him." The people knew him well. He had lived among them until only a year or so earlier. This was a well-known passage about the coming of the Messiah. Everyone was familiar with it. How would the hometown boy explain it?

Jesus simply said, "Today this scripture is fulfilled in your hearing" (Luke 4:21).

Apparently, it took awhile for the impact to sink in. Since the synagogue service was often informal and conversational, the congregation buzzed with comments. Perhaps some were whispering, *Look how he's grown!* or *Mary must be very proud of him,* but gradually it dawned on the people what Jesus was saying. He was claiming to be the Messiah. Now their mood shifted from hometown pride and amazement to blatant skepticism.

They had known him when he was running around playing tag in Joseph's carpenter shop. How could that rambunctious kid now claim to be the Messiah?

We have heard that you have done miracles in Capernaum, but we haven't seen any, they challenged him. *Show us your stuff.* Skepticism was now turning to hostility.

PART 2

● "I tell you the truth . . . no prophet is accepted in his hometown."

Luke 4:24

Jesus responded to the challenge of the people of Nazareth with this simple statement. Though it seems simple, it further angered the townspeople. It's hard for people to see greatness in those closest to them. A family member may achieve accolades for his achievements in business, but those closest to him know him as "just plain Joe."

Then Jesus went on. He told how the prophet Elijah had sought lodging from a widow in the pagan town of Zarephath, and how the prophet Elisha had healed the Gentile general Naaman. In other words, pagan Gentiles responded better to the prophets than God-fearing Jews.

> **IN THE MIRROR**
>
> Do you sometimes feel that the people in Jesus' time should have known more? Put yourself in their shoes. Would you have understood and believed that he was the Messiah, or would you have been part of the mob who wanted to throw him over a cliff?

Only twenty years earlier in Sepphoris, a half dozen miles from Nazareth, the Romans had struck down an uprising. It was a bloody massacre that the Nazarenes would never forget or forgive. Was Jesus saying that those bloody Roman soldiers were as good as they were?

Local boy or not, those were fighting words. The people were furious. They dragged him out to the ridge that surrounded Nazareth. Enraged, they intended to throw him over the cliff. Favorite son one minute; dangerous heretic the next.

Somehow, and the Bible doesn't explain how, Jesus "walked right through the crowd and went on his way" (v. 30).

PART 3

How could the people who knew Jesus best totally miss out on who he was? It makes you wonder whether we Christians can make the same sort of mistake. Does Jesus become so familiar to us that we stop learning more about who he is? Do we get a certain image of him set in stone and refuse to let him reveal anything different?

Maybe, like the Nazarenes, we need to take a fresh look at him. Jesus was announcing that his mission involved freedom for the prisoners, sight for the blind, releasing of the oppressed, and good news for the poor. He was focusing on the very people most of us wouldn't want attending our churches. That's right.

We tend to throw the doors open for beautiful people, the affluent, and the talented, while secretly hoping that the neediest folks move on to the church down the street. That's the exact opposite of Jesus' policies. As the apostle Paul wrote, God has chosen the foolish, the weak, and the lowly "so that no one may boast before him" (see 1 Cor. 1:27–29). How well do our churches reflect God's choices?

We are often tempted to mute the gospel message to make it more acceptable to people. Jesus didn't. He must have known the reaction he would receive, yet in front of his neighbors he announced himself as the fulfillment of prophecy. Couldn't he have warmed up the congregation with a few miracles first? That would certainly have given him a more sympathetic hearing. But he didn't dodge the issue. He hit it head-on.

Today the popular culture maintains that there are many different ways to God and that we can pick and choose our religion, cafeteria-style. It's okay to pick Christianity, according to this reasoning, as long as you acknowledge that every other faith is also a legitimate way to find God. But that's not how Jesus tackled the matter. In front of his neighbors, he announced his divinely appointed mission, and elsewhere he boldly said that no one could come to the Father except through him (John 14:6).

16
SEZ WHO?

Sez who?

That's the schoolyard taunt. The response is usually, "The teacher said so," or "My dad said so," or, if you are bigger than the taunter, "*I* said so."

It's important to be able to back up your words. When Muhammad Ali was boxing, he often boasted, "I'm the greatest." Then he went into the ring and whupped his challengers. Though he made fantastic claims, he was able to back up his words.

On one Sabbath day, after a feast in Jerusalem, Jesus healed a man who had been an invalid for thirty-eight years. Doing anything at all on the Sabbath, including a miraculous healing, was a no-no to the orthodox religionists, but when Jesus told the man, *Pick up your mat and walk,* that really sent them through the roof.

Sez who? they asked.

My Father said so, replied Jesus, but he said more than that. He said that he was doing the same work his heavenly Father was doing. They worked together. It was a Father-Son team. He identified himself completely with the Father.

Then he made this amazing statement:

● "I tell you the truth, whoever hears my word and believes him who sent me has eternal life and will not be condemned;

93

Monday: Read part 1 of this chapter. What four witnesses did Jesus cite?

Tuesday: Read part 2. How do you approach Scripture?

Wednesday: Read part 3. How does this week's study improve your relationship with God?

Thursday: What do you think your neighbors think about the Bible? How would you explain to them what you think?

Friday: What can you do differently to make sure you meet Jesus in Scripture?

Saturday: Reread John 5 today and ask God to give you a fuller sense of him as you read.

Sunday: Read Psalm 119:105–12. Praise God for being the great Communicator.

he has crossed over from death to life."

John 5:24

Sez who?

It was right for them to challenge such a remarkable statement. You don't want crackpots running around loose. Eternal life? Free from condemnation? Oh, come on, Jesus, get real!

Yes, it was an amazing statement for several reasons: First, Jesus was totally identifying himself with God the Father. Second, he claimed to be the giver of eternal life. Third, he declared that you could get eternal life simply by believing, in other words, by faith. And fourth, eternal life can be yours right now. You don't have to wait until you die. Eternal life for you can start right now.

In our sports lingo, we speak of football players crossing the goal line and of baseball players crossing the plate. Jesus says that those who hear his words and believe have already crossed the goal line, even though the game is not over yet. They have crossed over from death to life.

Sez who?

Jesus was ready for the cross-examination. Back in the Old Testament, in the book of Deuteronomy, Moses set up a judicial system that required two or three witnesses to verify a claim (Deut. 19:15). So Jesus spoke of four witnesses who could come to his defense (John 5:31–40).

First witness: the supreme Judge of the universe, God the Father himself. Jesus

W'S

Who: Jesus was obviously speaking to Bible experts. The Jews had a class of scribes devoted to the copying and preservation of God's law, and the Pharisees taught the law, according to their narrow interpretation.

When: At one of the three major feast times: Passover (early spring), Pentecost (late spring), or Tabernacles (fall). Jesus might be about a year into his public ministry.

Where: Jesus was visiting Jerusalem for the feast.

may have been recalling his baptism, when a voice came from heaven declaring, "This is my Son, whom I love; with him I am well pleased" (Matt. 3:17).

Second witness: John the Baptist. John called Jesus "the Lamb of God, who takes away the sin of the world" (John 1:29).

Third witness: Jesus' mighty works. John never did any miracles. He preached and he baptized, but he did no miracles. But now the accusers of Jesus were standing with a man in their midst who had been miraculously healed after being crippled for thirty-eight years.

Fourth witness: the Scriptures.

PART 2

● "You diligently study the Scriptures because you think that by them you possess eternal life. These are the Scriptures that testify about me, yet you refuse to come to me to have life."

John 5:39–40

If there was anything that the scribes and Pharisees knew, it was the Scriptures, what we today call the Old Testament. They knew all the jots and tittles; they knew all the laws and commandments; if they appeared on *Who Wants to Be a Millionaire* and the subject was Scripture, they would win without having to use any lifelines.

Those words of Jesus are perplexing, aren't they? He says, "You think that by [the Scriptures] you possess eternal life." Jesus was talking to people who had spent their lives immersed in Scripture. Was he now downplaying its importance? Was he implying that the Scriptures do not, in themselves, bring eternal life? Yes, that is exactly what he is saying. The Scriptures, in themselves, do not bring eternal life. Eternal life comes through believing in Jesus.

On the classic TV show *Dragnet*, Sgt. Joe Friday monotoned, "All I want are the facts, ma'am, just the facts."

"All I want are the facts," say students cramming for their finals on Shakespeare. If they have read CliffsNotes, and if they

CROSS REF

Compare John 5:30, 40 with Jeremiah 9:23–24.

can fill in the blanks with the correct answers, pass the exam, and emerge into the outside world, they think they have attained an education.

Some Christians read the Bible like that. All they want are the facts. They may even read the Bible from cover to cover—all 1,189 chapters—in twelve months, but if all they are getting from it is "just the facts, ma'am," that's not enough.

You will find Bibles in jails, hotels, hospitals, and courtrooms. Bible verses are on billboards and banners. The Bible remains a best seller year after year. And whenever the traditional renderings of familiar passages become old hat to you, a new translation is published. In the past century more than forty new English translations have come off the press. We are knee-deep in the printed Scriptures.

However, the problem isn't Bible ownership or even Bible readership but something deeper. It's very much like the problem of the Jewish leaders in the time of Christ.

They certainly were aware of the witnesses Christ presented in answer to their challenge. They had seen John the Baptist, they had heard of the miracles, and they knew the Scriptures. All three may have been dinnertime conversations in their homes. But they failed to realize that the purpose of all three was to point to Jesus and not to draw attention to themselves.

That's the problem we have today.

John the Baptist isn't around anymore, but there are a number of popular preachers. Do we focus more on the speaker or on the Savior the speaker speaks about?

We see some exciting miracles and fantastic accomplishments in the name of the Lord, and we support some of them with our giving. Organizations like the Salvation Army, World Vision, and Habitat for Humanity are giving cups of cold water to the thirsty in the name of Christ. But is our focus on the organization or on the Lord whom they represent?

Even when we look into Scripture, we often miss seeing Jesus. Instead of saying, "What can I learn about Jesus here?" we tend to say, "What's in it for me?" When we read Psalm 23:1—"The LORD is my shepherd, I shall not be in want"—we concentrate on the last six words and not on the first five. In a verse like Philippians 4:19—"My God will meet all your needs according to his glorious riches in Christ Jesus"—we can concentrate on how our needs might be met today and not on God's glorious riches in Christ Jesus.

PART 3

The Old Testament had a threefold character: It was *law* in a narrow sense; it was *promise*; and it was *testimony*. The purpose of it all was to build *relationship*. The Jewish leaders in Christ's day were concentrating on the first purpose—the law of God.

The law emphasized the do's and don'ts, but it brought no joy. The Old Testament is laced with promise, beginning in the early chapters of Genesis. The testimony of the Scriptures was that God is faithful. Admittedly, that was not easy to accept when you had Roman soldiers patrolling your streets and tax collectors taking your money to build another palace for Herod.

So without factoring in Jesus, the Jews found no joy in the law. And the more they immersed themselves in the commandments, the less joy they had. Without factoring in Jesus, the Jews found no hope in God's promises. Without factoring in Jesus, even the testimonies of God's faithfulness were matters of the long ago and far away, and the discouraged Jews found their faith dissolving.

And regarding relationship? This is what made Christ's remarks about his Father so shocking. How could someone talk about a relationship with the almighty God in such an intimate way?

Today we sometimes stumble along the same path when we fail to factor in Jesus. If we don't look for Jesus on every page of Scripture, it becomes a dead book. He makes all the difference. Without him, even the New Testament becomes a heavy yoke, a book without joy, hope, or faith. But with Jesus, when we are looking at its pages through the eyes of faith and expectation, it is also a book of warm relationship, vibrant with love.

Students speak of "cracking the books." Detectives speak of "cracking the case." The Pharisees of Jesus' day knew how to crack the book, but they didn't realize that to crack the case, to have it all make sense, they needed Jesus.

This week, make sure that you crack the Book and crack the case.

QUOTE TO NOTE

The Bible contains many thousands of promises. It is God's book of signed checks.

F. B. Meyer

17

WHICH IS EASIER?

A guy gets up at a talent show and says, "Hey, I do a great impersonation of Patrick Henry. Let me show you. *'Give me liberty or give me death . . .'* Isn't that great? It sounds just like him!"

Well, no, it's not great. *Maybe* it sounds just like Patrick Henry sounded, but we don't know. There is no way to know whether the impersonator is accurate or not, because it's impossible to verify.

That's the logic behind Jesus' comments to the Pharisees in Mark 2. But let's set the scene first.

Mark's Gospel hits the ground running. No stories about Jesus' birth in Bethlehem, no sermons. Chapter 1 gives us John the Baptist, Jesus' temptation, the calling of the disciples, and several healings. So by the start of chapter 2, Jesus is already drawing crowds.

He's teaching in Capernaum, not far from his hometown of Nazareth. Most of his disciples are from this area—in fact Jesus might be teaching in the very home of Peter and Andrew (see Mark 1:29). In any case, the place is packed.

Archaeologists have dug up some working-class homes in Capernaum, including one site they think could have been Peter's house. These were not spacious dwellings. So this could be

99

Monday: Read part 1 of this chapter. Do you need to seek forgiveness for some sin that is holding you back from experiencing fullness of life?

Tuesday: Read part 2. Notice how Jesus reads the minds of the Pharisees.

Wednesday: Read part 3. What did this healing prove?

Thursday: What can you learn from Jesus about forgiveness? Are you holding a grudge you have not been able to forgive?

Friday: Read the verses in the Cross Ref section. What do they teach about confession and forgiveness?

Saturday: Pray a prayer of confession of your sin and request healing in any area of life where you might need it.

Sunday: Read Psalm 32 and praise the Lord who is the great Forgiver.

IN THE MIRROR

Do you have a friend who needs your active faith to work on his or her behalf?

a crowd of thirty or forty people assembling to hear Jesus, with maybe more outside the door.

There's a paralyzed man in town who wants Jesus to heal him. He gets four men to carry him on his mat to the house where Jesus is teaching, but they can't get in. There's no room. Then someone has a bright idea: *Let's hit the roof!* Rooftops were flat in homes like this, often used as patios, places to chill (literally) in the cool of the evening. There was probably a staircase along the outside of the building. The roof itself would have been made of beams with a grid work of branches and earth creating a solid surface, so you wouldn't need a jackhammer to dig through it. The four friends of the paralyzed man set to work removing the earth and branches from the roof surface, and eventually they were able to lower the man on his mat down in front of Jesus.

Imagine the scene inside the house. At first, they may have thought the pawing on the roof was a stray dog or a goat. But then some clods of earth begin to fall on the folks in the front row. (We learn later that's where the Pharisees are sitting.) Suddenly sunlight streams through and this bed descends in front of Jesus.

Anybody else might have said all sorts of things on this occasion. "Hey, who's gonna pay for that roof?" Or "I just washed this robe!" But Jesus looked at the paralyzed man and said:

● "Son, your sins are forgiven."

Mark 2:5

It seems like a non sequitur, doesn't it? It doesn't fit the situation. What does sin have to do with it?

Everything, if you'd ask anyone else in that room. It was the common belief that sickness was a result of sin. Remember how the disciples asked about the cause of the blind beggar's situation. "Who sinned, this man or his parents?" (John 9:2). Sin and suffering were firmly linked in the minds of first-century Jews.

We're much more enlightened now, aren't we? Now we realize that sickness has no connection with sin, right? Well, yes and no. The connection is never automatic. We must never assume that sick or suffering people have brought their troubles on themselves. Jesus said as much in his response regarding the blind man, and Paul's "thorn in the flesh" is another example. Sometimes our struggles occur to demonstrate God's strength.

But sometimes bad behavior does result in bad health. There's not necessarily anything mystical about that. Party all night, and your body will suffer from the lack of sleep. Overuse of alcohol or drugs or even food will bring about negative physical consequences. Often guilt feelings can wear down one's body. On the other hand, scientists are discovering the medical benefits of prayer. So there can be a connection between sin and sickness.

> **CROSS REF**
>
> Read more about forgiveness:
> Colossians 1:13–14
> James 5:15–16
> 1 John 1:8–9

But whether or not the paralysis had anything to do with this man's behavior, Jesus saw that more than anything else, he needed forgiveness. And so Jesus offered it. This did not go over well with the Pharisees in the front row.

PART 2

What were these Pharisees and teachers of the law doing there? No doubt checking up on this maverick rabbi named Jesus. They had heard of his healings and wanted to see if he was for real. Someone said he was teaching at a house in town, so they hustled over and muscled their way to the front. Then the roof fell in and a man dropped down and Jesus uttered a phrase that only God himself could get away with.

Forgiveness required sacrifice, an animal's blood shed on the altar in the temple in Jerusalem. You can't just go around forgiving folks with mere words. "Why does this fellow talk like that? He's blaspheming! Who can forgive sins but God alone?" (Mark 2:7). Such were their thoughts, which Jesus read like a scroll.

● **"Why are you thinking these things? Which is easier: to say to the paralytic, 'Your sins are forgiven,' or to say, 'Get up, take your mat and walk'?"**

Mark 2:8–9

It's a good question. Which is easier to say? Think about it.

This is like the impersonation of Patrick Henry. It's easy for someone to say he sounds just like Patrick Henry, because no one knows how Patrick Henry sounded. There's no way to verify it. In the same way, it's easier to say, "Your sins are forgiven," because it's a spiritual transaction. That might be harder to *do*, but it's easier to *say*, because it's not verifiable. No one else will ever know if those sins have actually been forgiven. But if you say, "Get up and walk," and the guy remains motionless, it's pretty obvious you don't have the power you thought you had.

But if you command a healing and it occurs, then it's clear to everyone that you have great power—perhaps even the power to forgive sins. Throughout Jesus' ministry, his miracles functioned as signs, proof of his divine power. Yes, he had compassion on those he healed, but his main task was not healing. He was more concerned about the spiritual health of the people than their physical health. The miracles confirmed his message and his identity.

Jesus had these religious leaders right where he wanted them. He had led with the forgiveness card, and their response was basically, *Who do you think you are? What gives you the right?* Forgiving sins would be blasphemy, if Jesus were not accredited to do so. In their hearts, these Pharisees demanded proof, which Jesus was more than happy to provide.

PART 3

● "But that you may know that the Son of Man has authority on earth to forgive sins. . . ." He said to the paralytic, "I tell you, get up, take your mat and go home."

Mark 2:10-11

Jesus didn't finish his sentence, at least not with words. He was talking to the Pharisees and teachers, and he began with a purpose clause—*but that you may know*—but then he left them hanging. Instead of completing that thought verbally, he turned to the paralyzed man, who had been left hanging, literally. (Remember that he was suspended from the roof by his four friends.) Jesus let his actions finish the sentence. He commanded the paralytic to get up and walk, and that's exactly what happened. Imagine how the crowd must have parted to let this man walk—*walk!*—outside to join his joyful friends.

And what was the look on the Pharisees' faces? The miracle had spoken for itself. They had considered Jesus a blasphemer for forgiving sins. He claimed he had authority to do so. And just when they were about to write him off as just another big talker, his actions spoke even louder. He healed a man in front of their eyes. What could they say?

This was the first time Jesus used the title "Son of Man" for himself. It's an interesting choice, glorious and humble at the same time. Jesus was human but the ultimate human. And in fact Daniel had a vision of "one like a son of man, coming with the clouds of heaven. . . . He was given authority, glory and sovereign power; all peoples, nations and men of every language worshiped him" (Dan. 7:13–14). Certainly this was the identity and authority Jesus was claiming.

Flip back from Mark a couple of chapters to the Great Commission

CLUES TO USE

Faith often played a role in Jesus' healings. In this case, it was the faith of the paralyzed man's friends that prompted the miracle. "When Jesus saw *their* faith," it says (Mark 2:5).

at the end of Matthew. There Jesus announced, "All authority in heaven and on earth is given to me" (Matt. 28:18). He has authority over all of us, and he uses that authority to forgive our sins.

QUOTE TO NOTE

Paralyzed legs are not as big an issue with God as a paralyzed heart.

Calvin Miller

18

WHO'S AFRAID?

A cry in the night! A mother wakens. She knows the cry of her two year old. And it's not a cry of pain or hunger. It's a cry of fear.

She finds her way out of the bedroom, turns on the hall light, and shuffles into the child's room. Only a few hours before, this "terrible two" was acting up—an untamed, unmanageable bronco. Now he's terrified.

She picks him up in her arms. He's gotten big; not so easy to lift anymore. But now as he snuggles on her shoulder, she caresses him. "Don't be afraid, honey," she whispers. "I'm here. Don't be afraid."

What was it? she wonders. *Was it a fear of the dark? Was he afraid of being alone? Was it a bad dream?* Perhaps she will never know, because soon he is sound asleep in her arms.

"Don't be afraid. I'm here." Those words are repeated over and over again in the Bible, and the reason is simple. Like the two year old, we too are afraid of the dark; we too have bad dreams; we too are afraid of being alone.

Of course, there are other causes for fear. At the beginning of time, after Adam and Eve had eaten the forbidden fruit, they

Monday: Read part 1. What are some good reasons for fear?

Tuesday: Read part 2. Can you think of other times in the life of Jesus when people around him may have been afraid?

Wednesday: Read part 3. Why do fears often come in darkness? How does this relate to God as light?

Thursday: Read part 4. What is a strong antidote for fear, today as well as two thousand years ago?

Friday: Consider changing your fears into challenges. How will you do this?

Saturday: Examine yourself. Are there any fears within you that diminish the success of your Christian life? Ask God to remove these hindrances from you.

Sunday: Praise God for the assurance that he is with us always and we need not fear anything!

hid from God. Why? As Adam explained to God, "I was afraid." And at the end of time, with the whole earth in tumult, the Bible speaks of "men's hearts failing them for fear" (Luke 21:26 KJV). Yes, sometimes there are good reasons for fear.

But more often in Scripture, the Bible delivers a different message: "Don't be afraid." That's what God told childless Abraham in Canaan. That's what Moses told the Israelites with the Egyptian armies behind them and the Red Sea in front of them. That's what God told Joshua as the conquest of the Promised Land was about to begin. That's what Jonathan told his friend David who was being chased by Saul's army.

The prophet Isaiah repeats it often: "Don't be afraid, for I am with you. . . . Don't be afraid, for I myself will help you. . . . Fear not, for I have redeemed you. . . . Do not fear; your Lord will come to save you."

As the Christmas story begins, it is filled with "fear nots." "Do not be afraid, Mary. . . . Joseph, do not be afraid to take Mary. . . . Do not be afraid, Zechariah. . . . Do not be afraid, shepherds."

Then comes the ministry of Jesus. From beginning to end, Jesus was telling people, "Don't be afraid. I am with you."

PART 2

● "Don't be afraid; from now on you will catch men."

Luke 5:10

One day Jesus was talking to crowds of people along the shore of Galilee. As the crowd got larger, he stepped into a boat and continued his teaching from there. When he finished, he asked the fishermen to row the boat into deeper water and let down their nets.

Simon Peter knew better. He and his partners had been fishing all night and hadn't caught anything. But because Jesus had asked him to do it, he cast out the nets again. This time it seemed that he had come across a national convention of fish. His first reaction was to call his partners and ask for their help. His second was to recognize that Jesus was someone special. Then Peter saw his own sinfulness. "Go away from me, Lord; I am a sinful man!" (Luke 5:8).

It was a reaction of fear. He didn't know much about Jesus at this point, but from that miracle he knew that there was something supernatural about him. Right in the boat, among the fish still flopping around, Peter fell to his knees before Jesus and heard his cryptic assurance.

Don't be afraid? He had just seen a stunning miracle. This carpenter had overruled the laws of nature—he had challenged the laws of *fishing*—and Peter was a part of it. Yet Jesus spoke of something greater, something even more terrifying. God would use Peter to bring people into his kingdom.

Why shouldn't he be afraid? Because this mighty power had a purpose to it. Jesus was not some impulsive sorcerer who zapped anything in his way. He had a mission—bringing people into a relationship with God—and now he was inviting Peter along for the ride.

PART 3

● "Don't be afraid."

Matthew 17:7

Peter, James, and John once had a mountaintop experience, literally. Jesus took them up a high mountain, possibly Mount Hermon, north of Galilee, and suddenly they saw Jesus transfigured before them, his face shining as the sun. Miraculously

CROSS REF

Look up these verses on fear, if you dare.

Genesis 3:10

Psalms 19:9; 23:4; 27:1

Proverbs 1:7

Isaiah 8:12–13; 41:10

Matthew 27:54

Luke 12:4–5

Philippians 2:12

2 Timothy 1:7

Hebrews 2:14–15

Moses and Elijah appeared and began talking with Jesus, and a voice from a cloud said, "This is my Son, whom I love; with him I am well pleased. Listen to him!" (v. 5).

How would you have responded to that multimedia presentation? The three disciples fell facedown in terror. But Jesus came to them, touched them gently, and said: "Don't be afraid."

In this and other passages, Jesus doesn't scold people for being afraid. Fear is a perfectly understandable reaction to the transfiguration, to a daughter's death, or to a miracle. But Jesus seems to say, "You can stop being afraid now. There are things to do." Fear can paralyze us, but faith gets us moving again. Fear shuts us down, but faith opens us up to Jesus' teaching, to the possibilities of new miracles, to our own participation in his work. Fear for a moment, but then trust for a lifetime.

PART 4

● "It is I; don't be afraid."

John 6:20

One morning between three and six, the disciples were caught in a storm as they struggled to row across the Sea of Galilee. High winds, high waves, and pitch darkness added up to terror. They had been rowing for hours and they couldn't tell if they were making any headway or not. They must have wondered, *Where is Jesus at a time like this, now that we really need him?*

When Jesus had left them several hours earlier, he said he was going up on a mountainside to pray, and then probably he would walk around the end of the lake and meet them in Capernaum. If they ever got to Capernaum.

Suddenly they saw what they thought was a ghost walking on the water. Some shrieked; others were so terrified that they couldn't get a sound out of their throats. Was this the angel of death coming for them? They were goners, for sure.

And then they heard the words of Jesus, identifying himself and calming their fears.

When you sense the presence of Jesus, there is freedom from fear. Writing about this passage, St. Augustine said, "He came treading the waves; and so He puts all the swelling tumults of life under his feet. Christians—why afraid?"

Why afraid? Indeed.

The Greek word for fear is *phobos*, which gives us our word *phobia*. Today we recognize all kinds of phobias, from claustrophobia (fear of closed-in places) to agoraphobia (fear of open spaces). Everyone seems to have a different phobia. Some fear dogs or cats; others fear snakes or spiders; and usually these fears are irrational. At least, we can't understand why they strike terror to the core of our being.

Fear might be understandable for those in ancient times. They didn't have scientific explanations for everything. They didn't know much about thunder and lightning, about weather fronts and isobars. They had no penicillin, no Pepto-Bismol, no aspirin. But an inoculation or a pill doesn't conquer fear. If it did, we would have a fearless society today.

Yet people today are extremely fearful, and more than ever they need to hear the assuring words of Jesus: "Don't be afraid; I am with you." It is the message of the beloved twenty-third Psalm, "Even though I walk through the valley of the shadow of death, I will fear no evil, for you are with me." And it is the message of Jesus, when he says in the upper room, "Do not let your hearts be troubled and do not be afraid" (John 14:27), and his final words in Matthew, "I am with you always, to the very end of the age" (28:20).

Most fears today are not phobias. According to a *Wall Street Journal* survey, our top three fears are a fear of failure, a fear of loneliness, and a fear of death. Then come a host of other fears: rejection, pain, the unknown future, ridicule, impotence, old age, and loss of health.

Fear often descends on us when we realize we are not in control. The disciples in the boat in stormy Galilee had lost control of their situation. They thought they knew how to navigate in a storm, but when the storm grew larger than their navigational experience, they were terrified. Then came this ghostlike apparition alongside their boat. Now they were facing the unknown, the supernatural. But when "they were willing to take [Jesus] into the boat," Scripture says, "immediately the boat reached the shore" (John 6:21).

Life is a constant challenge, and there is no way to live it without an element of fear. A teenager leaves home and goes to college, facing the multiple fears of loneliness, rejection, an unknown future, and possible failure. A family leaves friends and moves to a new location. We begin new careers, we hunt for a new church, we struggle with a desire to go back to school for more education. Each has its own set of fears because of the uncertain future. As the Swiss physician and author Paul Tournier said, "Everything that has meaning in life is frightening."

Did the disciples ever get into a boat again? Of course they did. Life is an adventure, especially a Christian life. But for the Christian, life is an adventure with Jesus at our side, and that makes all the difference.

After Jesus left them and ascended into heaven, the disciples became missionary adventurers to the ends of the earth. Scary, oh yes. But you can be sure those disciples never forgot Jesus' parting words: "I am with you always, to the very end of the age."

And that is a strong antidote for fear, today as well as two thousand years ago.

QUOTE TO NOTE

Christ asserts that each single creature is distinctly under God's hand and protection, that nothing may be left open to chance.

John Calvin

19

WHO WANTS TO BE COMMITTED?

People hate to make commitments these days. And even if they make them, they have a hard time keeping them.

Professional athletes try to renegotiate their five-year contracts in the middle of their second year. Spouses break their "till death do us part" vows when the going gets rough. Many pastors are leaving the ministry. Churches find it harder and harder to get board members to agree to three-year terms of office. Sunday school teachers want a change of venue after one year. And here's a good-news/bad-news factoid: The number of short-term missionaries is up, while the number of long-term missionaries is down.

Yes, people hate to make commitments.

In his day Jesus must have thought the same thing. It wasn't that he didn't have followers. Remember those five thousand people he fed? They were all followers or at least potential followers. But tagging along is one thing; commitment is something else.

One day Jesus and his disciples were hiking along a road when a man, identified in Matthew as a teacher of the law, ap-

Monday: Read part 1 of this chapter. Consider the questions in "In the Mirror."

Tuesday: Read part 2. Consider the obligations in your life that might keep you from following Jesus fully. Should you reexamine these?

Wednesday: Read part 3. What do you think was wrong with simply saying good-by?

Thursday: What is your cross that you must take up daily?

Friday: Read Mark 10:17–31 about another person who had problems with following Jesus.

Saturday: When you spend time in prayer, ask Jesus about how you can follow him. What does he require of you?

Sunday: Read Psalm 51 and pay special attention to verses 16–17. Praise God with your whole heart.

proached them. Usually experts in the Old Testament law joined with the Pharisees to hassle Jesus, but this teacher was different. He wanted to join Jesus.

"I will follow you wherever you go," he said.

Wow! Not only a volunteer but an enthusiastic one. Jesus had personally invited his disciples, "Follow me," and they had. Their group included several fishermen, a former tax collector, and a political revolutionary. Now here was an educated teacher of the law wanting to join up. Wouldn't he make a nice catch for Jesus?

Apparently Jesus wasn't so sure.

● **"Foxes have holes and birds of the air have nests, but the Son of Man has no place to lay his head."**

Luke 9:58

What was Jesus doing?

For one thing, he was being realistic. Earlier in this chapter (v. 52), he had sent messengers ahead to see if they could find lodging for him in the next village. Suddenly "No Vacancy" signs started popping up all over the place. No room for Jesus. It seemed such an insult that James and John wanted to call down fire from heaven and destroy the whole town.

No room for Jesus. Sounds like a replay of the Bethlehem story, doesn't it?

An old gospel song says, "Out of the ivory palaces, into a world of woe; only his great eternal love made my Savior go." The

112

Son of God left the mansions of glory for the homeless shelters of this fallen world because love compelled him.

Did the enthusiastic volunteer share that love? Or would he, as an educated teacher of the law, insist on rooms at the Hilton?

PART 2

● "If anyone would come after me, he must deny himself and take up his cross daily and follow me."

Luke 9:23

Before the teacher of the law offered to follow him, Jesus had given this definition of discipleship. In other words, "If you want to follow me, you've got to follow me all the way." The "No Vacancy" signs come with the territory. You might as well know ahead of time what you are getting into. And it would seem that this young man, like the rich young ruler, probably went away sorrowful. The cost of discipleship was more than he wanted to pay.

But as the disciples walked along the road with the Master, they got another lesson in commitment. Jesus summons another tagalong: "Follow me."

The man responds, "Lord, first let me go and bury my father."

"Let the dead bury their own dead, but you go and proclaim the kingdom of God," Jesus says (v. 60).

IN THE MIRROR

The first man who desired to follow Jesus was evidently too attached to other things to commit himself to Jesus. What about you? Are you too rooted in your comfort zones to fully commit? Jesus makes it clear that the way may be rugged. Are you equal to the call?

Shocking! Didn't Jesus care about family commitments?

Nothing was more important to the Jew than a proper burial. Even the killing of a sacrificial lamb at Passover or the circumcision of a baby boy was not as urgent as a proper burial. But Jesus was saying that proclaiming the kingdom of God is not a "when it's convenient" kind of thing. Jesus was saying, *I know the priorities that have been set by the teachers of the law. I know that burial of a family member takes precedence over every ob-*

CROSS REF

On being a disciple:
Luke 14:26–27
Luke 18:18–25
Mark 3:31–34

servance of the temple. But I am saying that discipleship takes the top priority even over the burial of your father. That's how important discipleship is.

Of course, Jesus knew that this man was not caring for his father at that moment anyway. But that's beside the point. Jesus was emphasizing that discipleship radically changes your priorities. If it doesn't, you don't understand what discipleship is all about.

As for the dead burying their own dead, the implication is that people without any spiritual awareness are spiritually dead. The message of Jesus Christ brings life to the dying. What can be more important than that?

PART 3

● "No one who puts his hand to the plow and looks back is fit for service in the kingdom of God."

Luke 9:62

Another volunteer showed up with an excuse similar to that of the last one. He would follow Jesus, *but* he wanted to say good-by to his family first. (That little word *but* thwarts a lot of would-be disciples.) Yet Jesus saw this response as "looking back" and failing to plow ahead.

What was wrong with this request? It seems reasonable enough to say farewell to the family before traipsing off with Jesus. And this guy had Scripture on his side.

In the Old Testament, when the prophet Elijah was looking for a successor, he spotted a farmer named Elisha plowing with twelve yoke of oxen. Impressed, Elijah threw his coat on Elisha's shoulders, signifying his selection. Elisha responded positively but then added, "Let me kiss my father and mother good-by . . . and then I will come with you" (1 Kings 19:20)—basically the same request that Jesus' volunteer made. That delay didn't seem to bother Elijah at all. Why wouldn't it be good enough for Jesus?

In his classic *The Cost of Discipleship*, Dietrich Bonhoeffer says that although this would-be disciple "places himself at the Master's disposal," at the same time he insists on retaining "the right to dictate his own terms. But then discipleship is no longer discipleship, but a program of our own to suit ourselves. . . . Discipleship can tolerate no condition which might come between Jesus and our obedience to him."

In Jesus' terms, the farmer who looked back would not be able to plow a straight furrow. Instead, the good plowman had to look ahead, fixing his eyes on a marker in the distance. If a disciple started a habit of looking back, his forward progress would always be crooked.

That's what commitment is all about. That's what faith is all about. We do not set the terms; God does. It is up to us to accept or reject, not to haggle.

QUOTE TO NOTE

Christ has no velvet crosses.

Samuel Rutherford

20

BREAD IS TO BE EATEN

PART 1

Bread just isn't what it used to be. Today it's something that helps you hold peanut butter and jelly together without getting your fingers gooey. We eat bread without thinking about it. At a ball game, vendors sell hot dogs, never even mentioning the bun that contains the hot dogs. McDonald's and Burger King wax ecstatic about their burgers but say little about their bready containers.

In Bible times it was different. Dinner was announced—"Come and get it!"—and everyone understood that "it" meant bread. Of course, bread wasn't the only food you got at the table. Fish from the Jordan or the Galilee might be served pickled, dried, or fresh. Vegetables, including beans, onions, lentils, cucumbers, beets, lettuce, or peas, might be on the menu. Meat was a special treat. Fruit came as the dessert.

Poorer people ate barley bread, olives, and fruit. Sometimes they ate locusts as their meat dish. But bread was central.

The most time-consuming job that a homemaker had was making bread, which she baked at home every day. The grain had to be ground into meal and then mixed with water and salt to make the dough. For the mixture to rise, yeast had to be added—except during Passover and other religious holidays when unleavened bread was required. After molding the dough into flat loaves, it was baked in a small earthenware oven. Every day it was the same routine. Same-old, same-old.

A meal wasn't a meal if it didn't include bread. Bread was vital to the Israelites' daily existence.

EVERY DAY WITH JESUS

Monday: Read part 1 of this chapter. In what way do you "eat" of the living Bread, that is, Christ?

Tuesday: Read part 2. What do the humanity and divinity of Christ mean to you?

Wednesday: Read part 3. Is Jesus the "bread" of your life? In what way?

Thursday: Read part 4. When you partake of the Lord's Supper, what does that mean to you?

Friday: Consider the question in "In the Mirror."

Saturday: Ask the Lord to show you ways to take his living Bread and feed multitudes—or at least a few neighbors.

Sunday: Read Matthew 26:17–30. Praise God for his gift of Jesus.

So the Jews understood that Jesus was making a very audacious statement indeed when he said,

● "I am the bread of life. He who comes to me will never go hungry."

John 6:35

Funny thing about bread. It's not good for anything if it isn't eaten. Water, on the other hand, is useful even if you don't drink it. You can wash in it; you can swim in it; you can fish in it; you can put goldfish in it. But bread must be eaten.

Whether it's pita or pumpernickel, whether it's a bagel or a bun, it doesn't do you a bit of good if you just sit there and stare at it. If you stare for too long, it will get stale. It has to be eaten.

That's how Jesus got into trouble. When he said that he was the living Bread, many of his listeners probably scratched their heads and wondered what he meant. But when he suggested that the living Bread had to be eaten, they thought he had gone crazy. At this even some of his disciples "turned back and no longer followed him" (v. 66). Can you blame them? Doesn't that sound like cannibalism?

PART 2

Everyone who heard Christ's amazing statement, "I am the bread of life," probably understood it from their own background. Some homemakers who had just shoved some dough into the oven may have thought that he had a secret bread-making recipe. They would certainly be skeptical.

Pharisees and religious leaders started thinking about the Old Testament story of how the Israelites in the wilderness were fed each day with manna from heaven. They too were skeptical. *Who does this guy think he is? He sounds as if he thinks he is better than Moses.*

Bread was interesting that way. On the one hand, it was the most common of foods; on the other hand, bread was honored in the Old Testament tabernacle and temple in both the Holy Place and the Holy of Holies. In the Holy Place twelve fresh loaves were placed each Sabbath on the golden table. It was called "the bread of the Presence." In the tabernacle's Holy of Holies was a golden pot of bread (manna). For the Jewish worshipers, the bread in the tabernacle reminded them not only of the divine presence but also of the divine provision.

Bread: common and yet uniquely holy. Jesus: human and yet uniquely divine.

PART 3

● "Where shall we buy bread for these people to eat?"

John 6:5

That was the question that Jesus asked Philip when the crowd of five thousand–plus people surged around him. And that was the question that began the focus on bread.

You may remember the story. Peter's brother, Andrew, brought to Jesus a boy who had a lunch of five small barley loaves and two small fish. But how could this meager fare feed a crowd?

According to Luke, Jesus told the disciples to have the people sit down "in groups of about fifty each" (9:14). Then Jesus gave thanks, broke the little muffin-sized loaves, and gave the pieces to his disciples to distribute among the groups of fifty. When all the people had enough to eat, Jesus said to his disciples, "Gather the pieces that are left over. Let nothing be wasted" (John 6:12). They collected twelve basketfuls of leftovers. Amazing!

The people were impressed. This was the kind of political leader they wanted, one who could miraculously give them food to eat. Some wanted to make him king right there. Others said, "Surely this is the Prophet," the one Moses had predicted would come.

> **TO THINK ABOUT**
>
> Remember how the disciples picked up those pieces of leftover bread? Well, if you have tasted the living Bread yourself, you should be able to share some of the pieces with your neighbor.

The next day, on the other side of the Sea of Galilee, the bread discussion got going again. Gathering around Jesus, people asked for a sign, as if the previous day's miraculous catering wasn't enough. They thought it would be cool if he gave them manna as Moses had.

Jesus corrected them on two points. First, it wasn't Moses who produced the manna, but "my Father." Second, the true bread from heaven wasn't manna, but a person who actually came from heaven.

That sounded good to the crowd. "Give us this bread," they said.

PART 4

● "I am the living bread. . . . If anyone eats of this bread, he will live forever. This bread is my flesh, which I will give for the life of the world."

John 6:51

How could Jesus give his flesh as bread to eat? It sounded scandalous. People who had earlier wanted to make him king now wanted nothing to do with him. Some who had acclaimed him as Messiah were now completely baffled.

Scholars call this one of those "hard sayings" of Jesus. It still confuses people today. But what it means is simply this: Following Jesus' teachings isn't enough. Many people of all religions give a nodding assent to Christ's noble thoughts. Not good enough.

The key to this saying is its final phrase. Jesus was giving his flesh *for the life of the world*. That propels us forward to Calvary. When Jesus died, "giving his flesh" for us, the living Bread was broken. He became broken so that we could become whole. He gave his life so that we could receive it.

And how do we receive this life? How do we partake of this living Bread? Through faith. It is faith in the crucified Christ that opens the door of salvation for us. When we accept his sacrifice with faith and thanksgiving, it nourishes us.

Bread doesn't do you any good if you just stare at it. In the same way, it's not enough to look at Jesus from afar. You can admire his teachings or his exemplary life, but you will not receive the life he offers until you partake of him through faith. As you would pop a morsel of bread into your mouth, you must bring Jesus into your heart. The bread becomes part of you, as does Jesus.

That's why the Lord's Supper (eating the broken bread, drinking the cup) is such a powerful event within Christian churches. It is a vivid reenactment of our salvation. Jesus offers us his body and blood—sacrificed on our behalf at Calvary—and in faith we partake of it.

QUOTE TO NOTE

Physical food lasts only until the next meal, but a life lived in Christ truly sustains. It gives health to the outlook, strength to the character, and vitality to one's purpose.

F. Lagard Smith

21

INVITATION TO BURNOUT SUFFERERS

Until a half century ago, no one had ever heard about burnout. Employees worked hard, had aching muscles, and complained about their tyrannical bosses and their paltry paychecks. Sometimes their shoulders sagged, their bodies caved in, and their lungs collapsed, and sometimes they dropped dead on the assembly line. But they never complained about burnout.

At some point, people began griping about working too hard, and a new word was coined—*workaholic*. As psychiatrists began analyzing it, they classified many workaholics as type A personalities, people with activism and aggression built into their genes. Soon workaholism was recognized as a serious addiction, just like alcoholism. Some "work addicts" cracked up, had heart attacks, or became dangerous to themselves as well as to others. Others just had to get out of the rat race to survive—otherwise, they would suffer burnout.

As psychiatrists found more and more burnout sufferers, they were able to define this malady. Burnout, they concluded, is a state of mental and/or physical exhaustion caused by exces-

Monday: Read part 1 of this chapter. Are you burned out in any way? Read the words of Jesus in this chapter and let them minister to you.

Tuesday: Read part 2. What part do your emotions play in your stress level?

Wednesday: Read part 3. What makes Jesus' yoke easy?

Thursday: What can a church do to help its people avoid "religious burnout"?

Friday: Spend some time meditating on the "rest" God gives. Rest from what? How do we obtain it? Can we help our loved ones experience God's rest?

Saturday: Pray that God will help you manage the details of life as well as your church work in such a way that you will find rest for your soul.

Sunday: Read Jesus' prayer in Mathew 11:25–26. Praise God today for his revelation of himself to those who are childlike.

sive and prolonged stress. If you mix continuous overwork with stress and strain, and then stir in a good dose of irritation, you are bound to develop a serious case of burnout sooner or later. Doctors and nurses get it; ministers get it; schoolteachers get it; housewives get it; checkout clerks get it. In fact people in all walks of life get burned out.

Yes, we have identified far more cases of stress and burnout in modern times than there were two thousand years ago. But don't kid yourself. The followers of Jesus felt some of the same symptoms in their day. And that's why Jesus gave the invitation:

● "Come to me, all you who are weary and burdened, and I will give you rest."

Matthew 11:28

Paraphrasing it, *The Message* puts it this way: "Are you tired? Worn out? Burned out on religion? Come to me. Get away with me and you'll recover your life. I'll show you how to take a real rest."

Burned out on religion? Is that what Jesus meant, or was the paraphraser just making that up? Actually, in Greek, Jesus used the verb form of the same word he used in Matthew 23:4, berating the Pharisees for placing heavy *burdens* on people's backs. So it's quite possible that he had the same situation in mind here, that the religious leaders had overburdened the people with all the laws they had imposed. Aren't you glad that sort of thing doesn't happen today? Well, maybe it does. Recent census figures indicate that more and more people are getting burned out on religion. Their beliefs may still be quite orthodox, but they no longer want anything to do with the organized church.

Why? There may be many reasons, but sometimes it's that combination of continuous overwork in the church, the stress and strain of meeting everyone's expectations, and a strong dose of irritation. It all leads to church burnout.

> **CROSS REF**
>
> If you are weak and burdened, and if you respond to Jesus' invitation—*Come to me*—then you will find great meaning and comfort in the following verses:
> Philippians 4:13
> Philippians 4:19
> 1 Peter 5:7

The burnout candidate can see the symptoms mounting. First, he feels stressed; his wires feel taut; commitments overwhelm him. Then he feels ineffective, as if he's just spinning his wheels; he's not accomplishing anything worthwhile; it doesn't seem like fun anymore; he's not getting any emotional satisfaction from it. And finally he retreats from it all or totally collapses. He is burned out.

You can understand why some of the followers of Jesus may have felt this way. He had invited them to leave everything and follow him. It was a total commitment. Now they were with Jesus 24/7. And living with Jesus, they were subject to the same criticisms that he faced. The Pharisees were always carping at something. And Jesus was so unpredictable. His way of looking at things went counter to what they had known in their lives up until then. He was introducing them to a revolutionary kind of lifestyle.

PART 2

● "Take my yoke upon you and learn from me, for I am gentle and humble in heart, and you will find rest for your souls."

Matthew 11:29

Psychologists say you need to take several steps to guard yourself from burnout: (1) Get your priorities straight, (2) access

IN THE MIRROR

Are you discouraged, stressed, burned out? Here's an idea: Instead of begging God to change your situation, try thanking him for it. That might just change your attitude.

your emotions, (3) ask for help, (4) take a few action steps and then pull away to rest, (5) spend time with others, and (6) keep learning and growing. This was essentially the strategy that Jesus prescribed.

Immediately before Jesus had issued his gentle invitation, "Come to me," he had chewed out the citizenry of two cities with whom he had grown increasingly frustrated. "Woe to you!" he cried angrily. Don't be too surprised at this display of emotion. The Gospels show Jesus with a full range of feeling, including anger. The Bible teaches self-control, but that doesn't mean we must bottle up our feelings. Such repression can contribute to stress and eventually burnout.

In Matthew 11 we see Jesus not only accessing his feelings but also getting his priorities straight, or at least *keeping* them straight. His priority was God's kingdom. He was offering these cities the good news of the kingdom, and they didn't want it. That was truly upsetting. But instead of harping on those angry emotions, Jesus immediately went to his source of strength, the Father. He prayed.

"I praise you, Father," he began. Even though the people of those two cities—those who were supposedly "wise and learned"—had rejected his message, the Father had opened the hearts of "little children," the less sophisticated workingmen and women of his day, including the motley crew of close followers who became his disciples (v. 25). In other words, Jesus found something to thank the Father for, even in this time of frustration and disappointment.

No doubt the disciples went along with Jesus on this emotional roller-coaster ride. They had wanted to call fire from heaven to destroy an unresponsive village, so they probably shared Jesus' pique in this instance as well. Surely they learned something important here: that you can express your anger but then take it to the Father. Process your emotions through prayer. That leads to the kind of rest and relief that Jesus offers.

PART 3

● "For my yoke is easy and my burden is light."

Matthew 11:30

A yoke was the heavy bar placed on the necks of oxen as they plowed a field. It kept them connected to each other and to the plow. Now, wait a minute, you may be saying. How can Jesus offer rest and at the same time put a yoke on your neck? It doesn't make sense.

Lurking in the background in all the Gospel stories were the religionists of Jesus' day, those scribes and Pharisees. They were the ones who told you how to wash your hands and arms, the precise number of yards you could walk on the Sabbath, and how many days a week you were obligated to fast. That was a heavy yoke.

To please God, you had to obey 613 Old Testament regulations plus the new ones that the Pharisees were concocting. No wonder some folks were burning out! It was like taking a driver's test with a thousand-page manual to memorize. People were working hard to please God, and yet they were afraid that they couldn't remember all the requirements.

In contrast to the heavy yoke of the law, Jesus said, "My yoke is easy." What did he mean? Was he saying that we can behave any way we choose? Was he tossing out the whole idea of living by God's standards? No. Elsewhere Jesus indicates that disciple-ship is no cop-out. It's serious business. And yet the "burden is light." The sternness and rigidity of the law are replaced by the forgiveness and freedom of grace. Followers of the Good Shepherd soon find that their Master is "gentle and humble in heart." Besides being the great Savior, he is also the great For-giver. Instead of having 613-plus regulations of the law to make sure that we plow straight, Jesus has given us the Holy Spirit as our internal guide.

Often yokes did not fit the oxen well. Sometimes they were rough-hewn hunks of wood with splinters and rough edges, causing irritation to the oxen. But Jesus provides an "easy" yoke. The word usually means "good" or "kind." A "kind" yoke is one that fits perfectly.

So there's your choice. You can put in long hours plowing the fields with a rough-hewn yoke digging into your skin, all the time feeling that you are not meeting all the requirements, in which case you are a candidate for burnout. Or you can come to the Savior and bear the easy yoke of grace.

QUOTE TO NOTE

Here is the gracious invitation of the gospel in which the Savior's tears and smiles were blended, as in a covenant rainbow of promise.

Charles Haddon Spurgeon

22

BOCCE, ART GALLERIES, AND PARABLES

PART 1

Jesus got the attention of the people quickly. No doubt about it. All you have to do is turn water into wine, multiply a little boy's lunch to feed thousands of people, heal the sick, cast out demons, and things like that. Before long, people were following him like puppy dogs.

But then, what was the best way to teach this mob? They had come along for the ride, but Jesus wasn't interested in giving them a free pass. He wanted these people to walk with him, to understand what he was teaching, to grasp the ABCs of the kingdom of God. He wanted to transform the mob into practical disciples. How would he do that?

Jesus chose to teach the ABCs by telling stories—or, technically, *parables*.

● "The knowledge of the secrets of the kingdom of God has been given to you, but to others I speak in parables, so that,

Monday: Read part 1 of this chapter. Of all Jesus' parables, which one is your favorite? Why?

Tuesday: Read part 2. Think of your past life. Which kind(s) of soil have you been in the past, and which are you today?

Wednesday: Read part 3. How have people responded when you have shared God's Word?

Thursday: Read part 4. Doesn't Jesus want people to understand? What does it take for people to understand?

Friday: Be creative! Write your own parable. Use a truth, maybe a Scripture, and tell it in story form.

Saturday: When you pray, ask the Lord to apply this week's lesson to your life. Ask him for "ears to hear."

Sunday: Praise God as the One who has ears to hear our prayers.

'though seeing, they may not see; though hearing, they may not understand.'"

Luke 8:10

What's a parable? It has been defined as "an earthly story with a heavenly meaning." Not a bad definition to start with, but it's more than that.

The Italians have a lawn game called bocce. You throw a hard ball, about a third the size of a bowling ball, across your lawn, and then other players try to throw their balls alongside of it. The winner is the one who throws a ball closest to the first ball.

The Greek word for parable means "to throw alongside of," so you might want to imagine Jesus playing the game of bocce. He tosses out a story *alongside* some major truth so people will understand that major truth.

Remember the story of King David committing adultery with Bathsheba? The prophet Nathan came to him afterward and told him a parable. A wealthy man had lots of sheep, Nathan said, and a neighbor who was very poor had only one little lamb. When the rich man wanted to make some lamb stew, he took and killed his poor neighbor's lamb rather than one of his own. King David responded angrily at such evil and demanded that the rich man be prosecuted. Nathan said, "You are the man" (see 2 Sam. 12:1–10).

If Nathan had stormed into David's court accusing him of sin, David might have stonewalled him. But, like a bocce ball, the parable was thrown alongside the truth. David understood.

PART 2

One of the first parables Jesus told was the parable of the sower.

● "A farmer went out to sow his seed. As he was scattering the seed, some fell along the path; it was trampled on, and the birds of the air ate it up."

Luke 8:5

As Jesus continued the story, he told of other seed that fell on rock, and still other that fell among thorns. But finally some seed fell on good soil, grew healthily, and yielded a crop.

The story, like most of Jesus' parables, is a simple one, and everyone who heard it understood what Jesus was saying; at least they understood it on one level. It's likely that Jesus, the disciples, and the crowd that followed were walking down a path in the countryside that separated two fields. Jesus probably stopped to let the people get closer and then he told the story, pointing to the fields on either side of him and to the path on which they were walking.

After Jesus finished telling the story, some of the people probably were scratching their heads and saying, "We've been following him for two hours to hear him tell us that if you plant seed on a road, it won't grow? We knew that already. We thought we were going to get some words of wisdom!" They heard the words, but they didn't understand the message.

Parables are sometimes called Jesus' picture gallery. Jesus painted word pictures of lost sheep, farmers, shepherds, prodigals, and little seeds growing into big trees. In the four Gospels we have about thirty of these pictures. The problem, however, is the same problem you might have when you walk through an art museum. "That's a nice picture," you say, "but what did the artist mean by it?"

This is often what the disciples asked Jesus when he finished his parable-stories. "What does it all mean?" While there were many parables that Jesus didn't explain, he laid this one out in detail.

PART 3

● "This is the meaning of the parable: The seed is the word of God."

Luke 8:11

Each aspect of this word picture had a deeper meaning. The seed stood for God's message, which was disseminated among different types of souls, represented by different types of soils. This was a culture built on farming. People knew about seed and soil.

Seed sown on a path can't take root. It sits there until birds grab it for breakfast. In the same way, some people have their minds closed to the gospel, and their hearts are hard. They have decided in advance that God's message doesn't apply to them. In such cases, the devil can snatch away the message before it ever sinks in.

People would recognize the agricultural phenomenon of rocky soil. Seed might spring up quickly, without putting down roots. So in the heat of the day, those plants would die out for lack of nourishment. This soil, Jesus said, represents people who seem to accept his words but then "fall away." Initially, they make the right steps, but then come the tough times, and they pull back. Maybe they didn't count the cost. Their faith lacked depth.

The thorny soil, as Jesus explained, stands for people who respond well to the gospel but then their faith is "choked by life's worries, riches and pleasures." Other things crowd out what is most important. They don't have time for prayer or reading God's Word. They show great potential, but there is too much other stuff going on in their lives.

Finally comes the good soil that represents people who receive the Word and let it grow to maturity in their lives.

Why did Jesus tell this story? Two reasons: First, he wanted his disciples not to get too upset if their preaching didn't produce the results they thought it deserved. Not everyone will respond to the simple truths of the gospel. But second, he wanted the crowd to know that they couldn't be wishy-washy followers forever.

Both lessons apply to modern hearers as well. What kind of soil are we? Have we responded fully to the message of Christ, sinking down roots and drawing in nourishment? Or are we shallow believers, too distracted by the cares of this world? And as we seek to share our faith with others, we must be ready for the different responses we'll get.

PART 4

● "He who has ears to hear, let him hear."

Luke 8:8

Back to the art gallery. Some people emerge with smiles on their faces, talking excitedly about what they have seen, while others are in a fog, not understanding a thing. Still others are commenting, "You call that art?"

Parables conceal truth as well as they reveal truth. The Gospel of Mark suggests that they conceal truth to the outsiders but reveal truth to the insiders—to those who have ears to hear it.

We all have ears, don't we? Yes, but not everyone has spiritual ears, Jesus says. To hear spiritual things, you need spiritual ears.

Musically, some people have perfect pitch. They hear a note, they know what it is, and they know if it is sharp or flat. Most of us don't have that level of recognition, but that doesn't mean we can't be trained. Our musical ears can be developed.

Have you been developing your spiritual ears?

QUOTE TO NOTE

Are all the soils quite hopeless? . . . Oh, no . . . the fallow ground can be broken up; the rock can be shattered; the thorns can be uprooted; the desert may blossom as the rose. So those who go out, bearing precious seed, shall come again, bringing their sheaves with them.

G. Campbell Morgan

131

23

THE UNINVITED GUEST
WON THE PRIZE

PART 1

Jesus may not have had a "place to lay his head" (Luke 9:58), but he spoke at a lot of banquets. One of them was at the home of a Pharisee named Simon.

Imagine yourself accompanying Jesus to this banquet. Perhaps you've been to other festive occasions with Jesus, such as the wedding in Cana, where he turned water into wine. Maybe you were with him at the banquet that Matthew the tax collector hosted, the one that was attended by "a large crowd of tax collectors." That one certainly raised some eyebrows among the religious elite, who despised tax collectors for collaborating with the occupying forces of Rome.

If you ever attended a dinner with Jesus at the home of Mary and Martha, you probably found it more relaxing and, well, ordinary. Except of course after the raising of Lazarus from the dead. Eating a meal with a man who had been dead for several days was certainly not an everyday event.

But this banquet at the home of Simon the Pharisee had to rank high among the unusual events on Jesus' social calendar.

Many of the common folk in New Testament times lived in one-room, boxlike homes. If you had a two-room house, the two rooms would be separated by an open court generally about the size of a room, something like a modern carport. Sometimes latticework covered the court, but often it was open to the sky.

This open courtyard was the bragging point, the pride and joy of the upper class. It was their dining room; they often planted trees, shrubs, and flowers in it; some had cisterns or wells there. (It saved a lot of walking to and from the town well.) In cold weather they built fires there; in

Monday: Read part 1 of this chapter, and read Luke 7:36–50. Imagine yourself at that dinner.

Tuesday: Read part 2. What teaching method was Jesus using with Simon? Why?

Wednesday: Read part 3. Have you ever done anything extravagant for Jesus?

Thursday: Read part 4. Consider the question in "In the Mirror." How can you change your attitude?

Friday: This lesson is about the love this woman showed to Jesus. Read 1 John 4:7–21, and write down the various characteristics of love.

Saturday: Pray a prayer of confession, remembering the tears of the woman in this story.

Sunday: Praise God for his great love that reaches to sinners such as this woman . . . and even to us.

warmer weather they bathed there. But the open courtyard, like a carport, was often open to the street. So when the upper class had a banquet, people from the neighborhood would stand outside and gawk, especially if there was a celebrity guest attending.

Now if you had been a first-century Jesus-watcher, you would have been scratching your head about several things that evening. First of all, it seemed strange that Jesus was invited to a banquet in his honor at the home of a Pharisee. Pharisees didn't like to be linked with Jesus. (Remember the Pharisee Nicodemus who came to see Jesus in secret?) But it was customary for the leading resident of a town to invite a visiting dignitary to his house for dinner, and that invitation would stand whether he liked the visiting dignitary or not.

Around the banquet table in the courtyard, the guests did not sit on chairs but rather reclined on low couches leaning on the left arm with the head toward the table and the body stretched away from it. You always took off your shoes (sandals) before reclining on the couches, and that meant your bare feet would be sticking out in back.

The Bible doesn't say who the other guests were, but from their reactions to what took place, we can guess that they were Pharisees like Simon.

PART 2

A second unusual thing happened that evening. A woman of the streets came into Simon's courtyard with a jar of perfume. Now, it wasn't unusual for people to gawk or even enter a courtyard during a banquet, but for someone to have the nerve to come right up to an honored guest! And for a *prostitute* to do that! What gall!

She entered the courtyard with an alabaster jar of perfume and stood behind Jesus, at his feet. Soon she began weeping uncontrollably. Her tears fell on his feet, and she knelt, unbound her hair, and wiped his feet with it. Then she kissed his feet and poured her perfume on them.

Had she no shame? Jewish women didn't let down their hair in public. It was a sure sign of her profession as a prostitute.

No doubt the dinner conversation stopped. An awkward silence must have followed. The host wanted to see how Jesus would react, but Jesus did nothing. The Greek words describing what the woman was doing imply continuous action, so it wasn't something she did quickly before running out of the courtyard. She stayed there pouring her perfume onto his feet, wiping them with her hair, and kissing them. It must have been an embarrassing time for all the guests, as well as for the host.

Jesus knew what Simon was thinking. The host was wondering why Jesus didn't stop the woman. If he were really a prophet, Simon thought, he would surely know what kind of a woman she was. And frankly, it wouldn't take a very brilliant prophet to figure out that this woman had been the town prostitute.

Finally, breaking the extended silence, Jesus said, "Simon, I have something to tell you." He proceeded to do what he did so well—he told a story.

● **"Which of them will love him more?"**

Luke 7:42

Suppose two men borrowed money, Jesus said, and neither was able to pay it back. One of them had a debt of fifty thousand dollars and the other five thousand dollars. But instead of demanding repayment, the moneylender said he would forgive both men their debts. Which of the two would show the most gratitude?

Though it seemed an easy question, Simon answered it cautiously and perhaps reluctantly. "I suppose the one who had the bigger debt canceled."

Jesus acknowledged his correct answer and then asked another easy question: "Do you see this woman?"

But Jesus didn't wait for a reply. Of course Simon saw her. Everyone saw her; everyone had been embarrassed by her actions; everyone thought she had ruined this special evening.

But no, Simon hadn't really seen her. He saw the label people had placed on her because of her past. She was a sinner, a prostitute. He didn't see her as a person. He didn't see what she could become and was already becoming.

And here Simon felt the tables turning against him, as Jesus chastised him for his harsh attitude. "When I came into your house, Simon, you didn't give me water to wash my feet [which was customary for the host to provide], you didn't give me a kiss [the kiss of greeting was also customary], and you didn't anoint my head with oil [another duty of a host for an honored guest]." Simon hadn't performed his host duties well. Ironically, it was the woman of the streets who had done all that.

> ### IN THE MIRROR
>
> Jesus said to Simon, "Do you see this woman?" He first saw her "type," then he saw her social sins, but he never saw her as a person. He didn't see her repentance, her love, or her faith. Is there anyone in your life whom you condemn without really seeing them?

This underscored a major theme of Jesus' ministry. On another occasion, he had dared to say that prostitutes and tax collectors would enter God's kingdom ahead of the religious leaders. Why? Because gaining heaven was not about piling up one's own works of righteousness. It was about responding with love and gratitude to the merciful love of God.

PART 3

● "Her many sins have been forgiven—for she loved much. But he who has been forgiven little loves little."

Luke 7:47

Jesus knew the sordid life this woman had been living, but he also knew that God's grace was greater than all her sins. Then he drove home the difference between Simon and the woman. She had a lot of sins to be forgiven, and she responded with a lot of love. Simon considered himself very righteous. Since he felt he didn't require much forgiveness, if any, he felt no need to show much love to Jesus.

Does that mean that Simon and his fellow Pharisees were, in fact, righteous enough already? Oh no. None of us can meet God's standards on our own. And the Pharisees were certainly guilty of the sin of pride. This was why they found it so difficult to follow Jesus. Why should they repent when they had so little to repent of? Or so they thought.

But Jesus' story about the delinquent debtors changed the rules of the game. The righteous acts on which the Pharisees prided themselves amounted to a pile of filthy rags. Jesus was teaching that what really counts is whether we rely on God's forgiveness.

PART 4

● "Your sins are forgiven. . . . Your faith has saved you; go in peace."

Luke 7:48, 50

After chastising Simon, Jesus turned to the woman and declared her sins forgiven. No doubt the buzzing around the table started again. *Does he think he can forgive the sins of this disreputable woman? Who does he think he is? God?*

Jesus didn't seem to pay any attention to their chatter. Instead, he commended the woman for her faith and sent her on her way.

It wasn't her tears, and it wasn't even the love that she showed. Rather, it was her faith that saved her. Throughout Scripture, faith means far more than mental acceptance. It means trusting, relying, depending. This woman knew that she had no great accomplishments to offer God. But Jesus preached that God would forgive sin, and she clung to that message. Her extravagant act of love was the consequence of her faith.

It might seem that Jesus dismisses her with a common benediction, "Go in peace." But literally it means "Go *into* peace." This answers a question you may have about this woman and all the tax collectors and prostitutes who encountered Jesus. What happened next? Did they leave their sinful lifestyles?

We have only a few before-and-after pictures. Zacchaeus the tax collector restored the money he had swindled and then some. Matthew (aka Levi) left tax collecting to follow Jesus. And the challenge to the woman caught in adultery was "Go and leave your life of sin."

The forgiveness Jesus offers is never a blank check to sin all we want. It's the beginning of a new life, in which saving faith continues to empower us each day. To this woman and to all of us who acknowledge our sinfulness and receive God's grace, he says not only "Go in peace" but also "Go into peace." We enter a new life in peaceful harmony with our Lord.

24

CLEANUP TIME

PART 1

● "Why do you break the command of God for the sake of your tradition?"

Matthew 15:3

Two things that your mother probably told you:

1. "Wash your hands before coming to the table."
2. "Don't talk dirty."

You may find it hard to believe that those two things gener-ated a controversy between Jesus and the Pharisees, but they certainly did. The Pharisees came to Jesus, pointing their fingers at his disciples and saying, "They don't wash their hands before they eat!" No fooling. That's an exact quote (see v. 2).

In the first two years of Jesus' public ministry, his popularity ratings in Galilee soared off the charts. Although his hometown of Nazareth threw him out, others in Galilee wanted to make him king, especially after he fed the five thousand. Jesus' popularity alarmed both King Herod, who had been appointed by Rome to keep his thumb on the Jews, and the ultrareligious Pharisees, headquartered in Jerusalem.

The Pharisees were not bad guys wearing black hats. They were good guys, or at least they thought they were until Jesus came along. Not only did the Pharisees keep the Old Testament law, but they built fences around it—extra laws to keep you from accidentally breaking a law—and then they built fences around the fences. We see an example of this in the Matthew 15 controversy over hand washing.

Monday: Read Matthew 15:1–20 and think through the "W's."

Tuesday: Read part 1 of this chapter. What do we mean today if we say someone is pharisaical?

Wednesday: Read part 2. Think about what worship is . . . and what it's not.

Thursday: Read part 3. Who are you leading and where are you leading them?

Friday: Read part 4. Where does your righteousness come from?

Saturday: As you pray today, ask the Lord to point out to you anything that is unclean in your heart and ask for help in removing it.

Sunday: Read Galatians 3:26–29 and thank God for your freedom in Christ.

When your mother told you to wash your hands before coming to the table, she was saying that for sanitary reasons (and maybe because your little sister told her that you hadn't). But the Pharisees' concern was religious, not medical. They didn't know about germs or microbes. They had a different kind of pollution in mind.

Matthew 14 ends with crowds thronging around Jesus, coming from everywhere to get close to him. "People brought all their sick to him and begged him to let the sick just touch the edge of his cloak, and all who touched him were healed" (vv. 35–36). No doubt, when Jesus was busy healing these people, one of his disciples was nibbling on a peanut butter sandwich, or the first-century equivalent. So when the Pharisees arrived from Jerusalem to check up on Jesus, they didn't criticize Jesus; they picked on the disciples.

With all the diseased people coming to Jesus, you might think the Pharisees would be most concerned about the sanitary aspects of hand washing, but that wasn't the issue. What bugged the Pharisees was the breaking of their tradition.

Remember the song "Tradition! Tradition!" in *Fiddler on the Roof*? To the Pharisees, keeping tradition was just as important as keeping the scriptural injunctions. In the process of defining tradition, they were quite precise. When they said that the hands had to be washed, they meant that first the hands had to be lifted up so that water could run down to their wrists and beyond. If the hands were pointing downward, the water would run down the fingers and dirt might accumulate at the fingertips. Tradition even told you how much water you had to use to wash each hand. Then the process was reversed with more water, but with hands pointing downward. Of course, there was no Old Testament law that specified this, but some of the elders may have thought they needed to elaborate on the command "Sanctify yourselves" (Lev. 11:44 KJV), and the Pharisees were experts in elaborating.

Rather than answer the charge against his disciples, Jesus responded by saying that the Pharisees disobeyed Scripture and yet stayed within the boundaries of their traditions. And he offered an example. The Ten Commandments tell us to honor father and mother, but the Pharisees had a way around that. If a Pharisee had some money that he didn't want to use to support his parents, he could declare it *korban* (a gift devoted to God). In fact he could say that all his possessions were *korban* and thus escape all obligations.

Jesus saw through their hypocrisy. While they claimed that their traditions helped people keep the law of God, in actuality their extra laws provided loopholes that allowed them to break the law.

PART 2

● "You nullify the word of God for the sake of your tradition."

Matthew 15:6

While Jesus spoke this to the Jewish leaders of his day, it's a warning that the Christian church has struggled with throughout its history. It's easy for denominational distinctives and even local church traditions to become etched in stone. They may start out as helpful expressions of obedience, but soon they become more sacrosanct than the Word of God itself. And at some point we may become proud, act hatefully, or even commit violent acts to preserve our tradition.

> **CROSS REF**
>
> Read some of the first chapters of Leviticus to see what the law was like. Read Psalm 50:16 and compare it to Matthew 15:8–9.

Sometimes this occurs in the context of worship. We may observe certain forms of worship, resisting any variation. Yet Jesus said in John 4:24 that worship is a matter of "spirit and truth." Worship is relationship, not simply ritual. The Psalms erupt often with the challenge: "Sing to the Lord a new song." Traditional rituals can assist worship, but we must not be riveted to them.

After challenging their traditions, Jesus called the Pharisees hypocrites. He would use that term for them many more times before his ministry was completed. Here he quoted a prophecy from Isaiah, which seems to define hypocrisy: "These people honor me with their lips, but their hearts are far from me" (Matt. 15:8). To hear them talk, you'd think they put God first. But in fact, when they wanted to get around the clear commands of God's Word, they found a way to do it.

> **IN THE MIRROR**
>
> Do you hear Jesus speaking to you when he says, "You nullify the word of God for the sake of your tradition"? Think about your traditions. Have they lost their heartfelt meaning?

PART 3

● "If a blind man leads a blind man, both will fall into a pit."

Matthew 15:14

The Pharisees, supposedly the spiritual guides for the people, were themselves blind to the truth of God. What happens when one blind man leads another? They both fall into a ditch. That's what was going on in Judea, Jesus said.

In his Epistle to the Romans, Paul spoke to Jewish leaders, "If you . . . are instructed by the law; if you are convinced that you are a guide for the blind, a light for those who are in the dark . . . you, then, who teach others, do you not teach yourself?" (Rom. 2:18–21). That's essentially the same challenge Jesus was making.

It's also a lesson for all who study and teach the Scriptures. We must make sure we stay close to the One the Scriptures are all about, so that the eyes of our hearts may be enlightened (Eph. 1:18).

PART 4

● "The things that come out of the mouth come from the heart, and these make a man 'unclean.' For out of the heart come evil thoughts, murder, adultery, sexual immorality, theft, false testimony, slander. These are what make a man 'unclean.'"

Matthew 15:18–20

After Jesus discussed the ritual of washing your hands properly before eating, he also got into the question of clean and unclean foods, or as we would say it, kosher and nonkosher foods. Jesus summarized the matter by saying that the problem is not with the food that goes into your mouth but with the thoughts and actions that come out of your heart. (In the parallel account in Mark 7:21–22, he adds seven more evil things to the list: greed, malice, deceit, lewdness, envy, arrogance, and folly.)

Jesus goes beyond your mother's injunction, "Don't talk dirty." What comes out of the mouth *is* dirty, Jesus says, because the heart itself is dirty. While some of the matters on the list exhibit themselves in talk (slander, false testimony, and deceit, for example), other dirty matters are acted out (murder, adultery, theft), and still others may ferment in the heart for years (evil thoughts, malice, and arrogance) before erupting. But sooner or later they too will be acted out. As Jesus pointed out in his

142

Sermon on the Mount, those who hate are really murderers, and those who think lustfully are really adulterers. So none of us gets off scot-free.

That's why Jesus came, not to establish a new religion with new sets of rules and regulations, not to give a codebook or an operations manual. Jesus was concerned about clean hearts, not about clean foods. Many people can change their diet; many religious practitioners can change their rituals; but only Jesus can change your heart.

In Galatians 5:22–23 the apostle Paul gives a list of things that are in the Christian's heart when the Holy Spirit takes over. It's a different kind of list. "Love, joy, peace, patience, kindness, goodness, faithfulness, gentleness and self-control." If love, joy, peace, and so on are in the heart, there's no room for all that other dirty stuff.

25
IDENTITY COMPLEX

PART 1

● "Who do people say the Son of Man is?"

Matthew 16:13

It was time for the stretch run. Jesus had been teaching and healing, mostly in Galilee, for a couple of years. He was certainly famous by now, but for what was he known?

His enemies weren't sure what to do with him. He flouted their Sabbath rules and challenged their lifestyle. The people seemed to love him, but were they really understanding his cryptic stories? Was he just another flavor of the month, or would he make a difference long term?

Like modern business leaders, Jesus knew that he had to keep reviewing his core values. You might think that Jesus' disciples would have mastered the Master's message by now, but Jesus wanted to make sure they were on the same page.

He started with a public opinion poll. *What's the buzz? What are people saying about me?* Consider the multiple-choice answers they came up with.

John the Baptist. John had made a huge splash, baptizing in the Jordan and preaching repentance. His fame was already strong

144

when Jesus appeared on the scene. Shortly thereafter John was imprisoned and executed. You might excuse some folks for thinking the two preachers were the same man.

Elijah. The last verses of the Old Testament promise a return of the fiery prophet Elijah before the day of the Lord (Mal. 4:5). So apparently some saw Jesus as a prophet with cosmic significance, breaking four centuries of prophetic silence, ushering in a time of God's redemptive activity on Israel's behalf. They got some of that right.

Jeremiah or one of the prophets. Certainly Jesus' creative and authoritative preaching placed him in league with the prophets of old. But why is Jeremiah mentioned specifically? Often known as "the weeping prophet," Jeremiah bemoaned the corruption of Judah's leaders. He warned of judgment to come and yet spoke of God's "everlasting love" (Jer. 31:3). Jesus had been doing all of the above. And since there's no record of Jeremiah's death, some thought he might have returned as Jesus.

EVERY DAY WITH JESUS

Monday: Read part 1 of this chapter. How would you respond to Jesus' question? What do people in your community think about Jesus?

Tuesday: Read part 2. Imagine yourself with the disciples on this retreat. What are the sights, sounds, and sensations of the place?

Wednesday: Read part 3. What rocklike qualities do you have? What rocklike qualities could God develop in you?

Thursday: Take your own opinion poll by reading Matthew 27:19, 29, and 54. How did these people identify Jesus?

Friday: Reread Matthew 16:16–17. Have there been times when you have thought or said things that "were not revealed by man," things that seemed to be inspired by God? How did you feel on those occasions?

Saturday: Read John 11:27. How does Martha's confession of faith compare with Peter's?

Sunday: Read Matthew 16:13–20 again. Worship God today as the One who reveals truth about himself.

PART 2

● "But what about you? . . . Who do you say I am?"

Matthew 16:15

145

Consider the scene. Jesus was on a retreat with his disciples, up to the highlands north of Galilee, away from the crowds. This was where the Jordan River gathered its waters before flowing south into the Sea of Galilee and south again toward Jerusalem, eventually emptying into the Dead Sea. In the same way, this was the beginning of Jesus' ultimate journey—a final surge of Galilean ministry, then on to Jerusalem and to his death.

After taking his public opinion poll, the Master was ready with his follow-up question. "Who do you say I am?"

Simon Peter, seldom at a loss for words, spoke up. "You are the Christ, the Son of the living God" (v. 16). The answer was stunningly on target, so much so that Jesus suggested Peter was getting divine prompting. Still, Jesus blessed Peter for saying this and stated that he would build a new community on this confession of faith (or on Peter himself).

What was Peter saying? *Christ* is Greek for "Anointed One," same as the Hebrew word *Messiah*. From Isaiah 61:1 and other prophecies, some Jews were looking for a specially appointed Redeemer whom God would send to save them. While it was flattering to be identified with John, Elijah, and Jeremiah, this confession places Jesus far higher. He was not just a spokesman for the living God; he was God's Son. He would not just announce God's redemptive activity; he would bring it.

PART 3

● "On this rock I will build my church."

Matthew 16:18

You have to wonder how Peter felt when Jesus said this to him. He had never been shy about expressing his opinion, but he sometimes regretted his comments later. Perhaps he was worried that he had gone overboard again, claiming a status for

Jesus that bordered on blasphemy. Would Jesus rebuke him for overstating the case?

Scripture says that Jesus "blessed" Peter for saying, "You are the Christ, the Son of the living God." *Blessed* is the same word he used in the Beatitudes. It's not that he was praising Peter but that he was expressing how fortunate Peter was to get this message from above.

Then Jesus made a little joke. He punned on Peter's name to make an important point. *Peter* means "rock." Jesus stated that he would build a new community on this rock. What exactly did he mean by that? Well, that's a matter of interpretation. According to Roman Catholics, Peter himself is the foundation rock of the church. They see this verse as the establishment of Peter as the church's first leader, starting a succession of popes. But Protestants tend to say that the "rock" was Peter's *confession of faith*. The church has been built on the belief that Jesus is the Messiah, the Son of the living God. The biblical text can support either interpretation. And historically, the book of Acts shows Peter as the main man in the church's crucial early years. Perhaps this is what Jesus meant.

Maybe there's not as much difference on that point as it seems. Isn't it true that we are what we believe—especially what we believe about the Lord? It was Peter's trust in Jesus that made him a rock-solid leader of the church. The same can be true for us. As we let Jesus empower us, he transforms our character.

QUOTE TO NOTE

A man who was merely a man and said the sort of things Jesus said would not be a great moral teacher. He would either be a lunatic . . . or else he would be the Devil of Hell. You must make your choice. Either this man was, and is, the Son of God: or else a madman or something worse.

C. S. Lewis

26
THE CRUCIAL WAGER

● "If anyone would come after me, he must deny himself and take up his cross daily and follow me."

Luke 9:23

The chapter begins with the twelve disciples going out on a missionary foray and returning to Jesus with great jubilation. Then crowds gathered and Jesus fed the five thousand. It was awesome. After that, alone with his disciples, Jesus asked them, "Who do you say that I am?" and Peter gave his great confession, "The Christ of God."

What a string of fantastic events! Who wouldn't want to jump on the bandwagon? Who wouldn't want to be first in line behind the miracle-working Messiah?

But then Jesus told them what was ahead of him. He would have to suffer and die. Their balloons were punctured.

Not only was Jesus predicting his suffering and death, but he was also saying that those who would follow him would not have an easy time of it either. So much for the bandwagon. Who's first in line now?

To us a cross is almost like a good luck charm—but not in those days. The disciples knew the purpose of crosses. Galilee was known for its insurrections, and the Romans had executed hundreds of Jews, using this very instrument of torture. Often the condemned man would have to carry his cross to the execution site, suffering a final indignity before dying a cruel death. And now Jesus was asking his disciples to "take up" a cross each day? Did he want them to pick one up every morning after breakfast?

Don't spiritualize this statement too soon. Recognize the horror of it, the stark absurdity. Those who wanted to follow Jesus fully would have to put their lives on the line on a daily basis, suffering all sorts of indignity, cruelty, and perhaps even death.

Discipleship is something like enlisting in the military in a time of war. You are now taking orders from a new commander. In his classic, *My Utmost for His Highest*, Oswald Chambers often uses the word *abandonment*. It's a word that's not used much in the same sense anymore: "a complete surrender without restraint or moderation." That's what Jesus asks from his followers—abandonment to his direction.

Monday: Read part 1 of this chapter. What does the cross mean to you?

Tuesday: Read part 2. Think about last week. In what ways did you "deny yourself" to follow Jesus?

Wednesday: Read part 3. Which of your activities threaten to lose "the real you"?

Thursday: Jim Elliot had a mission. What's yours?

Friday: Consider the question in "In the Mirror."

Saturday: Pray for missionaries; perhaps you know some personally. They need our prayers for strength, patience, and safety.

Sunday: Read aloud Psalm 71:22–24 and rejoice in the Lord. Let your joy overflow to a neighbor and to others in your family.

IN THE MIRROR

How do you "take up your cross daily"?

When Jesus says we must take up our cross daily, he is saying that total commitment means never looking back, no matter how bad things look ahead of us. If we are walking with Jesus, we must go with him wherever he goes.

Can you imagine a soldier getting out of his bunk at reveille and saying, "I don't feel like being a soldier today; I don't want to fight any battles today; it's too dangerous"?

Jesus is saying that life as a Christian may be dangerous, and the closer we get to the front lines, the more dangerous it becomes.

PART 2

You say, "I like the part of Christianity that talks about love, joy, peace, and everlasting life, but this part about denying myself and taking up my cross daily—this part is scary."

149

● "For whoever wants to save his life will lose it, but whoever loses his life for me will save it."

Luke 9:24

That doesn't make sense—or does it?

This is the crucial wager: to try to save your life and avoid the cross or to lose your life in total abandonment to Jesus.

Jim Elliot was still a college student in 1949 when he confronted this verse and its crucial wager. Jim felt he had to give a clear-cut response to Jesus' challenge, so he wrote, almost as a commentary on the verse, "He is no fool who gives what he cannot keep to gain what he cannot lose."

When you come to think of it, the wager makes sense. Your earthly life is a perishable commodity; eternal life is imperishable.

Jim Elliot chose to offer himself in missionary service, using his temporal life to advance God's eternal kingdom. Five years later he was in Ecuador with four other young missionaries, trying to figure out the best way to bring the gospel to the Auca Indians, a tribe that had never heard about Jesus. Flying a small plane, they dropped gifts into an Auca village, indicating their peaceful intent. Eventually they landed in a clearing and made contact with the Aucas. But early in 1956, all five missionaries were killed by some of the tribesmen they were trying to reach for Christ.

> **CROSS REF**
>
> For a new perspective on death, read:
> Romans 6:5–10
> 1 Corinthians 15:31
> Philippians 3:10–12

This modern martyrdom made international headlines. What a waste! Five bright, young lives snuffed out. But Jim Elliot would be the first to correct the notion that it was a waste. This was no tragedy. He had won his wager. He had finally gained what he could not lose.

PART 3

● "What good is it for a man to gain the whole world, and yet lose or forfeit his very self?"

Luke 9:25

In Paris in the early 1500s, Francis Xavier was a professor of philosophy at the University of Paris during the day, but at night he was a playboy. Practically addicted to gambling, he found Parisian nightlife thrilling. Still, it left him empty. And then one night he met an old friend, who kept repeating Luke 9:25.

Xavier tried to walk away from the Bible-quoter, but finally he knelt and dedicated the rest of his life to his new Master. Soon he quit his professorship and was ordained to the priesthood. Then he went out as a missionary to India, Thailand, the South Sea islands, and Japan. Called the greatest missionary since the apostle Paul, he died in Thailand at the age of forty-six. It has been estimated that he brought more than a million people to Christ. Did Xavier take a gamble that night in Paris? And did he win or lose?

> **BOOK BIN**
>
> Want to read more about Jim Elliot and the Aucas? Read *Through Gates of Splendor* by Elisabeth Elliot and *The Journals of Jim Elliot*, edited by Elisabeth Elliot.

French philosopher/scientist Blaise Pascal was the author of *Pensées*, a collection of his brilliant thoughts. In it he writes about the crucial wager. "You must wager," he says. "It is not optional." He says that all humankind must make a wager first of all on whether God exists. If you wager that God is and act on it, "you gain all; if you lose, you lose nothing." What you wager is finite, says Pascal; what you stand to gain is infinite.

Our world is filled with people who have devoted their lives to "gaining the world." Rich people strive to get richer. Executives clamber up the corporate ladder. Power moguls seek more and more power. And yet, again and again, we see that worldly fortunes are won at the expense of something important. Jesus talked about losing one's "very self." The Greek word there is *psyche*, often translated "soul," but it can mean "personality" or even "the real you."

Only when you lose yourself in Jesus do you find "the real you." Only when you lose yourself in Jesus does your personality become complete. What a divine wager!

27

POSSIBILITIES UNLIMITED

Definition: *mountain*—an up between two downs.

However you look at it, ups and downs go together. On the mountaintops of life you feel exhilarated. Breezes blow through your hair, and on a clear day you can see forever. In the valleys of life, the stagnant air can crush you like a sumo wrestler. In life, our mountaintop visits seem way too short, while our time in the valleys seems interminable.

Again and again, the Bible moves from mountains to valleys and back again. Where did God give Moses the Ten Commandments? On Mount Sinai. But then Moses went down into the valley and saw the Israelites worshiping a golden calf. Where did Elijah call down fire from heaven to defeat the prophets of Baal? On Mount Carmel. But then he went down into the valley and had to flee the wrath of Queen Jezebel.

In the early verses of Matthew 17, Jesus is on the mountain with his disciples when Moses and Elijah appear and a voice from heaven thunders: "This is my Son, whom I love." The face of Jesus "shone like the sun, and his clothes became as white as the light." Talk about mountaintop experiences! This beats them all.

But then comes the valley. As Jesus, along with Peter, James, and John, walk the trail down the mountain, they see a crowd waiting for them. A man runs to Jesus and begs him, "Lord, have mercy on my son" (v. 15). His son was having frequent seizures, and besides that, he was plagued by a demon. The father went on to say, "I brought him to your disciples, but they could not heal him."

Those nine disciples who were left behind in the valley must have felt chagrined, embarrassed, and totally defeated. Previously, they had gone on mission trips with Jesus during which they had healed people and cast out demons; but now they were ineffective. How frustrating to be losers in front of a crowd of people!

Monday: Read part 1 of this chapter. Now read Matthew 17:1–5. What was Peter not getting?

Tuesday: Read part 2. Have you ever seen amazing results from faith-filled prayer?

Wednesday: Read part 3. Does your prayer life tend to be chatting or wrestling?

Thursday: What "mountains" in your life would you like to move?

Friday: Is anything greater than faith? See 1 Corinthians 13:13 to find out. Why is this true?

Saturday: Reflect on your own faith. Did any part of this chapter reveal to you the nature of your faith? Is there any way you could strengthen your faith?

Sunday: Praise God for his many answers to prayer. Try to think of several specific answers and thank him for those.

Here's a nugget of insight for you. Throughout the Gospels, when Jesus goes "up," he displays God's power, but when he comes "down," he overcomes our weakness. As his followers, we need to accompany him up to the mountaintops but also invite him to accompany us and give us answers in our valleys.

In this case, the boy was brought to Jesus, and the father explained that his son had had a problem from childhood. The situation was desperate; the son often threw himself into streams or fires. "If you can do anything," the father begged Jesus, "take pity on us and help us" (Mark 9:22).

● "'If you can'? . . . Everything is possible for him who believes."

Mark 9:23

Jesus zeroed in on the first three words the man said: "If you can." What tone of voice did the man use for these words,

CHECKOUT COUNTER

Check out Romans 5:1–2 to see what else our faith accomplishes.

and how did Jesus sound when he repeated them? We can't know for sure. But you can imagine that this father had probably consulted several rabbis and healers already, receiving no help. Then, hearing that Jesus was in the area, he sought help from the disciples, but they couldn't help either. Finally, when Jesus trekked down from the mountain, the father called out, "If *you* can do anything . . ."

Or was the emphasis on *If*? You couldn't blame the father for nearly giving up hope. Maybe no one could heal the boy, not even this wonder-working rabbi. But if he could . . . if he could . . .

Did this phrasing amuse Jesus, or was he just taking the opportunity to teach a lesson? In any case, he turned it back on the father. "Everything is possible for him who believes." The question was not whether Jesus had power to heal but whether the father had faith to believe that Jesus could heal.

The father responded immediately with an amazingly poignant cry: "I do believe; help me overcome my unbelief!" What an honest response! Like all of us, he was a big bag of faith and doubt. He did trust in Jesus, he really did, but he had been disappointed so many times before. Instead of pumping the purity of his own faith, he just laid it all out before Jesus. And despite the fact that his belief was mixed with some unbelief, Jesus healed the son.

PART 2

● After Jesus had gone indoors, his disciples asked him privately, "Why couldn't we drive it out?"

He replied, *"This kind can come out only by prayer."*

Mark 9:28–29, emphasis added

Jesus' disciples had just failed miserably, attempting to drive a demon out of a young boy. To their credit, they wanted to learn from their mistakes. *What did we do wrong, Jesus?*

These disciples had come to regard their healing powers as a gift of magic. *Hocus-pocus* and you're healed. It seems that the disciples had forgotten that it was God's power that did the healing, not their own. God is not a genie who comes out of a lamp when we utter our prayers.

Prayer and faith are both about *relationship*. We pray to "our Father" and we trust him to bring his kingdom into our world. Our prayers of faith don't create the power of healing—they merely open the door and invite our compassionate, powerful God to enter the situations of our lives.

> **DARE TO COMPARE**
>
> Mark's account of faith moving mountains is expanded and more dramatic. Take a look in Mark 11:22–25.

PART 3

● "If you have faith as small as a mustard seed, you can say to this mountain, 'Move from here to there' and it will move. Nothing will be impossible for you."

Matthew 17:20

That is real "possibility thinking." But what does it mean?

Think of the smallest seed you know. Well, the black mustard seed was the smallest seed that Palestinian farmers knew, and yet it could grow more than fifteen feet tall. In other words, Jesus was saying that you don't need a whole lot of faith to accomplish something in the kingdom of God. A little faith will do. It's not the quantity; it's the quality.

Can we really move mountains? Well, Jesus was talking in the shadow of the Mount of Transfiguration, so he may have gestured toward the mountain as he spoke. Yet the Jews knew the phrase "to move mountains" as a metaphor, even as we do when we say we have a mountain of work. Obviously that's the sort of thing he's talking about: mountainous situations, huge obstacles, Everests of aggravation. When the impossible is looming ahead of us, we need to come to God in faith and ask him to remove the mountain.

On several occasions in the Gospels, Jesus indicates that someone's faith has healed him or her. That gets us to thinking that we must drum up some otherworldly optimism to get our prayers answered. But this story from Matthew 17 is very instructive. Apparently the disciples were not acting in faith at

CROSS REF

Read more about faith:
Hebrews 11
Ephesians 2:8–9
1 John 5:4–5

all. Disconnected from their power source, they were completely ineffective. Yet the boy's father admitted that there was unbelief mixed with his faith, and still, his son was healed. Why? Because even with his so-so faith, he connected with Jesus, the Source of power.

Jesus reminds us that it's not how big our faith is but how big our God is. The smallest faith, even tinged with doubt, can open the door for great miracles, as long as it is humbly presented before our powerful Lord.

Jesus' words make it sound so easy, don't they? Nothing will be impossible, he said, but we struggle with mountains every day. Even the little potholes on our daily walk don't go away easily. Why don't all our problems miraculously vanish? Shouldn't our prayers be able to send them sliding into the sea?

That's the mystery of faith and the paradox of prayer. Praying in faith is both easy and hard. It's easy because we now have "access to the Father" (Eph. 2:18). It's hard because we struggle "against the powers of this dark world and against the spiritual forces of evil in the heavenly realms" (Eph. 6:12). It's easy because "no matter how many promises God has made, they are 'Yes' in Christ" (2 Cor. 1:20). It's hard because we see Old Testament heroes like Jacob wrestling with God and Job groping in darkness. It's easy because Jesus said, "Ask and you will receive" (John 16:24). It's hard because even Jesus in the Garden of Gethsemane prayed until "his sweat was like drops of blood falling to the ground" (Luke 22:44).

Today we need to practice prayer when it's easy and when it's hard. Easy prayers include our chats with God throughout the day. Jesus said, "I have called you friends" (John 15:15), and friends like to share whatever is on their hearts.

But the hard kind of prayer occurs when those mountains loom ahead of us, when we move from the chat room to the conference room, when we don't understand what the Lord is doing, when all the lights are off and we can't find the nearest switch.

Both kinds of prayer are important for our relationship with God. And we can prepare ourselves for our hard prayers in the darkness by remaining faithful with the easy prayers in the light.

28

TWO OR THREE

Chances are, you have seen this happen in your church. A offends B in some way. Perhaps Alice didn't invite Barbara to the big wedding. Perhaps Andrew connived to replace Bob as head of the stewardship committee. Perhaps Adam preached a sermon that Beth thought was critical of her. Perhaps Amy was gossiping about Ben. Yes, it's hard to believe, but all those things can happen within a church.

In any case, B feels wounded by A. And what does B do about it? He or she sulks, avoids A, or possibly says hurtful things to others about A. Walls go up between these two believers. They might go through the motions of Christian fellowship, but there is no genuine love anymore.

That's the situation Jesus confronts in Matthew 18, giving us amazingly detailed guidelines for making things right.

- "If your brother sins against you, go and show him his fault, just between the two of you. If he listens to you, you have won your brother over."

Matthew 18:15

157

Monday: Read part 1 of this chapter. What is the purpose of confronting someone else with a fault (Matt. 18:15)?

Tuesday: Read part 2. Is this "two or three witnesses" step easy to do or difficult? Why?

Wednesday: Read part 3. How should a "pagan or tax collector" be treated?

Thursday: Read part 4. Can you see the joy in verses 19–20?

Friday: What are the dangers of the confrontational approach Jesus recommends? What are the possibilities?

Saturday: Pray for unity in your church. Pray about any ill will you may have toward other Christians.

Sunday: Read Ephesians 4:1–6. As your heart lifts in praise, also pray that the Lord will help you "make every effort to keep the unity of the Spirit."

The process starts with a personal confrontation, probably the most difficult part of all. Many of us avoid confrontation at all costs. We will nurse our wounds privately and hold major grudges, but we won't simply talk to the person who wronged us. Yet our attitude just draws us into sin as well.

Jesus recommends the direct approach. Tell the person what the problem is, and see what he or she has to say. Maybe the offense was unintentional. Maybe you imagined something that never happened. In those cases, communication can usually clear up the conflict. An apology might be offered and fellowship restored. If there was an intentional trespass involved, then your rebuke might stir repentance.

PART 2

● "But if he will not listen, take one or two others along, so that 'every matter may be established by the testimony of two or three witnesses.'"

Matthew 18:16

Sometimes people just won't listen. You confront them with an issue, and they don't want to hear you. The Greek word here is graphic; literally it means "to hear sideways." You're asking someone to pay attention to your complaint, but they turn aside, continuing in the same direction they were going.

The next step in the confrontation process is to bring one or two others into it.
Jesus quotes from Old Testament court
procedures: "One witness is not enough
to convict a man accused of any crime or
offense he may have committed. A matter must be established by the testimony

<table>
<tr><td>CROSS REF.</td></tr>
<tr><td>Read more about
relationships:
   Matthew 5:23–24
   Philippians 2:1–5</td></tr>
</table>

of two or three witnesses" (Deut. 19:15). Of course this isn't a
court case, but the principle is a wise one.

Maybe you're just being too sensitive. Maybe you're misunderstanding the situation, and the other person hasn't really
wronged you at all. In that case, your "witnesses" will be able
to tell you that. But if there is a genuine offense, and if the
offender hasn't made things right, those extra witnesses lend
force to your case. Their involvement may give you perspective
on the case or may convince the offender to get things straight.
This is the church at work—in microcosm.

It's also interesting that private transgressions can remain
relatively private through this point in the process. You don't
go crying to the church board every time your feelings are hurt.
Thus many matters can be resolved discreetly, before they're
blown out of proportion.

PART 3

● "If he refuses to listen to them, tell it to the church; and if
he refuses to listen even to the church, treat him as you
would a pagan or a tax collector."

Matthew 18:17

What church? When Jesus said this, there was not yet a
church. It's possible that Jesus used a generic Aramaic word
for "assembly" and Matthew translated it as the specific Greek
word for church (*ekklesia*). Yet Jesus may have been foreseeing
the church that his disciples would become, which the next
few verses hint at. In any case, the next step in the process is
clear. If confrontation by "two or three" doesn't work, then
the whole community of believers must hear the matter. If

IN THE MIRROR

Are you at odds with another Christian? Do you need to confront the situation? How would you go about this?

the offender remains obstinate, he or she should be treated as someone outside the community.

You shouldn't stop loving the obstinate offender, but you should stop expecting the person to act like a believer. However, we should do all we can to love an unrepentant sinner back into the grace of God.

The goal of the whole process is back in verse 15: to win your brother over. It's not about gaining revenge or vindication but about restoring fellowship with the person and helping him or her get right with God. We join the Good Shepherd in leading the lost sheep back to the fold.

PART 4

● "Again, I tell you that if two of you on earth agree about anything you ask for, it will be done for you by my Father in heaven. For where two or three come together in my name, there am I with them."

Matthew 18:19–20

The football team is ready for its big game, but their star running back is hospitalized with a season-ending injury. Shortly before kickoff, he calls the locker room. "I'll be with you in spirit," he says.

"We're playing this one for you," the team replies.

Is that what Jesus is saying here? That he'll be with us in spirit if we play each day for him? Sort of, but there's much, much more.

What does it mean to come together in his name?

One name prophesied for him is Emmanuel, which means "God with us." Our gathering begins with the knowledge that he is indeed with us, that all the fullness of the Father dwells in Jesus, who dwells within us through his Spirit. God is not some absentee landlord but an important presence affecting every aspect of our lives.

Together, we bear the name *Christians*. The Christ people. Paul says, "Now you are the body of Christ, and each one of you is a part of it" (1 Cor. 12:27). We have different gifts, as any body has different parts, but together we do the work of Christ. The Greek name *Christ*, like the Hebrew *Messiah*, means "Anointed One." As Jesus began his earthly ministry, he described his anointing by quoting Isaiah 61—"The Spirit of the Lord is on me, because he has anointed me to preach good news to the poor. He has sent me to proclaim freedom for the prisoners and recovery of sight for the blind, to release the oppressed, to proclaim the year of the Lord's favor" (Luke 4:18–19).

When we gather in the name of Christ, we take on his anointing. We are mini-Messiahs, if you will, anointed to continue his ministry to the poor and oppressed, proclaiming freedom and the Lord's favor.

When Jesus says that anything we ask will be done for us, it's not a blank check for new cars or full bank accounts. The underlying assumption is that we are agreeing *in his name*, which means that we will receive what we need to do his work. There is great power in the prayer of two or three or two hundred. We commit ourselves as we pray, "Your will be done," and he gives us the strength and support to do his will.

QUOTE TO NOTE

There are two ways of being united . . . frozen together, and melted together. What Christians most need is to be united in brotherly love.

Dwight L. Moody

29
KID STUFF

The Bible never talks about how cute children are. Genesis to Revelation, you won't find a whisper of "Kids say the darnedest things." Oh, we get a few snapshots for the family album—young Samuel misunderstanding God's voice and waking up Eli, or the twelve-year-old Jesus dazzling rabbis in the temple—but generally children are not celebrated for innocence or beauty or ornery behavior. They are pretty much ignored.

Yes, children were seen as a blessing, but that's because they would care for you in your old age. In the meantime, they were extra mouths to feed, completely dependent creatures who couldn't contribute much to the family business until they grew up. As a young man, Timothy was told, "Don't let anyone look down on you because you are young" (1 Tim. 4:12). That's an apt phrase. Children were looked down on, figuratively as well as literally.

So when Jesus was surrounded by a crowd of parents bringing their tots to touch him, it's understandable that the disciples tried to turn them away. These fishermen-turned-henchmen weren't being ogres; they were just reflecting the attitude of the times. Jesus had to save his energy for the ministry that really mattered. After all, he was on his way to Jerusalem for a final showdown with the authorities. He couldn't be bothered with these halflings.

We can be thankful that Jesus didn't see it that way.

● When Jesus saw this, he was indignant. He said to them, "Let the little children come to me, and do not hinder them, for the kingdom of God belongs to such as these. I tell you the truth, anyone who will not receive the kingdom of God like a little child will never enter it." And he took the children in his arms, put his hands on them and blessed them.

Mark 10:14–16

PART 2

Let's get it straight from the outset. Jesus did not welcome these young'uns because they were cute. This was not a Precious Moments scene—kids with big eyes and tousled hair. Nor did he open his arms to them because they were innocent. Any parent knows that kids come with a built-in rebellious streak. "Don't do that," you say. You turn around, and they're doing it just the same, except perhaps with greater purpose. Among children, as with adults, "There is none righteous—no, not one."

So these kids brought nothing to earn Jesus' favor. Except this. They couldn't fend for themselves. Children must trust in parents for food and clothing and shelter. They are completely dependent, and that's the object lesson Jesus makes.

EVERY DAY WITH JESUS

Monday: Read part 1 of this chapter. We always need to pay attention when Jesus shows emotion. Here he is indignant. About what?

Tuesday: Read part 2. What characteristics of childhood are admirable?

Wednesday: Read part 3. How can you go about changing something basic about yourself?

Thursday: Read part 4. Who are the humble believers who would make your Hall of Fame?

Friday: Is there some area of your life where you're striving for prominence when you should be developing a humbler spirit?

Saturday: Pray for the children you know in your church or elsewhere.

Sunday: Read Hannah's prayer of praise in 1 Samuel 2:1–2. Pray it along with her.

IN THE MIRROR

What lessons do you need to learn from children?

The kingdom of God belongs to these little ones, says Jesus. Hmmm. Who else did he say the kingdom belongs to? In the Beatitudes, Jesus told us that the kingdom rested with the "poor in spirit" (Matt. 5:3), the humble, those who stake no claim on the kingdom but receive it in faith, as a gift. In other words, the childlike.

But here Jesus goes further. This isn't just some special waiver. It's not "Kids eat free!" This is a *requirement*. No one enters the kingdom without becoming like a little child. That's what puzzled Nicodemus, the Pharisee who came to interview Jesus in secret (John 3). Jesus insisted that he be "born again" if he wanted to see the kingdom. Nicodemus recognized the physical impossibility of a literal understanding of that metaphor, but what did Jesus actually mean?

Our modern world has gone through a love-hate relationship with the term *born again*. Somewhere along the line it came to mean "getting a whole new outlook on life," and that's probably part of it. But the central meaning must be something like the dependence we find here in Mark (and elsewhere). Unless we become dependent like little children, receiving what we're given, we have no place in God's kingdom. The Pharisees could print out their impressive résumés and trot out their character references. They could trumpet their good deeds until they were blue in the face. But none of that would get them past the bouncers at the gates of heaven. It's children who get to walk in free.

We keep trying to impress God by being more religious than everyone else. We think God will welcome us because of our many good deeds. But Jesus keeps telling us that's not the case. We must strip ourselves of all that pretense, becoming as naked as babies and just as helpless. All we can do is cry out to him, and he takes it from there.

PART 3

- At that time the disciples came to Jesus and asked, "Who is the greatest in the kingdom of heaven?"

  He called a little child and had him stand among them. And he said: "I tell you the truth, unless you change and become like little children, you will never enter the kingdom of heaven. Therefore, whoever humbles himself like this child is the greatest in the kingdom of heaven.

"And whoever welcomes a little child like this in my name welcomes me."

Matthew 18:1–5

The disciples were squabbling, as usual, about their places in the kingdom. Jesus would soon be making his move, setting up his new regime, and they were jockeying for the best positions—secretary of state, perhaps, or superintendent of fishingr rights. No doubt Peter, James, and John felt especially close to Jesus and assumed they deserved higher posts than, say, Bartholomew. They asked Jesus to settle the matter.

> **CROSS REF**
>
> Read more about God's view of children:
> Deuteronomy 11:18–19
> Psalm 127:3
> Isaiah 54:13
> Luke 9:48

Jesus was a master of the object lesson. "Look at the fields!" he said on one occasion, before teaching an important truth. Another time he referred to a stone pile at a building site. He was often talking about seeds and soil and plows and rain—the sort of things he and his disciples would pass as they walked through the countryside each day. This time he used a child to make his point.

First, Jesus called for a change. They had to adjust their way of thinking. It was the most natural thing in the world to assume that the most loyal disciples would earn the most important roles in the kingdom. Didn't Alexander the Great parcel out power to his generals? Wasn't the power in imperial Rome based on "who you know"? It was a reasonable way to think, but it wasn't the way of the kingdom.

"Change!" Jesus demands. "Become like little children." If you can't turn your thinking around, he warns, you don't belong in the kingdom at all. And how can you be a ruler in this kingdom if you don't know the first thing about it? The first thing is *humility*. Do you want to be the greatest in this kingdom? Here's how. Be as humble as this child.

News flash from the world of human psychology. Virtually all children have low self-esteem. Sure, there are a few spoiled brats out there, but even the best-parented children get frustrated by the fact that they're smaller, less adept, and more ignorant than older people. They struggle against these limitations every day. It's all part of growing up.

So what is Jesus saying when he places a child in the middle of these bickering disciples? Carve a dimple in your cheek so you can dazzle God with your cuteness? Hardly. He's saying that we all must recognize our limitations. We cannot barge our way into God's kingdom; we must be carried there by God's grace. And whatever greatness occurs in this new regime will be nothing of our own doing. It will be a gift of God.

PART 4

● "You know that those who are regarded as rulers of the Gentiles lord it over them, and their high officials exercise authority over them. Not so with you. Instead, whoever wants to become great among you must be your servant, and whoever wants to be first must be slave of all. For even the Son of Man did not come to be served, but to serve, and to give his life as a ransom for many."

Mark 10:42–45

The disciples were bickering again. In fact James and John had their *mother* come to Jesus asking for special consideration. Jesus acknowledged that it was the way of the world to woo and wield authority, but "not so with you." The followers of Jesus would have to be different. The greatest in God's kingdom would be a servant. Do you see the irony in that? To be great, you have to stop thinking about being great. This is an upside-down kingdom, where the first shall be last and the last first. Everything you thought you knew is turned on its head.

Some time ago, business analysts noted a particular phenomenon. It seemed that most companies took on the traits of their CEOs. If the boss was highly competitive, competition marked the whole operation. If there was creativity at the top or pride or prejudice, that spirit flowed through the ranks. Jesus describes a similar effect here. The "Son of Man" (Jesus' term for himself) was all about serving—not receiving service—and so his kingdom would need to reflect that same priority.

We don't always get that. Christians still elbow one another to gain power, within the church and in the world. It's tempting to think you can really make a difference by being in charge, but Jesus' caution rings in our ears: "Not so with you." If we're not humbly serving, we belong in some other kingdom.

A few years ago, as the millennium turned, many historically minded Christians took the opportunity to make lists of the most important believers since the year 1000. Who belongs at the top of that list? Martin Luther, who sparked the Reformation that changed the religious and social landscape of Europe? Thomas Aquinas, who codified Catholic thought? William Carey, who launched the modern missions movement? Or Billy Graham, who has preached to more people than anyone else?

Based on Jesus' teaching, all such attempts to identify important believers are rather futile, because God uses a much different yardstick. The greatest Christians are the humblest, and so you probably don't even know their names. We're thinking that Dwight Moody's Sunday school teacher might be on our list, or Gutenberg's printing assistant. How about the guy who carried William Tyndale's Bible translation back into England or John and Charles Wesley's mom?

And maybe the greatest Christian of the next millennium is the one who cleans out your church bathrooms or tends the nursery or refs the youth basketball games. We're not saying they *will become* great at some point in the future—that they'll finally get their break and leave the puking babies behind. No, we're saying they are great *now*, because they are serving in the spirit of the Son of Man.

QUOTE TO NOTE

[A child] has not yet learned to think in terms of place and pride and prestige. He has not yet learned to discover the importance of himself.

William Barclay

30
ON THE JERICHO ROAD

What if you were the program chairman of the local chamber of commerce and you heard that Jesus was coming to town? You might mention his name to your planning committee as a possible speaker for the leadership breakfast. After all, he is a rabbi who's been attracting quite a following.

But one member of your committee says, "Wasn't he the rabbi who was invited to Simon's house for dinner and a prostitute followed him in? I heard that he praised the prostitute and scolded Simon."

"Oh yes," someone else points out, "I know for a fact that in Capernaum, tax collectors and other notorious scumbags held a dinner for him."

"What about that extortioner down in Jericho who climbed a tree to get a good look at Jesus, and the rabbi invited himself to dinner at that rascal's house?"

"No, I don't think our club wants to be associated with the likes of him. When you ask Jesus to speak, you never know what to expect."

● "Do this and you will live."

Luke 10:28

Once a very respectable legal scholar asked Jesus, "Teacher, what must I do to inherit eternal life?" (v. 25). That might sound like a serious faith question, but it wasn't. It was a test.

Jesus turned the question back on the lawyer, since he was an expert in the law. "How do you read it?" Jesus was a master at answering a question with a question.

The lawyer responded

Monday: Read part 1 of this chapter. Why does God require of us that which is impossible to do?

Tuesday: Read part 2. Consider the question in "In the Mirror."

Wednesday: Read part 3. Who is your neighbor?

Thursday: Read part 4. Which of these five ideas is cutting-edge in your life? '

Friday: Is it possible to love others as Jesus loves us? How will you try?

Saturday: Pray today for more love for the people around you.

Sunday: Praise God today for his overwhelming love.

with a textbook answer, quoting Deuteronomy 6:5 and Leviticus 19:18. These were the same verses that Jesus himself used on another occasion when he was responding to the tests of Pharisees and lawyers. First, love the Lord with all you've got—heart and soul, mind and body. Second, love your neighbor as yourself. These verses summed up the Scriptures perfectly. So Jesus gave this scholar an A for his accuracy: "You have answered correctly. . . . Do this and you will live."

But if you are familiar with the rest of the New Testament, you may have a problem. *Do this and you will live?* But eternal life isn't achieved through righteous behavior. Didn't Paul say, "No one will be declared righteous in his sight by observing the law" (Rom. 3:20)?

The man knew how eternal life was *supposed* to be won— loving God and others thoroughly by keeping every bit of God's law. But he wasn't counting on the problem of sin, which made it impossible for anyone to be that good. Jesus knew the sneaky pervasiveness of sin; so eternal life required the grace of God.

Do this and you will live? Absolutely. But if you can't do all this, and none of us can, then we must throw ourselves on the mercy of the court, asking the Judge to supply his righteousness in place of our own.

● "A man was going down from Jerusalem to Jericho, when he fell into the hands of robbers."

Luke 10:30

You've seen "attack interviews" on TV, haven't you? The journalist sits across from some executive and delivers questions that sting: "How can you in good conscience continue to produce merchandise that poisons innocent children in Third World countries?" It happens sometimes in press conferences with politicians, and it was probably happening with Jesus in Luke 10. The questioner, a legal expert, was trying to trip Jesus up, getting him to say something contrary to the law of God, but Jesus defused the attack.

Jesus' questioner was completely neutralized on his first attempt. So, wanting "to justify himself," he asked a follow-up question: "Who is my neighbor?"

Lawyers specialize in definitions. The law says, "Love your neighbor," but how do you define *neighbor*? Is it the person who lives next door to you, across the street, down the block?

Of course Jesus wouldn't give a simple answer. He answered with a story about a traveler who got mugged on the road to Jericho.

No doubt, the lawyer knew the Jericho road very well; it was notoriously dangerous. And when Jesus said "going down," he wasn't kidding. Jerusalem is twenty-three hundred feet above sea level. Jericho sits near the Dead Sea, which is thirteen hundred feet *below* sea level. So the road dropped more than three thousand feet in about seventeen miles. It also had a lot of twists and sudden turns, as most mountain roads do. Because robbers lurked in the ravines, ready to pounce on solitary travelers, most people traveled the Jericho road in groups or caravans.

IN THE MIRROR

Over the past week, have you acted more like the priest and Levite, or more like the Good Samaritan?

The lawyer probably thought that the man was stupid for traveling the Jericho road alone. But he didn't say anything. He was waiting for Jesus' punch line.

As the story went on, the traveler was stripped, beaten, and left half dead. Then a priest came down the road, saw the man, and moved to the other side of the road to avoid getting too close to the wounded man.

The lawyer could understand that. How could the priest tell whether the man was dead or alive? If he were dead and the priest touched him, the law of Moses said that the priest would be declared unclean for seven days. That would mean that he couldn't serve God in the temple for that time. Didn't serving God have priority?

Then, Jesus says, a Levite hurried down the road. He too saw the man and moved to the far side of the road to remove himself from the situation.

The lawyer could understand that too. The Levites were helpers in the temple and might have the same ceremonial concerns the priest had. Besides that, it was dangerous to loiter on the Jericho road. Sometimes robbers used decoys. One of them would lie in the ditch and pretend to be injured, and his cronies would attack anyone who stopped to help. No, it wasn't safe for a person with the religious obligations of a Levite to take such a chance. The injured man had been stripped of his clothing, so you couldn't tell whether he was a Roman soldier, a tax collector, or even, God forbid, a Samaritan.

Jesus continued his story. A third traveler came down the road, a Samaritan. He approached the wounded man, applied first aid, put him on his donkey, and took him to an inn.

The lawyer no doubt nodded here, because there was only one inn on the Jericho road, and he knew just where it was.

But there was more. Not only did the Samaritan take him to the inn, but he stayed with him through the night, and when he had to leave the next morning, he gave the innkeeper enough money to pay for two months' lodging for the man. Then as he saddled up his donkey, he looked back at the innkeeper and said, *By the way, if that doesn't cover it, I will make it up to you when I get back this way again.*

> **DARE TO COMPARE**
>
> The story of the good Samaritan is a love story. Compare it to 1 Corinthians 13.

At first, the lawyer was probably thinking, "Nice story, but what does it have to do with my question?" Finally, Jesus got to the punch line:

PART 3

● "Which of these three do you think was a neighbor to the man who fell into the hands of robbers?"

Luke 10:36

The answer was obvious. The lawyer may have gulped before he replied. He couldn't bring himself to say the name of the half-breed heretics who had been thorns in the sides of true Jews for several centuries. So he simply said, "The one who had mercy on him."

This was a stunning turnabout. Jesus was not saying, "Look at this poor, outcast Samaritan. You ought to take pity on him." No, it was the Samaritan who took pity on the Jew. While the priest and Levite had the right theological answers, their focus on ceremonial cleanliness had kept them from doing an obvious act of love. Apparently this fellow Jew was not their neighbor, as long as he held the potential to make them ritually unclean. But the Samaritan had nothing to lose, as far as ritual cleanliness was concerned, and he treated the wounded man with more-than-neighborly mercy.

"You strain out a gnat but swallow a camel," Jesus once chided the Pharisees (Matt. 23:24). They had a way of nitpicking the details of the legal code but missing the main point. Why bicker about precisely who your neighbor is when someone needs help?

PART 4

● "Go and do likewise."

Luke 10:37

You never know what to expect when you try to engage Jesus in a nice, refined theological discussion. Theological discussions are mental exercises, but they aren't where the rubber meets the road. Jesus often ended his discussions with some variation on the imperative, "Go and do." His teachings got very practical. They were never purely theological.

And so he gives us the same challenge. Who are our neighbors? And how can we show mercy? Here are some ideas:

1. *Develop peripheral vision.* Like the priest and the Levite, we keep passing the needy one on "the other side." And since most of us are speeding along six-lane, divided superhighways, we never even see most of the need. We must wake up in the morning and pray, "Lord, help me to see someone by the side of the road today."

2. *Take the responsibility yourself.* Usually we rationalize our way out of doing anything. Perhaps the priest wondered if he should do something but looked back and, seeing the Levite coming, said, "I'll let him handle it. He probably knows more about first aid than I do." Take the responsibility yourself.

3. *Develop a "safety second" mentality.* The priest may have asked himself the question: "Isn't my life more important than his? He may be a drunken bum, for all I know." Too often personal safety is our only consideration—"Safety first!" While we shouldn't be reckless about our personal well-being, we may need to take some risks to show God's mercy.

4. *Forget about personal comfort or convenience.* Couch potatoes seldom make good neighbors. If they had stopped, the priest and the Levite might have been late for important business appointments in Jericho. And being a Good Samaritan may inconvenience us, but that's our calling as Christ-followers.

5. *Don't worry about the identity of the man in the ditch.* He could be a terrorist, a man dying with AIDs, or a pornographer. Is he your neighbor? Jesus says yes. Everybody loves the people who are lovable. We demonstrate true obedience when we show God's love to those most difficult to love.

QUOTE TO NOTE

Do not waste time bothering whether you "Love" your neighbor; act as if you did.

C. S. Lewis

31

LOST AND FOUND

● "'Rejoice with me; I have found my lost sheep.' . . .
  "'Rejoice with me; I have found my lost coin.' In the
same way, I tell you, there is rejoicing in the presence of
the angels of God over one sinner who repents."

Luke 15:6, 9–10

Have you ever lost anything and then found it again? Your
keys, a recipe, an important paper for school or work, a photo
from your family history, the address of an old friend, or maybe
the old friend? Some folks have impeccable filing systems. In a
few seconds they can put their hands on anything they own. The
other 99.9 percent of us lose things. We'd misplace our elbows
if they weren't tied on. Jesus uses this common experience to
give us a glimpse of heaven.

A shepherd loses track of one of his hundred sheep. What
does he do? He scours the hills and valleys, searching for the lost
creature. A woman loses a coin and sweeps her whole house
looking for it. (For many of us, the best housecleaning we ever
do is when we've lost something.) And when they find what
they lost, there is rejoicing—not just on the part of the shepherd
or the woman but by all the neighbors as well.

174

This rejoicing emerges as Jesus' main theme in these three "lost and found" stories of Luke 15. It's good and right and *natural* to rejoice when somebody finds something that was lost. Then why were the Pharisees grousing about the way Jesus "welcomed sinners" (Luke 15:2)? These religious leaders were ostensibly promoting a "back to God" movement, trying to make Israel righteous again. But they did so by vilifying everyone who didn't think as they did. "This man welcomes sinners and eats with them," they complained. So how did Jesus respond to their complaints?

He responded with three beautiful stories of losing and finding—and rejoicing.

Monday: Read part 1. It says in Luke 15:2 that the Pharisees muttered. Notice how Jesus knows what is in their hearts without really being told.

Tuesday: Read part 2. According to this part, what is the difference between law and grace?

Wednesday: Read part 3. In what areas of your life have you wandered from God?

Thursday: Read part 4. The older brother was angry. Why?

Friday: Consider the question in "In the Mirror."

Saturday: Pray for those who are lost. Name them and ask God to show you what you can do to reach them so they can be brought into the family of God.

Sunday: Read Psalm 51 today. Praise the Lord as you read and meditate.

PART 2

● "There was a man who had two sons. The younger one said to his father, 'Father, give me my share of the estate.' So he divided his property between them.

"Not long after that, the younger son got together all he had, set off for a distant country and there squandered his wealth in wild living."

Luke 15:11–13

You know this as the story of the prodigal son. It could very easily be called "The Forgiving Father" or "The Angry Brother." All three characters figure prominently in the story, but it starts with the younger son cashing out and sowing his oats in a faraway land.

CROSS REF

See Romans 8:15–16 for the difference between being a slave and being a son.

It has been pointed out that of the three lost items in Luke 15, the prodigal son is the most culpable. That is, the sheep strayed away because it didn't know better and the coin presumably had no say in the matter. Only the son was willfully lost. He took his early inheritance and squandered it in "wild living." This was a distinction the Pharisees would surely have made, but Jesus didn't. A lost person needed finding, whether he deserved to be lost or not. The Pharisees would have focused on what this boy deserved; Jesus saw only his need. And that, in one glimpse, is the difference between law and grace.

PART 3

● "When he came to his senses, he said, 'How many of my father's hired men have food to spare, and here I am starving to death! I will set out and go back to my father.'"

Luke 15:17–18

Sin is stupid. There's a whole stream of scriptural thought that says this, mostly in Proverbs but also in Deuteronomy and some of the prophets. Sinful behavior brings its own setbacks. You will reap what you sow. Crime doesn't pay!

And the prodigal finally sees that. He "came to his senses," realizing that he had been acting in a senseless manner, following his animal urges, much like the pigs he was feeding. So he hatches a plan to return home. He does not expect to get back what he lost. He knows he has squandered his place in the family, but perhaps there is some menial task he can perform in the household somewhere. He is swallowing his pride to become a servant. Even that would be far better than his current state of need.

● "But while he was still a long way off, his father saw him and was filled with compassion for him; he ran to his son, threw his arms around him and kissed him.

"The son said to him, 'Father, I have sinned against

heaven and against you. I am no longer worthy to be called your son.'"

Luke 15:20–21

The prodigal is still "a long way off" when his father sees him, which tells us the father was looking for him. We might imagine a story-behind-the-story: For weeks, months, maybe years, the father scans the horizon daily. *Will my son come home today?* When the son finally shows up, there is instant welcome. No game playing here, just a hug, a kiss, a robe, a ring, a feast. The boy can't even finish his prepared speech. He's all ready to become a servant, but he's being whisked back into sonship.

Every parable, of course, has a deeper meaning, and this one is clear. The prodigal's father is our heavenly Father, and the boy himself stands for every sinner who has wandered away. From our twenty-first-century perspective, that includes us. It is the greatest story ever. God loves us. God loses us. God finds us again. And there is great rejoicing.

PART 4

● "Meanwhile, the older son was in the field. When he came near the house, he heard music and dancing. . . .

"The older brother became angry and refused to go in. So his father went out and pleaded with him. . . .

"'My son,' the father said, 'you are always with me, and everything I have is yours. But we had to celebrate and be glad, because this brother of yours was dead and is alive again; he was lost and is found.'"

Luke 15:25, 28, 31–32

Everyone rejoices over the finding of what was lost—except for the older brother. *Why all this fuss over the kid who thumbed his nose at the entire household when he left? You're treating him like royalty, Dad, but what about me? Have I been wasting my time here, being loyal to you? Why don't you ever throw me a party?*

He's got a point. It really doesn't seem fair. Obviously this father has not studied up on reality discipline. Let the errant

IN THE MIRROR

Who are you in this story? Are you more like the son, the father, or the brother?

child experience the consequences of his misbehavior, and make sure you don't take your good kids for granted. The prodigal really does deserve to become a servant in this household, since he has already wasted his inheritance. Is the older brother wrong for bringing his father back to reality?

Well, yes. The older son might have all sorts of arguments about what he and his brother deserve, but the father is functioning on the higher reality of grace and love and joy. What exactly is the older brother's mistake? He is refusing to rejoice over the finding of his lost brother.

And if the son represents all sinners and the father represents God, who is the older brother in this story? The Pharisees, of course, who were hounding Jesus about hanging out with sinners. Jesus was rejoicing that these wayward souls were coming back to their heavenly Father, and he was inviting the Pharisees to join the party, but like the older brother, they "refused to go in." If such riffraff populated God's kingdom, they'd just as soon stay outside.

It's sad that there are still people like that, who insist on working their way into God's eternal banquet hall. Assuming that God operates on a merit system, they feel threatened by forgiveness and grace. But that's the theme of this ultimate party—that we who have been dead are alive again. We who were lost have been found.

QUOTE TO NOTE

You can never expect to be perfectly saved, till you know yourself utterly lost.

Anonymous

32
FORGIVEFULNESS

No, there isn't such a word as *forgivefulness,* but maybe you should write a letter to the dictionary people and suggest they include it in their next edition. It's pretty obvious what the word would mean. And when you think about it, forgivefulness is a quality that should characterize all Christians.

A lot of us are afflicted with *forgetfulness.* We forget to do certain things we're supposed to do—especially if we never wanted to do them in the first place. But Jesus suggested that his followers need to be infected with forgivefulness.

One day Simon Peter, who was full of more questions than a four year old, asked, "Lord, how many times shall I forgive my brother when he sins against me? Up to seven times?" (Matt. 18:21).

The rabbis had an answer for almost everything, and they were saying that forgiving someone three times was good enough. The fourth offense would not merit forgiveness. Peter no doubt thought that Jesus would go beyond the rabbis, so he suggested seven as a good number. Six times would be double what the rabbis taught, and then just to be safe, Peter asked, "Up to seven times?"

Jesus answered:

● "I tell you, not seven times, but seventy-seven times."

Matthew 18:22

179

Monday: Read part 1 of this chapter. How could a general attitude of "forgivefulness" affect a whole church?

Tuesday: Read part 2. Put into your own words the meaning of the parable of the king.

Wednesday: Read part 3. What are the privilege and duty of every Christian?

Thursday: Try writing your own parable about forgiveness.

Friday: Consider the question in "In the Mirror."

Saturday: In your prayer time, pray the Lord's Prayer slowly, thoughtfully.

Sunday: Praise God for his forgiveness as you read 1 John 1:7–9.

Maybe Peter didn't get it at first, but Jesus was alluding to something that happened in the early chapters of Genesis. After Cain killed his brother Abel, he worried that someone would come after him and kill him in vengeance. But God assured him, "Not so." If anyone would come after Cain to kill him, "he will suffer vengeance seven times over" (Gen. 4:15).

Then Lamech, one of Cain's descendants, killed a man who had hurt him. Lamech thought he deserved similar divine protection and more. He said, "If Cain is avenged seven times, then Lamech seventy-seven times" (v. 24).

But Jesus was reversing all of that. He wasn't interested in revenge; he was interested in forgiveness. And frankly, he wasn't interested in keeping score. He didn't want his followers to keep tally sheets on their refrigerators, hoping to get to seventy-eight, when they could say, "Now I can finally give you what you have been deserving all along."

PART 2

Forgiveness is easy to talk but hard to live.

Mr. Pecksniff, however, didn't think it was so hard. Pecksniff is an unsavory character in the novel *Martin Chuzzlewit* by Charles Dickens. What made Pecksniff so unsavory was his hypocrisy. Dickens calls him a "sleek, smiling, crawling abomination," who could slip into places of trust and honor. He was described as a perfect Judas, except that "after receiving his thirty pieces of silver, he has not the grace to go out and hang himself."

Pecksniff was humble, very humble, and very proud of his humility. He also bragged about his ability to forgive. "Forgiveness," he said, "is not incompatible with a wounded heart." And then he adds in melodramatic fashion, "With my breast still wrung and grieved to its inmost core by the ingratitude of that person, I am proud and glad to say that I forgive him."

IN THE MIRROR

Do you find it easy or difficult to forgive? If it's difficult, what can you do about that?

Yes, Pecksniff could boast about his forgiveness, but it was a forgiveness only in words. Real forgiveness has to go deeper than that.

To bring his teaching down to earth, Jesus told a story, a parable.

● "Therefore, the kingdom of heaven is like a king who wanted to settle accounts with his servants."

Matthew 18:23

A king was checking the accounts of his trusted civil servants. These men had huge responsibilities in the kingdom and apparently had access to the king's fortunes. One of them owed the king what Bible scholars have estimated to be over a billion dollars. He had probably embezzled it.

The king was wealthy, but a billion dollars is a billion dollars, so he ordered that the man, his wife, and his children all be sold at the slave auction. At best, that would bring only five hundred dollars apiece, a far cry from the billion dollars that was owed. But the civil servant got the point. He fell to his knees in front of the king and promised to pay back everything.

The king said, *Okay, I will cancel the debt. Let's call it a bad loan.*

But the servant still went to work on getting the money back to the king. Finding one of his coworkers who owed him a couple thousand dollars, he grabbed him, started to choke him, and demanded repayment. The fellow servant fell on his knees and groveled (just as the first servant had done before the king). *Be patient,* he begged.

No way, said the first servant. *Off to prison with you.*

181

When the king heard about it, he was livid. He called his ser-vant on the carpet, saying, "You wicked servant. . . . I canceled all that debt of yours because you begged me to. Shouldn't you have had mercy on your fellow servant just as I had on you?" (vv. 32–33).

PART 3

● "Shouldn't you have had mercy on your fellow servant just as I had on you?"

Matthew 18:33

Some parables, such as the parable of the sower and the seeds, are like allegories, where almost everything has a double meaning. But most parables, like this one, are meant to convey a single truth.

So what is the single truth in this parable? The fact that the great King of the universe has forgiven all our sins in Jesus Christ and that makes any wrong done to us seem trivial. How can we withhold forgiveness from anyone when we have been forgiven a billion times more?

> **CROSS REF**
>
> Read more about mercy and forgiveness:
> Matthew 5:7
> Matthew 6:14–15
> James 2:13

In Luke the Lord's Prayer reads this way: "Forgive us our sins, for we also forgive everyone who sins against us" (Luke 11:4). This parable then is a commentary on that section of the Lord's Prayer.

Every Christian has a privilege and a duty. The privilege is in knowing that we are forgiven. As far as the east is from the west, that's how far God has removed our sins from us (Ps. 103:12). "I will forgive their wickedness," God told Jeremiah, "and will remember their sins no more" (Jer. 31:34). That's the good news; that's our privileged position.

But our duty is to forgive. Because of his love, he forgives us, and because we live in the awareness of his love, we can love others and forgive them. If we don't forgive, we can't love, we can't have fellowship, and we can't have friendship. But if we learn to forgive as he has forgiven, then we can have true fellowship with God as well as with our brothers and sisters in Christ.

No, forgivefulness is not easy, but as we realize that our billion-dollar debt to God has been forgiven, then it isn't too hard to forgive the debt of a few pennies that someone owes us.

QUOTE TO NOTE

Nothing is more contradictory than a Christian who will not forgive.

Calvin Miller

33

THE LIGHT SWITCH

It was the closest thing to a fireworks spectacular that the Hebrew calendar contained. Held every fall, the Feast of Tabernacles or Booths (*Sukkot*, in Hebrew) was a fun time, a time of rejoicing in God's goodness for the harvest, and a time of remembering how tough life used to be.

For a week Hebrew families lived in simple booths made out of tree branches and boughs. It was camping out, Israelite style, and the kids loved it. During the week, the parents taught their children about how their forefathers had camped out in the wilderness for forty years. One week of it in cramped quarters was okay, but forty years? No, thank you.

God had led the Israelites by day with a cloud and by night with a pillar of fire, and the Feast of Tabernacles was an annual reminder of his guidance and protection. During the feast, all the worshipers and their families gathered in the temple for an evening ceremony called the Illumination. Jewish families crowded into galleries, specially built for the occasion; the children could hardly wait. In the center of the temple's Court of the Women stood four gigantic candelabra.

Finally, darkness came, and then the candelabra burst forth with light. It was almost as if a light switch had been turned on.

You can imagine the screams of delight from the children and the clapping and shouting of the adults. Soon came dancing and psalms of praise. Long into the night the festivity continued.

It was on a night such as that when Jesus seemed to turn on another light switch, saying:

● "I am the light of the world. Whoever follows me will never walk in darkness, but will have the light of life."

John 8:12

Imagine walking home after the revelry in the temple court has ended; the dancing has stopped, and the brilliant light of the candelabra has been extinguished. It is now dark, pitch dark, and you have to find your way to your little shack, a shack like all the others, in a big city you don't know very well. Everything is over now, but still ringing in your ears is that voice you heard in the temple: "the light of the world . . . never walk in darkness . . . the light of life."

You find your booth, grope inside to find the little earthenware lamp, take it outside, and light the wick to give a little light for your family. You can see other little pinpoints of flame, but they are vain attempts to dispel the darkness. Around the ancient world people had always sought light in their darkness; now someone in the temple was shouting to all that he was the Light of the World.

In the ancient world the image of light and darkness was more vivid than it is today. Today our big cities are engulfed in light throughout the night. Before Thomas Edison it was different. Electricity allows us to take light for granted, but it should be no surprise that biblical writers use light (and darkness) as a powerful theme.

EVERY DAY WITH JESUS

Monday: Read part 1 of this chapter. Imagine yourself in that ancient celebration.

Tuesday: Read part 2. How does truth set you free?

Wednesday: Read part 3. Why do you think Jesus said, "Before Abraham was, I am"?

Thursday: How would you describe the freedom Jesus gives us?

Friday: As you consider your friends and neighbors who don't know Jesus, what are they enslaved to? How could the truth of Jesus set them free?

Saturday: Thank Jesus for light, truth, and freedom. Ask for his help in understanding these things.

Sunday: Praise God as you read Psalm 43:3–4.

CHECKOUT COUNTER

Check out Exodus 33:18–23 to see Moses and the glory of God. Now read what Paul has to say about God's light and our freedom in 2 Corinthians 3:12–4:6.

John seems especially fond of this image. Throughout his Gospel, his Epistles, and Revelation, he refers to light more than thirty times. He writes of Jesus as "the true light that gives light to every man" (John 1:9). This light "shines in the darkness, but the darkness has not understood it" (v. 5). In the last chapter of Revelation, John speaks of an eternal home with "no night" and no need of a lamp or sun, "for the Lord God will give them light" (Rev. 22:5).

If you had heard Jesus in the temple, calling himself the Light of the World, you might have been reminded of a prophecy from Isaiah: "Arise, shine, for your light has come" (Isa. 60:1). You couldn't help but think that Jesus was claiming to fulfill that prophecy. And you might have wondered if the religious leaders were making the same connection.

They were. And they didn't like it.

PART 2

● "You will know the truth, and the truth will set you free."

John 8:32

Everyone from Eastern gurus to Harvard profs has appropriated this verse for their own purposes. The gurus say, "Once you get our Knowledge with a capital K, you will enter into oneness with the Infinite, and our truth shall set you free."

When Harvard was founded in 1636, it adopted John 8:32 as its motto. In the school's original Rules and Precepts, the third point was "Seeing the Lord giveth wisdom, every one shall seriously by prayer in secret seek wisdom of him," and the fourth was, "Every one shall so exercise himself in reading the Scriptures twice a day."

After Jesus' audacious "light of the world" claim, the authorities challenged him. How could he make such claims? He entered into a debate with some of them, with a crowd of his supporters listening in. To these curious observers he said, "If you hold to my teaching, you are really my disciples. Then you will know the truth, and the truth will set you free."

It's a promise and a challenge. Jesus was inviting the curiosity seekers to step up to the next level, not just hearing his words but *holding to* them. If they followed his teaching, then his truth would bring them freedom.

That might be hard for some modern folks to follow. Don't we live in a free world, and aren't we adding a new freedom to the list every decade? Freedom of speech, freedom of worship, freedom of the press, freedom to congregate, freedom of choice, freedom to vote for the candidate of our choice, freedom to do what we want when we want. What do you mean, *free*?

> **CROSS REF**
>
> Read about truth:
> John 8:31–32
> 2 John 4

And that's what the first-century audience asked. *We're not slaves. We're Abraham's descendants and we have never been slaves to anyone.*

Who were they trying to fool? They had been slaves in Egypt for more than four hundred years, they had been captives in Babylon for seventy years, and now they were under the Roman thumb. Had they flunked history? Not necessarily. It seems they were grasping the spiritual nature of Jesus' comment. He wasn't promising to lead a revolution against the Romans. He offered a freedom of heart, of spirit, of life. And they insisted that they already had this inner freedom as children of Abraham.

But Jesus saw a greater oppressor. "Everyone who sins is a slave to sin" (v. 34).

It's true. We humans are addicted to sin. We have rehab centers for physical addictions, but we wrestle unsuccessfully with our compulsion to sin. Yes, we are slaves, and we need deliverance.

The first step in getting out of our addiction to sin is to admit our slavery. The second step is to recognize that we can't do anything to free ourselves. The third step is to ask for help from the One who can. Jesus said that he could help.

PART 3

● "If the Son sets you free, you will be free indeed."

John 8:36

The crowd was getting worked up. Maybe they had been on his side when the debate began, but Jesus' challenging words seemed to trouble them. For one thing, they didn't like the idea that they were addicted to sin. Then they really had a hard time when Jesus said, "You belong to your father, the devil" (v. 44). That was more than they could take.

After calling Jesus demon-possessed, they asked, "Who do you think you are?" (v. 53). In response, Jesus made two startling claims. The first was, "Abraham rejoiced at the thought of seeing my day; he saw it and was glad" (v. 56). He was speaking as if he and Abraham were buddies. Abraham was the great patriarch of the nation, and yet Jesus was acting as if he was even greater than Abraham. "You are not yet fifty years old," they scoffed, "and you have seen Abraham!" (v. 57). Now they knew that he was either crazy or demon-possessed.

Jesus answered with his most stunning declaration yet.

● **"Before Abraham was born, I am!"**

John 8:58

No longer were these the ravings of a lunatic; this was blasphemy. Jesus was identifying himself not only as the Messiah but also as the incarnate God. Angrily the crowd hurried to pick up stones and rocks to hurl at him, but Jesus slipped away.

Why did they feel they had to stone him? That last sentence. *"Before Abraham was,"* constituted a claim to preexistence, a quality belonging only to God. And then he didn't say, "I was." He said, "I am."

"I am." This was how God identified himself to Moses at the burning bush. Moses was to tell the children of Israel: "I AM has sent me to you" (Exod. 3:14). Jesus was taking on himself the hallowed name of God.

Now the entire chapter ties together. Early in the chapter Jesus says: "I am the light of the world." Now at the end of the chapter, Jesus says, "Before Abraham was, I am."

The light switch has been turned on. God in the flesh has arrived.

34

THE LIGHT SWITCH SEQUEL

PART 1

Discussion starter: Why do bad things happen to good people?

Follow-up question: Why do good things happen to bad people?

Second follow-up: Why do things happen?

Such questions became the basis of best sellers in the 1980s and 1990s, but of course, people have been asking the same questions for millennia. In the Old Testament, Job asked the first question, and his friends were more than ready with answers. As they saw it, the fact that catastrophe plagued him proved that he wasn't a good guy after all.

In the Psalms, David asked both questions 1 and 2. *Why are all those bad guys living in the lap of luxury while I am running for my life?*

The minor prophet Habakkuk had a different twist on the question: *I can understand, Lord, why you have to punish us, but why are you going to use the despicable Babylonians to do it? The stuff we do is child's play compared to their atrocities.*

So it's no surprise that these questions resurface in the teachings of Jesus.

● "Neither this man nor his parents sinned . . . but this happened so that the work of God might be displayed in his life."

John 9:3

189

Monday: Read part 1 of this chapter. People often ask, "Why did this bad thing happen?" How did Jesus answer?

Tuesday: Read part 2. What do you think the neighbors were thinking? What about the Pharisees, the parents, the man?

Wednesday: Read part 3. How would you answer the question in John 9:35?

Thursday: Read part 4. What was Jesus saying about blindness and sin?

Friday: What miracles have you observed in your life? How have you responded?

Saturday: Pray for eyes to see God's miracles, for eyes to see those who need your testimony of miracles he has done for you, and for eyes to see his glory.

Sunday: Praise God as you read Psalm 146. Especially note verse 8.

Scene 1: It's a Sabbath morning, not long after Jesus had declared himself to be the Light of the World and the fickle crowd had picked up stones to kill him. Jesus was walking with his disciples, perhaps outside the temple gates. It was here that beggars congregated and clamored for alms.

The disciples pointed to one blind man. Evidently they knew that he had been blind from birth. So they asked why. *Who sinned? This man or his parents?* There was no doubt in their minds that the answer had to be one or the other. The Jewish rabbis taught that where there is suffering, there must be sin. It was possible for an embryo to sin in the mother's womb, they said, though the cause of the blindness may have been the parents' sin. So the disciples' question was a logical one.

The answer, however, like many of Jesus' answers, surprised them. If it was a multiple-choice quiz, Jesus answered, *None of the above.* It wasn't his sin or that of his parents, but something else was going on here—"the work of God."

Then Jesus repeated that he was the Light of the World, and as long as he was in the world, he was going to keep on doing what he had come to do. One of the things the Messiah was supposed to do was to bring sight to the blind.

The disciples viewed the situation as a discussion question. But Jesus didn't spend much time with philosophical questions. He looked at the situation and saw an opportunity to help. The disciples were looking for human causes; Jesus was seeking divine results. The disciples stepped away from the problem; Jesus stepped into it.

PART 2

Right after reminding the disciples that he was the Light of the World, Jesus got down and dirty—literally. He spat on the ground, made mud, and placed it on the blind man's eyes.

● "Go . . . wash in the Pool of Siloam."

John 9:7

Scene 2: This is where the blind man's story begins. No, actually it's where the story of the blind man ends, for as soon as he obeys Jesus and washes in the pool, his sight is restored. He is no longer "the blind man." He goes home, and his neighbors can't believe it's the same guy. "He only looks like him," some said. Not having a driver's license or anything to prove his identity, he told the amazing story of his healing.

"Where is the man who healed you?"

"I don't know."

Scene 3: Rather than praise God for the miracle, the neighbors were suspicious; things like this weren't supposed to happen on the Sabbath day. A lot of medical quacks were traveling the countryside; miraculous healings were often claimed; it was prudent to investigate. Following good investigative procedure, the neighbors took the formerly blind man to the Pharisees to get an official opinion. When the man repeated his story, the Pharisees knew that they had

> ### CLUES TO USE
>
> Ever wonder why Jesus spat on the ground to heal the blind man? Scholars tell us that in the ancient world, saliva represented the essential being of a person. In deep sympathy, Jesus was sharing himself with this man.

grounds for a criminal charge. Whoever did this had healed on the Sabbath. In the process, he had made clay, and that involved work; furthermore, their tradition stated that it was fine to apply medication from the throat downward, but not upward. This was upward. In addition, Jesus had applied saliva to the man's eyes, and their legal interpretations expressly forbade doing that on the Sabbath. It was clear to see that a major crime had been committed.

Scene 4: Next, the parents were called in for questioning. They were scared stiff. They didn't want to tangle with the Pharisees.

All we know, they said, *is that he is our son and that he was born blind. If you have any questions, ask him; he is old enough to answer for himself.* In other words, keep us out of it.

Scene 5: Back again to the formerly blind man. All the Pharisees can get out of him was this masterful response: "One thing I do know. I was blind but now I see!" (v. 25).

They kept coming at the poor fellow. *What did the healer do? How did he do it?*

But his testimony was simply, *I was blind but now I see.* Testimonies don't have to be elaborate. They don't need to be couched in theological language. Just say what Christ did for you. This man might not have known whether Jesus was the Light of the World, or all the implications of that idea, but he could easily say, "Jesus is the light of *my* world." In fact that guy ought to be getting royalties from John Newton. The great hymn "Amazing Grace" quotes him almost verbatim: "I once was lost but now am found, *was blind but now I see.*"

The man wasn't cowed by the insults and attacks of the Pharisees. In between their jabs, he parried with, "Do you want to become his disciples, too?" (v. 27) and "If this man were not from God, he could do nothing" (v. 33).

The Pharisees had heard enough. They threw him out of the synagogue.

PART 3

Back on the street again, the man didn't care about the Pharisees or his neighbors—he just wanted to find the man who had healed him. As in the closing scenes of many Lone Ranger films, he must have been asking, "Who was that masked man?" What did his healer look like? He had never seen Jesus' face. Where would he begin to look?

As Scripture puts it, it was Jesus who found him.

Scene 6: We're guessing the man went back to the scene of the crime, the temple gate. Jesus found him and asked him this simple yet profound question.

● "Do you believe in the Son of Man?"

John 9:35

"Who is he, sir?"

"He is the one speaking with you," said Jesus.

The man fell at Jesus' feet and worshiped him. "Lord, I believe," he said.

The religious leaders had attacked this man, his neighbors had turned him in to the authorities, and his parents had separated themselves from him. He was no longer welcome in the synagogue. He couldn't even go back to work as a blind beggar because now he had sight. Where could he go? He didn't know it, but the Son of God was already looking for him, and when the Son of God goes looking for someone, you can be sure he will find him.

"Do you believe?"

Sometimes it's only when we have nowhere else to turn that we fall at his feet and say, "Lord, I believe." And the searching Son of God accepts us.

PART 4

● "For judgment I have come into this world, so that the blind will see and those who see will become blind."

John 9:39

Stare at the sun and you'll go blind. Isn't that interesting? It illumines our world, but it also has the power to blind us. As the Light of the World, Jesus came to restore sight, to make things clear to us. But of course some would turn away from this light, preferring the darkness of their own pride, hate, or lust. This is the "judgment" Jesus was talking about—a turning point, a watershed, a moment of decision.

Scene 7: The Pharisees appear again. (Are they tailing him in the hopes of gathering incriminating evidence?) They hear Jesus talking about sight and blindness, and they take offense. *Are you saying we're blind too?* They're baiting him.

Jesus decided to play it coy. "If you were blind, you would not be guilty of sin; but now that you claim you can see, your guilt remains" (v. 41).

193

Yes, they were blind. They were as spiritually blind as this fellow had been physically blind. But the difference between them and the formerly blind man was in *awareness of their blindness*. They weren't; he was. If these Pharisees recognized their blindness and came to Jesus for spiritual healing, he could free them from their sin. They didn't.

In the longtime favorite invitation hymn "Just as I Am," one verse begins: "Just as I am, poor, wretched, blind." We can be saved only when we recognize that we cannot save ourselves. Only when we admit that we are blind and indeed have been blind from birth—only then will the Light of the World shine in our hearts and give us sight.

35

SHEEPISH

● "I am the good shepherd. The good shepherd lays down his life for the sheep."

John 10:11

Everything you need to know about sheep you learned in Sunday school. But not quite everything. You probably learned "The Lord is my shepherd" from Psalm 23. You probably saw pictures of Jesus as the Good Shepherd holding a little cuddly lamb in his arms. You probably pasted cotton balls on outlines of a flock of sheep and felt the softness.

But there's more.

No animal is mentioned in the Bible more often than sheep. Genesis 4 says that "Abel kept flocks," and the last chapter of the Bible, Revelation 22, mentions "the throne of God and of the Lamb." In between, you find the story of God stopping Abraham from slaying his son Isaac; a ram caught in a thicket was the substitute sacrifice. In Egypt on Passover night, the Israelites were told to kill a lamb and sprinkle the blood on the doorposts of their houses. The preeminent offering in Jewish sacrifices was the sheep, so when John the Baptist announced that Jesus was "the Lamb of God, who takes away the sin of the world" (John

Monday: Read part 1 of this chapter. Think of the vulnerability and dependency of the sheep.

Tuesday: Read part 2. What did Jesus mean when he called himself the Gate?

Wednesday: Read part 3. When have you been "surprised by joy"?

Thursday: Read part 4. Consider the question in "In the Mirror."

Friday: Can you find other "I am" statements in John's Gospel? Taken together, what do these metaphors teach you about Jesus?

Saturday: Pray today for the "other sheep" Jesus mentioned (John 10:16). Do you know some who should be in the flock of Jesus?

Sunday: Let your heart praise God as you read the beautiful Psalm 23.

1:29), there was no doubt about what he meant.

The most famous biblical shepherd, of course, was David, who killed a lion and a bear to protect his flock. It was he who penned the beloved Psalm 23 and verses like "We are his people, the sheep of his pasture" (100:3).

After David, sheep were never quite the same. Before Psalm 23 was written, the mention of sheep was always taken literally. When the Bible mentioned sheep, it meant the flesh-and-blood woolly creatures. But after David, the prophets began talking in figurative language about how *we* are like sheep. Like stupid sheep (and sheep have never scored very high on IQ tests), we all "have gone astray," Isaiah said; "each of us has turned to his own way" (Isa. 53:6). Unlike dogs and cats, sheep get lost easily, so Jeremiah compares his people to sheep that "wandered over mountain and hill and forgot their own resting place" (Jer. 50:6). But it's Ezekiel who puts it all together. The problem isn't simply with the stupid sheep that are "scattered over the whole earth," but it's the fact that no one searched or looked for them (Ezek. 34:6). Ezekiel blames the shepherds in no uncertain terms. Then he talks about *God* becoming a shepherd: "I myself will search for my sheep and look after them" (v. 11).

In John 10, immediately after healing the blind man and calling the Pharisees "blind leaders," Jesus talks about unworthy shepherds in the same way that Ezekiel had done hundreds of years earlier. He calls them strangers, thieves, and robbers—not very nice epithets for distinguished spiritual leaders, but they didn't get it.

Who's he talking about? they probably asked one another. *Certainly not us.*

● "I am the gate; whoever enters through me will be saved. He will come in and go out, and find pasture."

John 10:9

When you read *gate*, what do you think of? Probably not a sheep gate. Shepherds weren't fussy about gates and doors. Sometimes they herded their flock into a cave for the night, and the shepherd would lie down to sleep at the opening. In that way the shepherd was a literal gate.

You can apply the truth of Jesus as the Gate in many different ways. The Gate provides sheep (that's us) with security, because nothing can get in to harm us. It would have to come in through the Gate. And he gives us contentment and fulfillment, because through him we walk in and out to the pastures, to nibble away at the green grass.

But Jesus applied the concept like this: First, he is the exclusive way to salvation. Today there's a lot of competition in the religious marketplace, and your friendly next-door neighbors may claim they know another gate that works for them. It's tempting in our multicultural society to go with the flow and not make waves. And Jesus could have said to the Pharisees, "I am simply offering an option. Some may find salvation your way, but some may prefer my way." But that's not what he said. He claimed exclusivity.

> **FACTOID**
>
> John 10 contains two of the seven great "I am" statements of Jesus that appear in John's Gospel.

Second, he spoke of sheep stealers, those who sneak over the fence "to steal and kill and destroy." Obviously he was hitting at the Pharisees, but today this applies to those who twist Scripture and delude the sheep. Cults are attractive because they offer a new angle on Scripture, provide a warm and fuzzy flock, and are led by an exciting charismatic leader. Such a leader, Jesus said in strong words, is a thief.

PART 3

● "I have come that they may have life, and have it to the full."

John 10:10

Jesus was placing himself in stark contrast to the sheep steal-ers. He was all about life, while they robbed the people of the joy of life. Centuries earlier, in his famous shepherd psalm, David had written, "My cup overflows," but it seems the Pharisees had forgotten that. Can you imagine one of those legalistic Pharisees saying, "Follow me, and you will have life to the full"? Where the Pharisees offered guilt, Jesus offered grace. Where the Phari-sees offered fear, Jesus offered freedom.

Fulfillment? Jesus will fill your cup full to overflowing. Yes, he was a "man of sorrows, and familiar with suffering" (Isa. 53:3). Yes, he told his followers that they must forsake all and take up their cross. But then, as C. S. Lewis discovered, a new convert is "surprised by joy," and that's the start of a new life, a life to the full.

How does Jesus provide this surprisingly full life? He "lays down his life for the sheep." He is the Good Shepherd who risks his neck to save the single sheep who has gone astray. The hired hand runs away when a wolf threatens the flock—what can you expect from a "temp"?—but the Shepherd cares for the sheep.

Are stupid, wandering, exasperating sheep worth it? Why would any shepherd, especially a good shepherd, lay down his life for some dumb sheep? Because he loves us, that's why. Does it make sense? Of course not, but God doesn't ask us to understand why he loves us; he simply asks us to accept that love.

PART 4

● "I am the good shepherd; I know my sheep and my sheep know me."

John 10:14

Sheep may be dumb, but one thing they know, and that is their shepherd's voice. If you put a half dozen flocks into one fold for the night, when Shepherd A comes calling the next morning, only his sheep will follow him, and when Shepherd B gives his distinctive call, only his sheep will follow him.

But the other side of it is that the shepherd knows his sheep. To us, every sheep looks like another, a potential lamb roast. But that's not how the shepherd sees them.

> **IN THE MIRROR**
>
> In the early morning, the shepherd goes to the fold where all the sheep in the area have been kept overnight. He calls and only his sheep come to him. They know his voice. How well do you know the voice of Jesus, the Good Shepherd? How do you know when he is calling?

There are millions of Christians around the world, but the Good Shepherd knows you individually and loves you and watches over you. Sometimes that's hard to believe, but it's true. You might think that when Jesus looks out over the ramparts of heaven, he says, "Ah, they all look alike. Like sheep, they are prone to wander; will they ever learn?" But no, he knows you by name, he knows all about you, and he loves you anyway.

The last book of the Bible looks forward to that day when "a great multitude [of people—sheep] that no one could count, from every nation, tribe, people and language, [are] standing before the throne and in front of the Lamb" (Rev. 7:9). Amazing what the Good Shepherd can do!

QUOTE TO NOTE

You may be a very lame, and timid, and worthless sheep; but you were purchased by the Shepherd's blood, because he loved you so. He will deliver you from the lion and the bear, and bring you in triumph to the fold.

F. B. Meyer

36

EVERYTHING

He had fallen in love. A teenage boy was gaga over a girl who lived down the street from him. "I will do anything for you," he wrote in a note that he passed to her in history class. "I will climb the highest mountain, swim the deepest ocean, just to see your face. I would ford a raging river to be with you, or trek through the most dangerous jungle, all for your love. And I'd like to come over and see you Saturday . . . if it doesn't rain."

We're like that in our spiritual lives, aren't we? We use lofty language in our songs and praises—"All to Jesus I surrender!"—but we often shirk our prayer time if it's inconvenient. We think of ourselves as fully devoted disciples, but our time and money are precious, sometimes too precious.

A man like that came to Jesus one day with a good question: "Good teacher, what must I do to inherit eternal life?" Jesus' response seems coy.

● "Why do you call me good? . . . No one is good—except God alone. You know the commandments: 'Do not commit adultery, do not murder, do not steal, do not give false testimony, honor your father and mother.'"

Luke 18:19–20

The main point here is about goodness. Clearly, the man considered *himself* good, and he had also attributed goodness to this rabbi. With his response, Jesus raised the bar regarding goodness. *Talk about goodness! Only God is completely good all the time. If you want to inherit eternal life, you'll have to share in his goodness.*

You might think that Jesus is saying that this man can earn eternal life by keeping the commandments, but Jesus is actually setting the bar of goodness at God-level. This whole story actually *supports* the idea of salvation by grace and not through the law. Theoretically, a person who perfectly kept all of God's commandments would win eternal life. But as Paul says, "There is no one righteous, not even one" (Rom. 3:10).

Lots of people in our world, even in our churches, consider themselves "good enough." They live their lives by the Ten Commandments and try to maintain high moral standards. In general, they assume that God will weigh their good deeds against their few indiscretions and welcome them into heaven. But their logic is faulty.

Many couples have discovered the damage that one little lie can cause. "Hey, I tell the truth 99 percent of the time. Why is this one untruth such a problem?" Because 99 percent isn't good enough. Trust depends on 100 percent assurance. One partner needs to know that the other is completely committed to truth telling.

Monday: Read part 1 of this chapter. Consider the question in "In the Mirror."

Tuesday: Read part 2. Is Jesus saying you get to heaven by way of the commandments?

Wednesday: Read part 3. Do you think this is saying that every Christian should be poor?

Thursday: What is the most valuable thing you possess? If you were to ask Jesus the same question as the rich young ruler asked, what might he say?

Friday: What treasure are you storing up in heaven?

Saturday: Pray today about your finances. Ask God to help you put money in the proper place in your life.

Sunday: Praise God as you read Psalm 107:1–9.

IN THE MIRROR

Jesus saw that the young man had himself rather than God at the center of his life. Can even our "good" deeds indicate that we are self-centered? Can we be proud of our obedience?

201

We all fall short of that 100 percent level. The young ruler who came to Jesus, like so many today, took pride in his own moral caliber—but still he sensed that something was missing. Jesus rattled off a few of the Ten Commandments, and the man insisted he had kept them all his life.

So Jesus had to raise the bar one more time.

PART 2

● "You still lack one thing. Sell everything you have and give to the poor, and you will have treasure in heaven. Then come, follow me."

Luke 18:22

Rich Christians feel uneasy about this verse. On the other hand, those who are active in ministry to the poor tend to quote it a lot. "See?" they say. "Jesus wants us to give everything to the poor."

On the defensive, the wealthy believers respond, "Jesus was only saying that to this one man, and that's because he knew this man loved his possessions so much. It's not a rule for everybody." (As if the rest of us aren't in love with our possessions.)

> **CROSS REF** ·
>
> How do you think the rich young ruler would respond to Matthew 6:19–24?

That debate might distract us from the full force of this text, so let's put it aside for the moment and see what Jesus was trying to teach this young man.

What was the man looking for? Eternal life. Now that's certainly a noble pursuit. He sensed that he was missing something in his life and that Jesus might help him find it. So far, so good.

How did the man expect to get eternal life? By doing something. "What must I *do*?" he asked. And when Jesus mentioned the commandments, the man proudly announced that he had kept them. No doubt he felt he had done most of the work necessary to get to God's kingdom. He had amassed 24,000 frequent-flier miles; just a little more would earn him a ticket to eternity.

But Jesus didn't give him some minor task. He went for broke, so to speak, asking for an ultimate commitment. If the man did this, it would change his life completely. He would lose his status, his home, perhaps some friends. This decision would put the man right where God wanted him—in a state of complete dependency. He would no longer be able to trust in his own material resources; it's reasonable to think that he'd also learn to trust in God's spiritual resources rather than his own.

Unfortunately, the man couldn't see the beauty of that situation. The glitter of all his goods blinded him; he couldn't imagine living without them. He chose to trust in his wealth and good deeds rather than in God's blessings. Matthew concludes his account starkly: "When the young man heard that saying, he went away sorrowful: for he had great possessions" (Matt. 19:22 KJV).

PART 3

● "How hard it is for the rich to enter the kingdom of God! Indeed, it is easier for a camel to go through the eye of a needle than for a rich man to enter the kingdom of God. . . .
"What is impossible with men is possible with God."

Luke 18:24–25, 27

Jesus chooses to use another image absurd enough for *Saturday Night Live*. He has already depicted people with planks in their eyes trying to remove specks from the eyes of others. And later he would mock the Pharisees for straining gnats out of their soup while swallowing camels. Some commentators have suggested that the "eye of a needle" refers to a narrow city gate in Jerusalem, but there's no need to make it that realistic. Jesus was intentionally being silly. You just can't thread a needle with a camel. That's how difficult it is for rich folks to get through the pearly gates.

This was not only an absurd picture but also an outrageous idea. In that society, the rich had the inside track on God's kingdom. Wealth was seen as an indication of God's blessing, as long as it wasn't earned dishonestly (like the wealth of tax collectors). The point is, everyone expected that the rich would get the best places in heaven. If *they* didn't make it to heaven, then no one could. This attitude is reflected in the disciples' response to the camel joke. In apparent disbelief, they asked, "Who then can be saved?"

And that's when Jesus provided the key to this whole story: "What is impossible with men is possible with God." Rich people will try to use their riches to save themselves. That won't work. When you're loaded, it's hard *not* to try to buy your way into God's good graces. When you don't have to trust God for your daily bread, how can you learn to trust him for your eternal destiny?

The question still comes up: What about rich Christians? Should they sell everything they have and give it to the poor? It's not a bad idea, but those who would make it a requirement for salvation are on the wrong track. The only requirement is that we humble ourselves enough to trust in God's grace. Jesus challenged the rich young ruler to do that by selling his holdings. It turned out that the man's holdings were holding him.

That's not an uncommon situation. All of us should be wary of the hold that our wealth has on us. Does it keep us from trusting God as we should?

QUOTE TO NOTE

The poorest man I know is the man who has nothing but money.

John D. Rockefeller Jr.

37
THE MOST HATED PROFESSION

PART 1

● "Two men went up to the temple to pray, one a Pharisee and the other a tax collector."

Luke 18:10

Does anyone love a tax collector? Be honest. Have you ever sent a Christmas card to a tax collector or called him up on the phone to sing "Happy Birthday"?

If you're looking for a profession that will give you cheers and applause, don't choose tax collecting. The approval rating for a Mafia hit man is probably a notch higher than that for a tax collector.

And that's the way it has always been. It was certainly that way in the time of Jesus, and folks at that time had good reason to think of tax collectors as scumbags—because most of them were. People had to pay four different kinds of taxes—property tax on land, personal property tax on everything else, a head tax, and finally a customs tax on goods transported over land and sea.

The Romans were directly responsible for collecting the first three kinds of taxes, but the fourth kind was farmed out to the highest bidder, and Jews who wanted money more than a

Monday: Read part 1 of this chapter. How do you interact with people at the bottom of the social ladder?

Tuesday: Read part 2. Is it wrong to thank God for our spiritual growth? When does that become pride?

Wednesday: Read part 3. Do you think Jesus was aware of what his going to Zacchaeus's home would do to his reputation?

Thursday: According to Luke 19:10, what was Jesus' mission? Where do you fit into that?

Friday: Consider the question in "In the Mirror."

Saturday: Pray humbly today for anyone you know who is lost and needs Jesus as Savior.

Sunday: Praise the Lord as you read Colossians 3:12–15.

decent reputation would bid high for it. These tax collectors were stationed in tollbooths along main crossroads, bridges, and entries into towns and marketplaces. While customs taxes were normally 5 percent of the value of regular goods and 12.5 percent of luxury items, the tax collectors had to make a profit, so they either invented some taxes or else overvalued the goods to get more money to put in their pockets.

Many Jews refused to accept change from a tax collector. They considered it dirty or unclean money. If they didn't have the exact amount, they would wait until another traveler came along and borrow it.

So Jews had three things against tax collectors: (1) As a rule, they were dishonest; (2) as employees of the occupying Romans, they were traitors; and (3) no one likes to pay taxes anyway.

Yes, most of the tax collectors were scumbags. But who is the first nonfisherman disciple we meet? None other than Matthew, the tax collector. He ran the tollbooth on the Damascus-Capernaum-Ptolemais road, a dream location for any tax collector. No doubt he was a thorn in the side of many merchants who commuted along that road.

Well, that's the background you need for the following stories, and it may help you see why tax collectors were outcasts—although usually wealthy—and were grouped with prostitutes and incorrigible criminals on the bottom rung of society.

But Jesus didn't look at them as scumbags. He looked at them as people in need of salvation, just like the rest of us.

PART 2

So Jesus tells a story about the two extremes on the Jewish religious ladder: the Pharisee at the top and the tax collector at the bottom. According to the Gospel of Luke, the story was addressed "to some who were confident of their own righteousness and looked down on everybody else."

Two men went to the temple to pray—the Pharisee and the tax collector. The Pharisee is described first. He stood and "prayed about himself" (Luke 18:11), which is not unlike the rest of us most of the time. He thanked God that he wasn't like some awful sinners, and he named robbers, evildoers, adulterers, and "even this tax collector." Then he bragged to God about how often he fasted and how much he gave to the temple.

The tax collector, on the other hand, knew he deserved nothing from God.

●   "He would not even look up to heaven, but beat his breast and said, 'God, have mercy on me, a sinner.'

"I tell you that this man, rather than the other, went home justified before God."

Luke 18:13–14

Both men went to the temple; both prayed; both acknowledged God. If you had asked him, the Pharisee may even have admitted he was a sinner, but as he prayed he was looking around, comparing himself with others, telling God that he was more worthy of his blessings than others. If you look hard enough, you can always find people more sinful than you are.

The tax collector wasn't looking around. He was praying to God and he wasn't concerned about anyone else. In his prayer, "God, have mercy on me, a sinner," the Greek could just as well be translated, "*the* sinner." His standard is not the morality of other people or even the morality of the Pharisees. He could have boasted that he was not proud like the Pharisee over there. But his standard was God.

He went home justified, the text says. Like the prodigal returning home, he cried out, *I am the sinner. Lord, be merciful.* But then God put his divine arms around him and said, *Welcome*

207

home, my child. You are loved. You may be the sinner, but you have come to the right place, because I am the Savior.

PART 3

● "Zacchaeus, come down immediately. I must stay at your house today."

Luke 19:5

In the next chapter of Luke's Gospel, Jesus comes to Jericho on his way to Jerusalem. Here he meets Zacchaeus, another tax collector, a favorite in children's Sunday school stories.

If Matthew was located in a tax collector's heaven on a main highway north of Capernaum, think of the spot that Zacchaeus had. Jericho was the center of a great agricultural region and was the winter resort capital of the area. All the commerce going to Jerusalem and west to the Mediterranean passed by his toll-booth. The Romans were erecting one magnificent building after another in Jericho, and all of that brought lucrative traffic through Zacchaeus's territory. The Bible says three things about him: (1) he was the *chief* tax collector, which means he had others reporting to him; (2) he was wealthy; and (3) he was short.

> **CROSS REF**
>
> Read about humility:
> Proverbs 3:34
> Isaiah 57:15
> 1 Peter 5:6

> **IN THE MIRROR**
>
> When you come before the Lord in prayer, do you sound more like the Pharisee or the tax collector?

In early America, when schoolkids learned their ABCs, they learned little Bible poems for each letter. For the last letter of the alphabet, they learned "Zacchaeus he / did climb a tree / his Lord to see." That is just about all that most people know about Zacchaeus.

Who hasn't gone to a parade or cavalcade to see a dignitary come by? Maybe it was a governor or a president or a returning war hero. You stood on tiptoes to get a better look. When you were very young, your father would put you on his shoulders after you had pestered him with "I wanna see; I wanna see" a dozen times. Then you saw, and everyone cheered and you clapped your hands.

Now, suppose that dignitary stops the cavalcade, looks in your direction, calls out your name, and says, "Hey, come join me in my limousine; I want to stay at your place tonight."

Wow!

That's what happened to Zacchaeus. Remember, not only was he too short to see over the crowd, but since he was a tax collector, no one wanted to have anything to do with him. If he had tried to push his way to the front, he would soon have been in the middle of a major scuffle. So he climbed a tree to get a better look. Then he saw Jesus looking up at him. He heard Jesus call him by name. Jesus was inviting himself to dinner.

Various versions use different words to translate how Zacchaeus responded: *gladly, delightedly, joyfully.* You get the idea.

> ### CHECKOUT COUNTER
> Paul was an example of a law-abiding Pharisee. Check out Philippians 3:8–9 to see what he says about his changed attitude.

You can also guess what the crowd was thinking. *There are lots of respectable people in Jericho. Why would Jesus have anything to do with such a scumbag? I guess you know someone by the company he keeps. And if he chooses to party with a scumbag, you know what that says about him.*

By this one action, Jesus had turned the crowd against him. He had come into town a hero; he would be leaving it a traitor. Why did he befriend the most hated man in town? Jesus had an answer for that.

● **"For the Son of Man came to seek and to save what was lost."**

Luke 19:10

Zacchaeus didn't initiate the interaction. The tax collector didn't come running to Jesus saying, "I'm going to be good from now on; I'm going to give back everything I swindled." No. Jesus called him first. Then after the tax collector had an encounter with Jesus, he promised to give half of what he owned to the poor and to pay back fourfold anyone he had cheated.

Jesus has a way of changing people—that's what conversion is all about. After Jesus saw the evidence of Zacchaeus's conversion, he said, "Today salvation has come to this house." And it was the house of a despised tax collector.

38
GOOD, BETTER

In our Christian lives, there are lots of good things we can do, but Jesus keeps calling us into a life that's "better," "abundant," "beyond."

We see such a comparison in the brief story of Mary and Martha. Jesus visited their home in Bethany, just outside Jerusalem, with his disciples. Martha played hostess and scurried around the house, "distracted by all the preparations that had to be made." And she was irked that her sister Mary just sat at Jesus' feet. "Lord," she complained, "don't you care that my sister has left me to do the work by myself? Tell her to help me!" (Luke 10:40).

It's hard to blame Martha for feeling that way. Like it or not, in that day a woman's place was in the kitchen. It was rare for rabbis to teach women. But aside from gender issues, Mary was certainly a cohostess of this gathering. Common courtesy would suggest that she pitch in to help her sister. But Jesus didn't send Mary away. In fact he used the opportunity to teach these sisters some "family values."

● "Martha, Martha, . . . you are worried and upset about many things, but only one thing is needed. Mary has chosen what

Monday: Read part 1 of this chapter. If you were in a play, which role would fit you better—Martha or Mary? Why?

Tuesday: Read part 2. We celebrate resurrection once a year. It no longer astounds us. But think of what this meant to Martha.

Wednesday: Read part 3. Do you invest yourself in situations that result in God's glory?

Thursday: What "tomb" might Jesus be calling you out of?

Friday: Is your life filled with good things but not the best things?

Saturday: Ask God to help you choose the "better" way, as Mary did.

Sunday: Read 1 Corinthians 15:12–21. Praise God for Jesus' resurrection from the dead.

is better, and it will not be taken away from her."

Luke 10:41–42

Perhaps you've imagined that Mary was sitting quietly before Jesus, intently listening to each word. Maybe, but how would you characterize Jesus' teaching? He was always saying funny things, telling humorous stories, and spinning clever witticisms. It's likely that Mary and the disciples were laughing out loud as Jesus regaled them with tales of the kingdom. And so, Martha, elbow-deep in oil and flour, kept hearing bursts of laughter from the other room—and surely she recognized her sister's voice among the others.

"Don't you care?" Martha asked Jesus. *Of course* Jesus cared about *Martha*, but not about all the things she cared about. She had many cares at the moment, and it didn't help that Jesus had descended on her home with his entourage in tow. *Martha, Martha*, he said, repeating her name to slow her down or just to capture her attention. Then he told her how she was feeling—"worried and upset."

Modern counselors call this "active listening." Jesus was mirroring her emotions. If nothing else, he was saying, *Yes, Martha, I do care, and I know just how you feel, but let me teach you something here.*

Martha's service was very nice, but it wasn't absolutely necessary. Jesus said that when you get right down to it, only one thing really matters—and that's what Mary had chosen to do.

It's great to serve lentil soup to this traveling rabbi and his dozen devotees, but there's something even more important—finding life in his words.

PART 2

Some time later, Jesus received word from Mary and Martha that their brother Lazarus was quite ill. But instead of rushing to the bedside of this friend, Jesus waited two days. By the time he had traveled to Bethany, Lazarus had been dead for four days. Martha greeted him with a scolding. "If you had been here, my brother would not have died." Then, perhaps rethinking her tone, she added, "But I know that even now God will give you whatever you ask" (John 11:21–22).

"Your brother will rise again," Jesus assured her. It sounds like the sort of platitude we say to grieving relatives—we'll see the dearly departed again in heaven. Martha claimed that promise in a generic way, repeating the sentiment: "I know he will rise again in the resurrection at the last day" (v. 24). But then Jesus, as he did so often, took the conversation to another level.

● "I am the resurrection and the life. He who believes in me will live, even though he dies; and whoever lives and believes in me will never die. Do you believe this?"

John 11:25–26

Martha must have been a multitasker. While she was whipping up the tuna casserole for Jesus and company, she had to have had an ear out for his teachings. Maybe Mary had to concentrate by sitting right in front of Rabbi Jesus, but Martha must have learned plenty listening in from the kitchen. How else could she respond to Jesus as she did?

"Yes, Lord," she answered, "I believe that you are the Christ, the Son of God, who was to come into the world" (v. 27). *Christ*, of course, means the Messiah, the

DARE TO COMPARE

Compare Martha's statement of faith in John 11:27 with Peter's in Matthew 16:16.

prophesied Savior of Israel. Martha knew that Jesus was no mere teacher but the divine Deliverer. And now he was talking about resurrection.

We actually see three kinds of "life" in this story. Of course there's the physical life that Lazarus had lost. Then there's also the generic "life after death" that Martha referred to. But Jesus was talking about a third kind of life. His mission as Messiah was all about life. He was breathing the Spirit into dusty souls. He was waking people up to God's will. He was bringing God's kingdom into vibrant reality. And he would eventually break the power of sin through his death and smash the chains of death through his resurrection.

This life-in-Jesus happens both now and in the future. It's an eternal life that starts in this life. The one who trusts in Jesus will continue to live "even though he dies"—that is, physically. The one who lives his life depending on Jesus will never die spiritually. In Jesus, we have power in this world and hope for the next.

It's good to believe in life after death. Many do, and they don't think much about it until some tragedy occurs. Jesus was talking about something even better, an abundant life that doesn't shrink in the face of physical death.

PART 3

Jesus went to the grave of his friend and wept. The precise cause of his weeping is a mystery. Yes, people cry at funerals, but didn't Jesus know what he was about to do? Perhaps he wept over the unbelief of the other mourners, or maybe he was bemoaning the power that death had always held over mortals. In any case, he asked that the grave be opened.

Martha protested that the four-day-dead corpse would have a sickening odor. Miracle or no, she had guests to care for. Jesus challenged her to trust him and "see the glory of God" (v. 40).

● "Lazarus, come out!"
John 11:43

If we see footage of a political candidate, say, tutoring a young child, most of us are jaded enough to understand it as a photo op. We know the scene was staged. Still, it's a sign for us, a kind of hieroglyphic showing us that this candidate cares about education. Or at least he cares that we care about education.

The miracles of Jesus were signs, proving his power and authority as a deliverer sent from God. But they weren't just photo ops. Scripture makes clear that these miracles were also acts of love and

> **CHECKOUT COUNTER**
>
> For more on resurrection, check out John 5:19–30 and 6:39. Also see 1 Thessalonians 4:13–5:11.

compassion. Jesus was sent to free people from spiritual death and soul sickness, but his redemption also extended to the physical realm. He delighted in the wholeness of body and spirit.

And so he strode to the tomb of Lazarus, had the stone rolled away, and called into the darkness, asking his friend to come out to play. "The dead man came out," the Gospel says, and he still wore the grave clothes. But this was no zombie; Lazarus was very much alive. This was the best sign yet. The healings had been great, but a resurrection! This was a powerful testimony to Jesus' identity.

Throughout this story, Jesus had been talking about glory. The sickness and temporary death of Lazarus occurred for the glory of God and God's Son (v. 4). And yes, Jesus received acclaim from this event, but there was a different kind of glory on the horizon. This resurrection made Jesus even more dangerous, and so the authorities jumped into action, seeking a way to kill him. This trip, with this miracle, was a giant step toward the cross, where Jesus would ultimately be glorified (12:23–24).

Jesus still calls people out of their tombs. You walk past spiritually dead people every day. Oh, their Day-Timers are filled with meetings and activities, and maybe their weekends are crammed with parties, but their hearts are as dead as Lazarus until they hear that call from somewhere beyond them: "Lazarus, come out!" The Son of God summons them with his life-giving power. Will they step out into his light?

QUOTE TO NOTE

The mystical and practical are both required in Christ's service.

F. B. Meyer

215

39
CATCH-22

PART 1

Catch-22 by Joseph Heller ranks among the best war novels of the twentieth century. In the novel a pilot named Orr tries to feign insanity to avoid another flight over enemy territory. Then he confronts Catch-22.

According to Catch-22, if you are concerned about your safety in the face of real and immediate danger, that's a sure sign you are sane. If Orr proved he was crazy, he would be grounded. But if he asked to be grounded because he was afraid of the danger, they would say that he was acting rationally. It was a Catch-22 situation. Orr couldn't get out of it. If he flew another mission when he didn't have to, he was crazy; but if he didn't want to, he was sane. No matter what he did, he would end up flying a bomber over dangerous enemy territory.

The Pharisees had never heard of Catch-22, but that was exactly the kind of trap they dreamed up for Jesus. They were sure they had concocted a no-win situation for the rabbi from Nazareth. And fittingly, it is all told in Matthew, chapter 22.

Apparently, the leading Pharisees didn't want to be recognized, so they sent some of their disciples along with some Herodians to ask Jesus a question. As you can guess by the name, the Herodians were supporters of Herod, who was appointed to his office by

Caesar. The Pharisees, on the other hand, detested Herod and his Roman bosses. But both parties wanted to get something on Jesus.

It looked like an innocent meeting. They began with flattery. "Teacher, . . . we know you are a man of integrity and that you teach the way of God in accordance with the truth. You aren't swayed by men, because you pay no attention to who they are" (v. 16). In other words, *Jesus, you tell it like it is, and you are respected for it.*

Then came the trick question, the Catch-22. "Is it right to pay taxes to Caesar or not?" (v. 17).

If he said yes, the Pharisees would denounce him as a traitor to his people. If he said no, the Herodians would report him to Herod, and he could be executed for treason. No way out.

Jesus saw through their trickery. He asked for a coin they used to pay the tax. They brought the coin to him (a denarius, equal to a day's wage), and he asked: "Whose portrait is this? And whose inscription?" (v. 20).

"Caesar's," they answered.

● **"Give to Caesar what is Caesar's, and to God what is God's."**

Matthew 22:21

It was a simple yet amazingly profound answer. Even though they hated the Romans, the Pharisees were benefiting from Rome whenever they used a Roman coin. So Jesus said it was proper

Monday: As preparation for this week's lesson, read Matthew 21:45–46. What were the Pharisees thinking?

Tuesday: Read part 1 of this chapter. Notice that Jesus answers questions with a question. Clever dodge or teaching method?

Wednesday: Read part 2. Why do you think Jesus rebuked most often those in the higher strata of life, that is, the religious leaders and the rich?

Thursday: Read part 3. Augustine said, "Love, and do what you will." Does that accurately sum up Jesus' teaching or not?

Friday: Consider the question in "In the Mirror."

Saturday: Many modern worship songs express love for Christ. Choose one and make it your prayer today.

Sunday: Read Deuteronomy 6:4–9 and express your wholly devoted love for the Lord.

to give back to Caesar what belonged to him, as long as you gave God what is rightfully his. Somehow Jesus took this no-win question and . . . he won. He turned the question back on the askers, challenging them to be less concerned about money and more concerned about honoring God with their lives.

The same challenge comes to us. Check your wallet and you'll find slips of paper with images of Washington, Lincoln, and other great national figures. The government prints that money and runs the economic system, so, hey, let them take their fair share. We are not robbing God when we pay taxes to our "Caesar."

But whose image do *you* bear? According to Genesis 1:27, we were made in the image of God. So if we should give back to Caesar what bears his image, shouldn't we give back to God what bears his image? That is, ourselves.

PART 2

● "You are in error because you do not know the Scriptures or the power of God."

Matthew 22:29

The TV program *Jeopardy* challenges contestants to give quick answers to difficult questions. Jesus knew all about jeopardy quizzes. On this particular day he was in constant jeopardy with one question after another.

The second question that day came from the Sadducees, who were just as strict as the Pharisees in interpreting the laws of Moses—except they did not believe in angels, demons, the resurrection of the dead, or a future life. The only part of the Old Testament they really believed was the Pentateuch, the first five books, the books of Moses. They thought they had a Catch-22 question for Jesus too.

They told a fantastic story of a man who died childless. According to Deuteronomy 25:5–6, the brother of a deceased man was obligated to marry the widow and have children for him.

218

Well, the man had seven brothers and each brother died after marrying the widow and still there were no children. In today's world you would suspect foul play—was the widow poisoning her husbands to collect the insurance?—but that would spoil the Sadducees' story. And you can tell they put a lot of thought into this one.

Since you believe in heaven, Jesus, whose wife will she be up yonder? Another $64,000 question. They really didn't want an answer. They just wanted to show how silly the idea of resurrection was.

Jesus gave his answer in two parts, and once again he challenged the askers, criticizing their ignorance of God's Word and his power. First, Jesus asserted that the resurrection body would not be the same as the physical body. Here Jesus differed from the Egyptians, who mummified the dead, believing that the next life would be material and physical, and also from the Greeks, who believed in the immortality only of a disembodied soul. Of course, he differed from the Sadducees too, who didn't believe in a resurrection at all.

Second, he quoted from Exodus, one of the books of Moses that the Sadducees considered authoritative. There God identified himself to Moses by saying, "I am the God of Abraham, the God of Isaac and the God of Jacob" (Exod. 3:6). God didn't say, "I *was* their God," in the past tense, but rather "I *am* their God," in the present tense. Jesus based a crucial point on that grammatical detail.

● **"He is not the God of the dead but of the living."**

Matthew 22:32

Abraham, Isaac, and Jacob had passed away centuries before God introduced himself to Moses. But by saying, "I *am* their God," the Lord was suggesting that they were still alive and well, though in some other kind of existence. The Sadducees must have quoted that verse many times. They would proudly say they worshiped the God of Abraham, Isaac, and Jacob. But they had never before seen that the verse proved what they had always disbelieved—the resurrection.

We probably wish that Jesus had said a lot more about the resurrection body, but he said just enough to squelch the Sadducees. The onlookers "were astonished at his teaching" (v. 33). Apparently they realized he had won another round of *Jeopardy*.

PART 3

The third round was still to come. The Pharisees returned in full force with a legal expert leading the charge. "Which is the greatest commandment in the Law?" he asked Jesus (v. 36). The Pharisees may have debated the question themselves in their temple chambers, but Scripture says that they asked it to test Jesus.

It might seem like an innocent question. All Jesus had to do was pick one of the Ten Commandments, right? But the Pharisees had counted 613 commandments in the books of the Law. Some 365 were things you shouldn't do, and 248 were things you should do. Each one was just as important as the rest. Another Catch-22. Call one law the greatest, and you're dissing 612 others.

● **"'Love the Lord your God with all your heart and with all your soul and with all your mind.' This is the first and greatest commandment. And the second is like it: 'Love your neighbor as yourself.'"**

Matthew 22:37–39

Masterfully, Jesus selected two verses from the books of Moses: Deuteronomy 6:5 and Leviticus 19:18. These verses had been in Scripture for hundreds of years, so Jesus was not expounding a new teaching here; he was just setting priorities. Love for God, neighbor, and self is essential for a fulfilling life.

In building a lifestyle, love must have top priority. Love ties the package together. Without love, it all falls apart and shatters into little bits. Love is the oil that makes Christianity work. Without it, our faith clanks and wheezes and grinds to a halt.

Yes. Jesus was amazing in his ability to answer trick questions, but he wasn't primarily concerned with wriggling out of Catch-22 situations, nor was he aiming to show up his adversaries. He was always doing more—teaching, telling the truth about God, and challenging his hearers to give themselves fully to their Creator.

40
WHERE ARE YOU GOING?

PART 1

A man has been transferred to a new office in a distant state. His suitcases sit by the front door. Suddenly his three-year-old son grabs him around the legs and asks for the tenth time, "Where are you going, Daddy?"

The father picks him up and hugs him. He can't even describe what the new place is like. The child is too young to understand.

"Can I come with you?"

"No, you can't come now, but after I get our new home ready, I'll be coming back for you and Mommy."

"Why can't I come now?" the boy asks. "I'll carry your bags."

"Do you think you can?" The father smiles at the little tyke, knowing that the youngster can't even lift them. The child is worried and the father knows it, so he speaks words of assurance and comfort. "Don't worry. It won't be long. I'll be back soon."

That is almost the same conversation that Jesus had with Peter and the other disciples in the upper room, as told in John 13:36–38. Simon Peter had been with Jesus just about as long as that little boy had been with his father, so if some of Peter's responses seem childlike, you'll have to forgive him. Or maybe you should praise Peter and the other disciples for the simple honesty of their expressions.

The beginning of John 14 is a favorite passage for those who have lost a loved one (second only to Psalm 23). Of course, it was starting to dawn on the disciples that they were losing a loved one. Jesus offered assurance to his worried friends.

EVERY DAY WITH JESUS

Monday: Read part 1 of this chapter. Why were the disciples troubled?

Tuesday: Read part 2. Consider this: Jesus is both the destination and the route.

Wednesday: Read part 3. What did Philip really want from Jesus?

Thursday: Read part 4. How is it possible that we (or anyone) can do even "greater things"?

Friday: Consider the statements in "In the Mirror." How do they make you feel?

Saturday: As you pray today, thank the Lord for the Holy Spirit and his work in you.

Sunday: Read Psalm 139:1–10, 23–24. Praise the Lord for his eternal presence.

● "Do not let your hearts be troubled. Trust in God; trust also in me. In my Father's house are many rooms; if it were not so, I would have told you. I am going there to prepare a place for you."

John 14:1–2

A place for you! A room reserved—in addition to the inheritance that is reserved for you (1 Peter 1:4)! Not a bad retirement plan.

PART 2

Only a day earlier, Jesus had sent two disciples ahead to prepare a room to celebrate the Passover meal. The two disciples did not know where they were going, but Jesus told them to follow a man carrying a jar of water, and they followed him to the upper room. Somehow that room had been prepared for them. Now Jesus said he was going ahead of them to prepare a place.

In John 2 Jesus called the temple in Jerusalem "my Father's house." The outside

IN THE MIRROR

Jesus said, "I will come back and take you to be with me that you also may be where I am" (John 14:3). You will never be alone if you have trusted Jesus. He has a place ready where he can be with you for all eternity.

of the temple contained little shelters that housed pilgrims who came from a distance to worship. The disciples knew all about these "rooms" and probably had sometimes stayed in them. So the idea of "rooms" in "my Father's house" was not completely new to them. But this was different, and they knew it.

Jesus said they knew the way to the place where he was going, but that confused Thomas. If he were in a classroom, he would have raised his hand. *Lord, we don't know where you're going,* he said, *so how can we know the way to get there?* (see 14:5).

● "I am the way and the truth and the life. No one comes to the Father except through me."

John 14:6

The words *way, truth,* and *life* are sprinkled throughout the Old Testament. The psalmist said, "Teach me your way, O LORD, and I will walk in your truth" (Ps. 86:11). The writer of Proverbs often mentions the "way to life." Jesus is the fulfillment of all those verses.

Nothing can be as bewildering as being lost in a foreign city. You can't read the street signs, and you're not sure you know how to ask directions. Life can be like that. Sometimes even God's road map, the Bible, doesn't make sense to us. Yet Jesus, who is the Way, is also *Immanuel,* God with us. He is both our Way and our Guide.

He is also the Truth. But truth is more than a recitation of facts. You can know the truth about Jesus without knowing him as the Truth. You can believe historical facts about him and acknowledge the truth of his teachings without accepting the embodiment of Truth in your life.

As far as truth for daily living is concerned, Jesus went on to tell the disciples that the "Spirit of truth" would be coming soon (John 14:17), and they would also have the Scriptures to guide them in truth (17:17).

CHECKOUT COUNTER

Jesus said, "I am . . . the life." Check out these verses to see what he meant:
Romans 6:22–23
Galatians 2:20
Colossians 3:2–4

224

He is also the Life. Throughout his Gospel, John reminds us of this repeatedly (more than forty times). And this is not ordinary life but life eternal, abundant life, joyful life, a life worth living.

John 14:6 is packed with amazing claims. Jesus said he was not just *a* way, but *the* way. Make no mistake. Jesus claimed exclusivity. The only way to get to God the Father is through Jesus the Son.

In his first Epistle, John summarizes it this way: "God has given us eternal life, and this life is in his Son. He who has the Son has life; he who does not have the Son of God does not have life" (1 John 5:11–12).

PART 3

But the disciples still had questions. This time it was Philip who asked for more information: "Lord, show us the Father and that will be enough for us" (John 14:8).

Can you imagine the mental loop-de-loops going on in the disciples' heads? They had seen Jesus' miracles and followed him, convinced that he was some kind of prophet. They had heard his teaching and believed that he spoke on God's behalf. Peter had finally confessed that Jesus was not just a prophet but the very Son of God, the promised Messiah. And now Jesus was saying, "If you really knew me, you would know my Father as well" (v. 7). Did Jesus have the power to reveal God the Father to them in a dazzling new way? That's what Philip was asking for, and Jesus began his response by saying, "Anyone who has seen me has seen the Father" (v. 9).

● **"Believe me when I say that I am in the Father and the Father is in me."**

John 14:11

Another amazing claim! Undeniably, Jesus identified himself with God. John's Gospel made this point from the start, talking about Jesus as the Word, which "was God" and yet "became flesh and made his dwelling among us" (1:1, 14). Still, Jesus was establishing himself as a separate person in the Godhead.

Some folks think that Christians made up the idea of the Trinity later, after Jesus' time, but it's all right here. In fact John 14:16 speaks of all three persons of the Trinity, each separate and yet one: "I will ask the Father, and he will give you another Counselor to be with you forever." So Jesus is God, but he is not the Father or the Holy Spirit.

PART 4

● "Anyone who has faith in me will do . . . even greater things than these, because I am going to the Father."

John 14:12

How would the disciples respond to this remarkable promise? They thought of themselves as followers of the Messiah, but after their Messiah was gone—wherever he was going—what were they? Just a ragtag bunch of Galileans, more at home catching fish than changing the world.

Little did they realize that in a few months, they would be healing people in Jesus' name. In a few years, they'd be standing up to the authorities in the power of Jesus. And within a generation or so, the gospel of Jesus Christ would be spread to the ends of the known world and—surprise, surprise—*they* would be the instruments of that world evangelization.

"Who, us?" they probably asked themselves. It's surprising what the Holy Spirit can accomplish through the most unlikely candidates.

But notice that Jesus' promise involves not only his twelve disciples (and at this point it was down to eleven) but "anyone who has faith in me." That means you. So if you consider yourself an unlikely candidate to be a world-changer, think again. That's just the sort of person God uses.

41

PASSING THE PEACE

Peace is a wonderful word, but it's frightfully overworked. The dictionary gives more than a dozen definitions for it. It seems that every day we read about peace talks starting, and the next day we read that the talks have broken off. In many churches, members "pass the peace" by saying, "May the peace of the Lord be with you" to the people beside them. Then they pass the plate.

In New Testament times, the Roman government brought a *pax Romana*, which meant that you'd better not start an uprising, or else. The Messiah came with a different kind of peace. Isaiah prophesied that the Messiah would be called the Prince of Peace (Isa. 9:6), and the shepherds heard the angelic host proclaiming, "Glory to God in the highest, and on earth peace" (Luke 2:14). Once, Jesus said, "Peace, be still" to a storm, and the storm ceased.

But now, in the upper room, the disciples, who had spent more than three years with the Prince of Peace, were feeling downright jittery. Something was brewing, and they weren't at all peaceful. They probably wished that Jesus would say, "Peace, be still," to them and calm their inner storm. That's exactly what he did.

● "Peace I leave with you; my peace I give you. I do not give to you as the world gives. Do not let your hearts be

227

Monday: Read part 1 of this chapter. What causes you to be afraid? How can Jesus help?

Tuesday: Read part 2. What are those four "legs" that peace stands on?

Wednesday: Read part 3. How can we bring glory to God?

Thursday: Consider the question in "In the Mirror."

Friday: Read Galatians 5:22–23. Is there anything you can do specifically to bear more of the fruit of the Spirit?

Saturday: Pray today for more love for the Lord. Pray for a passion for him.

Sunday: Read Psalm 91. Praise the Lord as your refuge.

troubled and do not be afraid."

John 14:27

Jesus had a lot on his mind. Even as he spoke, he knew that Judas was betraying him; he knew that his arrest was imminent; he knew that crucifixion was ahead of him; and he knew that these beloved disciples would forsake him when the going got rough. Yet he wasn't thinking about himself. He was thinking of his disciples and their inner turmoil. So he bequeathed them peace. He was passing his peace to them.

Jesus said that his peace was a different kind of peace than the world gives. The world defines peace as the absence of war or trouble. If you want peace, you get away, you escape to an island in the South Pacific where balmy breezes blow. That's the kind of peace that refuses to face things. But that's not the Jesus brand of peace. He sends peace in the midst of trouble, even if the dark clouds of crucifixion are overhead. The world's brand of peace depends on circumstances; Jesus' brand of peace is independent of circumstances.

In Romans, Paul speaks of making peace with God, and that of course is vital. Because of Christ's death on the cross, we can know peace with God. We are reconciled to God through the death of Christ. But here Jesus is talking about the peace *of* God that his followers can enjoy.

How do you make God's peace a reality in your life? In these verses in John 14, Jesus mentions four legs for peace to stand on. First, *realize that you have a loving heavenly Father who is all-powerful.* When you couple his power with his love for you, the combination is awesome. Second, the disciples were told that the Holy Spirit would soon be coming and that he would be an ever-present guide and a personal tutor. *So cultivate the awareness of him in your life.* Third, although Jesus was leaving them physically, he would still maintain a spiritual relationship with them. *You can count on Jesus to help you become an effective disciple.* Fourth, *you need to have a close relationship with the Word of God.* The Word is a gift to you; your job is to obey it.

> **CROSS REF**
>
> Want to know about peace? See the book of Isaiah:
> 9:6–7
> 26:12
> 59:8

Your peace can rest securely on those four legs.

PART 2

Though Jesus was leaving the disciples, he was promising to maintain on ongoing relationship with them. How could that be?

● "I am the vine; you are the branches. . . . Apart from me you can do nothing."

John 15:5

In Israel almost everyone had grapevines growing in their backyard. So even though most of them were fishermen, the disciples knew exactly what Jesus was talking about. In fact the vine was the symbol of the nation. When the Israelites made their own coins, which they did for a short time, the symbol of a vine was stamped on them.

> **IN THE MIRROR**
>
> What can you do to make sure you are "plugged in"? Think about your life right now and define any changes you need to make so that you will bear more fruit.

All through the Old Testament, Israel is likened to a vine. The psalmist wrote, "You brought a vine out of Egypt; you drove out the nations and planted it. You cleared the ground for it, and it took root and filled the land" (Ps. 80:8–9). Isaiah wrote, "The vineyard of the LORD Almighty is the house of Israel" (Isa. 5:7).

So when Jesus told his disciples, "I am the true vine, and my Father is the gardener"(John 15:1), it was a shocker. By using the word *true*, he was implying that Israel had only been an imperfect foreshadowing of what he would bring.

And that wasn't all. Yes, he was the vine, but his followers were the branches. Isaiah tells of God looking for good fruit from the old vine Israel, "but it yielded only bad fruit" (Isa. 5:2). Now it was up to the disciples, this frightened bunch of Galileans, to bear good grapes in God's vineyard.

Yes, it was both good news and scary news. The good news was that they were somehow to be joined to Jesus despite the fact that he was leaving them. The scary part was the responsibility to be fruitful.

The disciples knew that vines grow fast and need constant pruning. Fast growth seemed great, but they probably didn't like the thought of the pruning. They knew that vines like to creep along the ground and need to be trained to grow on trellises or forked sticks. Training for the disciples would be important, so they couldn't get too attached to the ground. They also knew that the wood of the vine is not good for anything. Although wood was sometimes brought to the temple to stoke the altar fires, it was stipulated that vine branches could not be brought. To get rid of them, you had to build a bonfire in your backyard and burn them. The disciples didn't want to become worthless vine wood.

The relationship of the vine and the branches is the key. In John 15:4–10, one word is repeated ten times: *remain*. The King James Version uses *abide*. Probably a better modern translation would be "plugged in." Jesus says that the only way you can be an effective disciple is to stay plugged in to him; after all, he is your source of power.

PART 3

And what's the purpose of being plugged in? What's the purpose of being a branch attached to the vine? Grapes, big bunches of luscious grapes.

● "This is to my Father's glory, that you bear much fruit, showing yourselves to be my disciples."

John 15:8

Fruit is another word that keeps popping up in these verses (eight times in verses 2–16). That only makes sense. When a branch remains connected to the vine, it produces fruit. It is the inevitable result of a plugged-in life.

But what kind of fruit is this?

For one thing, it is the fruit of the Spirit that Paul talks about in Galatians 5:22–23. God's Spirit produces characteristics such as love, joy, and peace in our lives. (Yes, peace.)

Second, it is the fruit of the Vine, that is, Jesus himself. That means we continue the priorities that Jesus stressed, especially love (see verse 9). It was a love that showed compassion to the poor and the despised, to tax collectors and prostitutes, to Samaritans and Gentiles.

Third, it is a contagious kind of fruit. Paul speaks of the spread of the gospel as the fruit of his labor (Phil. 1:22). If you are truly plugged in to Jesus, you won't be able to keep it under wraps for long.

Want to bring glory to God? Of course you do. Then stay plugged in and bear some fruit.

42

FRIENDS, LOVERS, AND HATERS

We prefer warm fuzzies to cold shoulders. That's why we love Bible verses like "The Lord is my shepherd" and "In all things God works for the good of those who love him." But what about a verse like "If anyone would come after me, he must deny himself and take up his cross daily and follow me"? You don't usually see that on a kitchen wall plaque.

In John 15 Jesus balances warm fuzzies with cold shoulders. Verse 9, for instance, says, "As the Father has loved me, so have I loved you." That's a very warm fuzzy. Verse 18, on the other hand, says, "If the world hates you, keep in mind that it hated me first." That's a cold shoulder.

But why did Jesus have to give both? Why couldn't he continue in the warm fuzzy vein? Early in this Last Supper conversation with his disciples, he had comforted them with "Do not let your hearts be troubled" (14:27). We love that verse, and the disciples needed it because Jesus would soon be leaving them; they were insecure and uncertain about the future. But Jesus knew that the

232

future for his followers would not be a walk in the park, so they needed to know about the cold shoulders too.

All through this conversation, Jesus was talking about the importance of obeying his commands. It's how you stay plugged in. But what commands should we obey? He gives one as the top priority:

EVERY DAY WITH JESUS

Monday: Read part 1 of this chapter. Whom do you find hardest to love?

Tuesday: Read part 2. What does it mean to you to be Jesus' friend?

Wednesday: Read part 3. What was God's purpose in choosing us?

Thursday: Read part 4. What sort of difficulties have you had with "the world"? How do Jesus' words reassure you?

Friday: Consider the question in "In the Mirror."

Saturday: Pray for your friends, and ask God for help in being a good friend to others.

Sunday: Read Philippians 1:3–6 and praise the Lord for his work in your life.

● "My command is this: Love each other as I have loved you. Greater love has no one than this, that he lay down his life for his friends."

John 15:12–13

Well, that's not hard, you say. *I can love other Christians.* But would you lay down your life for them?

The disciples were an interesting mix. Start with a base of several fishermen, two of whom were called Sons of Thunder because of their fiery dispositions. Then mix in one hated tax collector, a pawn of the Romans, who probably levied fees on those same fishermen—and stir in Simon the Zealot, who belonged to the terrorist party seeking to overthrow the Roman government. That's a recipe for disaster.

Now Jesus is saying that if you want to stay plugged in to him, you have to love the whole bunch of them. Can you imagine the disciples saying under their breath, *I guess I can love them, but I don't have to like them*? But then Jesus talked about laying down your life for your friends. Oh boy, that's going too far.

If we are all part of one body, the body of Christ, we may need some rehab therapy. Our muscles need to be coordinated. A body part is not free to choose what other body parts it wishes to respond to, and neither is a Christian free to pick his or her spiritual friends.

● "You are my friends. . . . I no longer call you servants. . . . Instead, I have called you friends."

John 15:14–15

Suppose you had a high school teacher, Mr. Meisenheimer. Now you have graduated and you play with this guy on a summer softball team. "Call me Bob," he tells you between innings. "Drop that Mr. Meisenheimer stuff. That's for school. We're friends now."

The disciples were graduating, and now they were invited to think of Jesus in a whole new way. Earlier that evening Jesus had referred to his disciples as servants, as orphans, and as "my children." Now he calls them "my friends." What an honor—to be a friend of the Son of God!

Have you ever been able to do a favor for someone because you had a friend who had influence? Maybe someone needed a job and you had a friend who was an employment manager. Or maybe someone wanted tickets to a game and you could say, "I have a friend who plays on the team. I think he could get you in." It helps to know the right people, they say. The disciples knew the right Person. And we do too.

But friendship is not primarily for favors; it's for intimacy. The master-servant relationship was always a barrier. A servant could never get very close to his master. But friends share good times together and bad times as well. They are always talking together. Sometimes they can even get mad at each other, but they know their friendship will be strong enough to handle it.

IN THE MIRROR

Do you have a friend for whom you would lay down your life?

Friends are for sharing, and that's a point that Jesus makes. "Everything that I learned from my Father," he says, "I have made known to you" (v. 15). And he wants you to share with him. The "whatever you ask in my name" part of it is mind-boggling. But it's a two-way street. First, we listen to what he wants to share, and then we share with him.

234

PART 3

● "You did not choose me, but I chose you and appointed you to go and bear fruit—fruit that will last."

John 15:16

Sometimes we think that we are the ones who did the choosing. "Of all the religions in the world, I chose Christianity. Of all the possible Saviors in the world, I chose Jesus. Isn't Jesus lucky to have me!"

No, that's not the way it works. Usually there is a moment of decision on our part, but Christ's call comes first. "Follow me," he called to the fishermen. "Follow me," he called to Matthew. "Follow me," he called to Philip. And "Follow me," he called to you.

Looking back on your life, you can probably see how he was drawing you in his direction even before you were aware of him. He told Nathanael, *Before your friend Philip told you about me, while you were still under the fig tree, I saw you* (see John 1:48).

Yes, you were chosen. Remember how they chose up teams when you were a kid? Two captains took turns choosing their players, but the choosing wasn't an end in itself. The players were chosen for a purpose. They were chosen to play ball.

Jesus says that you were chosen to be on his team for a purpose, to go and bear fruit—to play ball for him. Jesus says, Come, and then he says, Go.

PART 4

We are both ambassadors and advertisements. We are appointees of the King, chosen to represent him in a hostile world. Wherever we go, we are a commercial for Christ.

A hostile world? Oh yes. That's the cold shoulder part. We've talked about the warm fuzzies—the fact that you are in a family of love, that you have friendship with Jesus, and that you are chosen and appointed. But there's a challenge too. And for that challenge Jesus offers us a strange reassurance.

● "If the world hates you, keep in mind that it hated me first."

John 15:18

Anyone who proclaims the same message as Jesus proclaimed should not be surprised when persecution comes. Sooner or later the opposition will rear its ugly head against you. But you're in good company. Jesus endured the same opposition and came through it victoriously. As we remain plugged in to him, his victory becomes ours. John spoke of this in his first Epistle: "Everyone born of God overcomes the world. This is the victory that has overcome the world, even our faith" (1 John 5:4).

43

GUESS WHO'S COMING TO DINNER

Vicki wanted to throw a surprise birthday party for her roommate, Rebecca. She found a place for the party and invited a dozen of Rebecca's best friends. All the arrangements were made. Vicki's biggest fear was that someone would spill the beans, but no one did. Rebecca knew absolutely nothing about it. In fact, on the day of the party, Vicki came home from work to find a note: "Hey, I decided to visit my parents for a few days. I'll be back Monday. See ya then. R."

When Rebecca returned, Vicki served her a frozen piece of cake with a candle in it, then showed her a videotape of the party they had thrown for her. *Surprise!*

Surprise is a major theme of Jesus' teaching, especially his parables. Sometimes God surprises people with his goodness, and sometimes people seem to surprise God by rejecting his goodness. And often we're surprised when we see the sort of people God invites to his parties.

- "Then he said to his servants, 'The wedding banquet is ready, but those I invited did not deserve to come. Go to the street corners and invite to the banquet anyone you find.'"

Matthew 22:8–9

237

Monday: Read part 1 of this chapter. What "street corner" were you on when Jesus invited you to his banquet?

Tuesday: Read part 2. The powerful, rich religious leaders usually reacted in anger to Jesus' teaching. What might have been their motives? Does that still happen today?

Wednesday: Read part 3. Is Jesus your cornerstone, stumbling stone, or humbling stone?

Thursday: Today try your hand at making up a parable. What role does Jesus play?

Friday: Consider the questions in "In the Mirror."

Saturday: Pray for those who have refused the invitation to God's banquet.

Sunday: Read Revelation 19:5–10 and sing hallelujah to the Lord!

Imagine that the president of the United States invites you to a state dinner. Whatever your politics, it's a great honor. You're going to find a way to attend.

Jesus envisioned the same sort of invitation, but it was a king throwing a wedding reception. Surprisingly, the A-list invitees sent their regrets. They had business to attend to or they had family responsibilities. Those might not be bad reasons for skipping your bowling night, but if you're ditching the king's party, those excuses are pretty lame.

The king was incensed. He instructed his servants to go out to the streets and invite anyone they could find. One way or another, his banquet table would be full!

It's clear that Jesus was standing up to the religious leaders. It was time to make his strongest challenge to the authorities who had opposed him every step of the way.

God had invited people to his heavenly banquet. You might say it was Jesus himself who delivered the invitations. But the leaders spurned the invitation. They had busied themselves with religious activity to the point that they couldn't take the time to kick back and party—even if the host was God himself. And so Jesus took the invitation to the "street corners," inviting anyone and everyone to the feast. That's why "sinners"—tax collectors and prostitutes and their ilk—were entering God's kingdom first (Matt. 21:31). The leaders were invited too, but apparently they had other plans.

The parable was obviously aimed at those leaders, but there are several things we can learn from it. First, *God loves a good party.* Jesus frequently depicts the kingdom of heaven as a festive gathering. Second, like those leaders, *we can sometimes get so busy doing good things that we ignore God's invitation to do better things*—like hanging out with him. Third, *God's invitation is always free of charge*. We don't have to pay to attend, but our attendance itself is a display of gratitude. And finally, *we are guests in the house of grace*. God gets to invite anyone he wants, without our say-so.

IN THE MIRROR

Do you feel the rejection in this lesson? How sad when no one comes to your party. Have you ever felt like that? If so, have you taken this to the Lord in prayer? He knows just how you feel.

PART 2

● "But when the tenants saw the son, they said to each other, 'This is the heir. Come, let's kill him and take his inheritance.' . . .

"Therefore I tell you that the kingdom of God will be taken away from you and given to a people who will produce its fruit."

Matthew 21:38, 43

Before the banquet parable, Jesus had told another story with a similar theme. A landowner rented his vineyard to tenants, who then refused to pay rent. One messenger after another was sent to collect, and the rebellious tenants beat each one. Finally, the owner sent his son, assuming that he would command the respect of the tenants, but that just incited them to greater violence. They killed the son.

On other occasions, Jesus had bemoaned Israel's treatment of the prophets, those messengers sent to get Israel to pay God the honor due him. During his last week in Jerusalem, Jesus heard the rising drumbeats of opposition. He knew that he—the Son—was headed for a violent death.

Some might see the parable of the tenants as a picture of God's dealings with the Jews. Because of their rebellion, the kingdom of God would be "taken away" and given to the repentant Gentiles. (Paul develops this theme in Romans 9–11.) But in Jesus' immediate situation, he seems to be talking about the Jewish *leaders*, the ones who had been dogging him throughout his ministry. They were supposed to tend the vineyard of Israel, but they did not produce the fruit of repentance or true obedience. As a result, their leadership was being discredited, and God was welcoming into his kingdom anyone at any level of society who showed the fruits of repentance. The poor, the needy, and eventually the Gentiles would be welcomed into God's banquet.

Are these parables of a vineyard and a banquet just allegories of God's dealings with Israel, or might they have some application to Christians today? Sometimes we forget that it is God's vineyard and not our own. In an effort to maintain our own standards, we can erect fences to keep out sinners who seek to know God. And like those invited to the banquet first, we may take for granted our relationship with God. If we spent more time with him, we might learn more about his concern for the poor in spirit, the strugglers, the sinners. Instead of fighting them, we might welcome them.

PART 3

- "Have you never read in the Scriptures: 'The stone the builders rejected has become the capstone; the Lord has done this, and it is marvelous in our eyes'? . . .

"He who falls on this stone will be broken to pieces, but he on whom it falls will be crushed."

Matthew 21:42, 44

It's quite likely that Jesus was looking at real stones when he quoted from Psalm 118 about the stone that the builders rejected. The temple complex was in the midst of a lengthy rebuilding project, and masons would have been moving about, dressing and finishing certain stones for placement. Limestone blocks would have been shipped in from various quarries throughout the area but builders on site would decide which stones to put where. Limestone cleaves rather easily, which made it nice to work with but also made it crucial to watch for flaws. You wouldn't want a stress-bearing block to split in two.

As he often did, Jesus used his real-life surroundings to make a point, and the biblical quotation he chose actually summed up his whole ministry. The psalmist was speaking of a surprising situation in which a stone that the builders saw

> **CHECKOUT COUNTER**
>
> Check out Psalm 118:22. Early Christians applied this passage to Jesus, as in Acts 4:11 and 1 Peter 2:7.

as flawed ended up as the most prominent stone in the structure.

Jesus himself is that stone. He wasn't the kind of Messiah the leaders were looking for. Maybe some had high hopes early on, but he spent a lot of time with sinners, and he never showed enough respect for the leadership. Though the "builders" of Israel rejected him, there was a surprise coming. In fact the surprise is that their rejection created the situation that made him the cornerstone—that is, his crucifixion. As tragic as that event was, it turned out to have a truly marvelous effect.

The New Testament writers played around with this image of Christ as "stone." He's the "living Stone" for Peter, who sees a living Temple being built up around him (1 Peter 2:4–8). Other passages repeat the picture of Jesus as the cornerstone on which the rest of the church is built (Eph. 2:20). But Jesus is also shown as a "stumbling block" (1 Cor. 1:23; Isa. 8:13–15). Many would continue to trip over the idea of grace. We might call him a "humbling stone," because after you trip, you must take a lower view of yourself. And that's exactly where God wants us: sprawled out, or on our knees, needing him to help us up. Tripping over this stone might break you to pieces, as Jesus says, but he routinely mends broken souls. In Jesus' word picture, the tragedy occurs when someone refuses to be humbled and instead gets "crushed."

This is the Lord's doing, Jesus says. God has placed a stone in Zion, that is, the very crucifixion of the rejected Messiah. If you don't like the idea of a "criminal" Savior, a "friend of sinners" who suffers capital punishment, you might trip over this stumbling stone, but then you have the opportunity to build your life on it.

QUOTE TO NOTE

How easy it is to read Jesus' rebuke of others and fail to see that he may be looking into our eyes when he says it.

F. Lagard Smith

241

44

SOMEONE'S COMING

Sometimes you feel sorry for Bible translators. No matter how many years they have studied Greek and Hebrew, some words defy translation. Take the Greek word *parakletos*, for example. You can tell that translators had problems with it because almost every Bible version translates it differently. It's the word that Jesus used in John 14–16, referring to the Holy Spirit. Everyone agrees that literally it means "one who is called in or beside." But that's a long and awkward phrase to use every time the word *parakletos* appears.

The King James Version translates it "Comforter," the New International Version has "Counselor," Moffat's version says "Helper," Phillips says "one who is coming to stand by you," the New English Bible likes "Advocate," and *The Message* uses "Friend."

You get the idea. Some Bible scholars just give up and use the word *Paraclete*.

In Greek courts, an accused person might call in a *parakletos* to stand alongside him and speak on his behalf. This person was his advocate or defense attorney. So a paraclete was a helper in court.

To prepare for the ancient Olympics, personal trainers were called in to work with the athletes and get them in shape for competition. They were also called paracletes. And believe it or not, there were some people in ancient times who needed counseling. If a person was in over his head and didn't know which way to turn, he would call in a paraclete for some guidance.

And there is at least one other usage from the ancient world. When soldiers were going off to war, there were paracletes (cheerleaders?) encouraging them to Fight, Team, Fight! In Greek literature the verb form of this word sometimes means "to encourage someone to think or remember." A *parakletos* then could also be an encourager or a reminder.

Jesus refers to the Holy Spirit as the *parakletos* several times in these three chapters. What did he mean by that? Defense attorney or personal trainer? Guidance counselor or cheerleader? Or all of the above?

● "And I will ask the Father, and he will give you another Counselor to be with you forever—the Spirit of truth. . . . You know him, for he lives with you and will be in you."

John 14:16–17

These verses are so packed with meaning that it is easy to skip over some of the goodies they contain. Did you catch the word *another*, implying that Jesus was the first Paraclete for the disciples? Now Jesus was introducing the disciples to his replacement.

243

The Holy Spirit is called the Spirit of Truth. Why is this important? First, because Jesus has just identified himself as "the Truth" (v. 6), so now the Spirit is identified with Jesus in the dissemination of truth. In addition, the disciples needed the assurance that they would continue to know Truth with a capital T. They were not scholars of systematic theology, but they would soon be going to the ends of the earth as witnesses of Jesus Christ, running up against all kinds of false philosophies and religions. They would be miserable failures if they didn't possess the Truth.

PART 2

The Holy Spirit would be with the disciples "forever." Jesus had spent about three years with them, and even then he couldn't be with them continuously. But the Holy Spirit would never leave them.

In the Old Testament the Holy Spirit operated on an ad hoc basis. That is, he came on individuals for a particular time to help them do great things. For instance, we are told that the Spirit of the Lord came on Samson in power, but that was temporary. Now, the Spirit dwells within Christians permanently. That makes a big difference.

● "The Counselor, the Holy Spirit . . . will teach you all things and will remind you of everything I have said to you."

John 14:26

How did Matthew remember the Sermon on the Mount? How did John remember these Last Supper teachings of Christ in John 14–16? It wasn't because of their remarkable intellects. Jesus doesn't give IQ tests before he calls us. No, it was the Holy Spirit who recalled to their minds what needed to be put into the Scriptures.

And the Holy Spirit provides more than a divine memo pad. He also carries a divine flashlight. We often read passages in Scripture and say, "Huh? What's that mean?" That's when the Holy Spirit shines his flashlight in our

> **CROSS REF**
> More on the Spirit within:
> Galatians 4:6
> 1 John 3:24

hearts and helps us understand. Paul wrote to the Corinthians how "God has revealed [the secret things] to us by his Spirit. The Spirit searches all things, even the deep things of God" (1 Cor. 2:10).

● "When the Counselor comes . . . he will testify about me. And you also must testify."

John 15:26–27

The Paraclete does not talk about himself; he talks about Jesus Christ. Whether you like the image of a courtroom advocate, a personal trainer, a guidance counselor, or a cheerleader, notice something they all have in common. They all focus on someone else. That's true of the Holy Spirit as well. The focus of the Spirit's attention is on Jesus Christ and on you.

What assurance do you need? What deeds can you do? What do you need to be reminded of? In what direction do you need to go? It's the Holy Spirit's job to make things happen within you, around you, and through you.

"And you also must testify," says Jesus. It is your testimony that the Holy Spirit uses. Just because the Holy Spirit is helping, that doesn't mean you are off the hook. You are the one on the witness stand. The Holy Spirit will empower you, but you are the one who must testify. And remember that in court the only valid testimony is a first-person experience.

PART 3

● "But when he, the Spirit of truth, comes, he will guide you into all truth. . . . And he will tell you what is yet to come."

John 16:13

Jesus didn't tell the disciples everything. He left some things for the Holy Spirit to tell them. The apostle Paul shares some of these things in Romans 8, when he writes about how, by the Spirit, "we cry, '*Abba*, Father'" and how "the Spirit himself testifies with our spirit that we are God's children" (vv. 15–16).

Obviously the Paraclete can talk tough as a prosecutor, while still whispering tender assurances to God's family. You can see why, after Jesus ascended into heaven, the disciples could hardly wait for their Counselor to arrive.

QUOTE TO NOTE

When we rely on organization, we get what organization can do. When we rely upon education, we get what education can do. When we rely upon eloquence, we get what eloquence can do. When we rely on the Holy Spirit, we get what God can do.

A. C. Dixon

45
THE UNLIKELY GLORY

Imagine you parachuted into Papua New Guinea to bring the gospel to a recently discovered head-hunting tribe. Your only contact with mission headquarters would be by means of a small radio transmitter attached to your Bible.

You preach and teach for a couple years. A dozen tribesmen are converted, and now it is time for you to be airlifted out of the jungle. You are concerned about these dozen tribesmen, because their fellow tribesmen have become increasingly hostile. You talk frankly with them about the future.

Well, maybe you have guessed by now that this imaginary story is supposed to parallel the situation of Jesus with his disciples in the upper room (and you also see a number of flaws in the analogy). But you can imagine how frightened those primitive Papuan disciples would be, realizing that their teacher would soon be leaving them.

Then you can also imagine how disturbed the first-century disciples must have been in that upper room. That's why Jesus took so much time with them.

● "I have told you these things, so that in me you may have peace. In this world you will have trouble. But take heart!

Monday: Read part 1 of this chapter. What "trouble" have you been having?

Tuesday: Read part 2. How did the cross bring glory to God?

Wednesday: Read part 3. What four things did Jesus ask for? Are those prayers still being answered among us today?

Thursday: Read part 4. How are we sanctified?

Friday: What is "the world" into which you are sent? How can you fulfill God's purpose in this world?

Saturday: Pray for God's protection against the power of Satan. Make this personal; name the sin that troubles you.

Sunday: Read Psalm 24:7–10 and praise God, the King of Glory.

I have overcome the world."

John 16:33

Jesus' words sound nice; we repeat them to one another and to ourselves when the going gets rough. But that last line, "I have overcome the world." Wasn't Jesus stretching things a bit?

Here he was in the upper room with twelve (make that eleven) cowering followers. The next day he would be crucified and buried in a borrowed tomb. His handpicked disciples would soon be running away. How can he say that he had overcome the world?

Isn't he an unlikely overcomer? Early in the Gospel of John, Jesus is introduced as the Lamb of God. Lambs are not known as the most ferocious of creatures. Yet in the last book of Scripture when the Beast makes war against the Lamb, who wins? "The Lamb will overcome them because he is Lord of lords and King of kings—and with him will be his called, chosen and faithful followers" (Rev. 17:14).

But that's in the future. What about today and tomorrow? In our daily battles, does the Lamb of God always come out ahead?

John writes in his first Epistle, "This is the victory that has overcome the world, even our faith" (1 John 5:4). Faith looks to the future. Faith connects the present conflict to the future outcome. Faith gets us through a horrendous Friday, because we know that Sunday's coming. There will be trouble today—Jesus assured us of that—but he has a firm grip on the future.

Jesus was addressing eleven men who would all suffer greatly for their faith. Ten of them would die for Jesus. Like the Lamb of God they loved, these martyrs gave their lives for the future kingdom of God. Yes, in this world they faced trouble, big trouble. But Jesus had already won the ultimate victory, and they knew it.

> **CHECKOUT COUNTER**
>
> Check out Philippians 4:7, an assurance that goes very nicely with John 16:33.

PART 2

After Jesus shared his parting words with his disciples, it was time to give his final report to mission headquarters. Certainly he had been in constant contact with the Father throughout his ministry, but this was a more formal and more public prayer, the longest recorded prayer of his ministry. The Lord's Prayer is certainly better known, but that was a model he gave his disciples. This prayer in John 17 is a personal prayer of Jesus the High Priest. This is truly the Lord's prayer.

In the first part (verses 1–5), Jesus focuses on himself and his relationship with the Father. In the next part (verses 6–19), he prays for this frightened handful of disciples who would be commissioned to overcome the world in his name. In the last part (verses 20–26), amazingly, he prays for *us*. Really! "I pray also for those who will believe in me through their [the disciples'] message," he says, "that all of them may be one."

A key theme at the start of this prayer is *glory*.

● "And now, Father, glorify me in your presence with the glory I had with you before the world began."

John 17:5

It was zero hour. As Jesus put it, "Father, the time has come." You might remember that at the beginning of his ministry, he had told his mother, "My time has not yet come" (2:4). But now his time had come.

Jesus' mission was nearly completed. Only a few days before, when some Greeks came to see him, Jesus announced, "The hour has come for the Son of Man to be glorified." Then he spoke about his death and said, "For this very reason I came to this hour. Father, glorify your name!" Stunningly, a voice from heaven thundered, "I have glorified it, and will glorify it again" (12:20–28).

You might think that the death on the cross would be the last act in this sacrificial drama. But it wasn't. In Philippians 2, Paul wrote about Jesus leaving the glories of heaven, descending to earth, and dying. That was the divine plan. Then Paul tells how the Father would exalt Jesus "to the highest place," back to the glories of heaven again (v. 9).

In the upper room on crucifixion eve, Jesus knew that the only way to bring glory to the Father was through the cross. And so he prayed that the Father would receive glory in this last lap of his earthly journey. There could be no detour around the cross. Indeed the cross was the purpose of it all. So there was heavenly glory at the start, the glory of the cross in the middle, and then the return to heavenly glory after his ascension. The circuit would be completed.

PART 3

● "My prayer is not that you take them out of the world but that you protect them from the evil one."

John 17:15

Jesus knew what his disciples would be up against, but he didn't pray that they would have the power to become invisible in dangerous times or to be equipped with ray guns to zap their opponents. No, he prayed for four things for his followers: (1) that they would be "one as we are one," (2) that they might have "the full measure of my joy," (3) that they would be protected from the evil one, and (4) that they might be "truly sanctified."

Oneness among the disciples? Not likely. They had been squabbling continually. *Joyfulness?* Do you expect people on the government's most-wanted list to be happy? *Protection from the evil one?* With Jesus leaving them, they were Satan's prime targets. *Holiness?* You've got to be kidding. These are rough and tough Galilean fishermen, not priests and Pharisees.

Jesus knew how huge his request was. He also knew that his Father's power was greater.

PART 4

● "Sanctify them by the truth; your word is truth. As you sent me into the world, I have sent them into the world."

John 17:17–18

The Greek word translated "sanctify" has three different meanings: to make holy, to set apart for sacred service, and to equip for service. The second meaning is what happens as missionaries are commissioned to go out, and the third may be what happens in a church officers' training retreat, but the first is done only through the atoning death of Christ on the cross, the work of the Spirit of Truth, and the ongoing cleansing work of the Word.

In the Old Testament a priest would ceremonially cleanse himself before offering a sacrifice for the sins of the people. In verse 19 Jesus says, "I sanctify myself, that they too may be truly sanctified." So Jesus is praying that all three meanings of the word *sanctify* might be fulfilled in the disciples' lives.

But Jesus was not praying just for his disciples; he was also praying for us, all who would come to faith through the disciples' message—"that all of them may be one." He wanted unity, but what kind of unity? He compared it to the unity that he and the Father shared. It is not assimilation, losing all individuality as we are swallowed up in a monolithic organization. No. The unity Christ prays for is a unity of relationship, a unity that love glues together, a common mission ("to let the world know"), and humility.

Love, mission, and humility. Those three qualities certainly characterized Jesus Christ. They should be the hallmark of any church body and the glory of every Christian.

QUOTE TO NOTE

The Gulf Stream maintains its warm temperatures even in the icy water of the North Atlantic. If Christians are to fulfill their purposes in the world, they must not be chilled by the indifferent, godless society in which they live.

Billy Graham

46
ARE WE THERE YET?

The family piles into the minivan for a journey to another state. The parents are a bit worried about the long ride with the kids, but they've brought oodles of games and activities. Of course, about ten minutes into this voyage, one of the children chirps, "Are we there yet?"

Chances are, you've been in that situation, as a parent or as a child. Why is it such a common occurrence? Because we all want to reach our ultimate destination, and because children have little sense of time or space.

Think about it. In their minds, what needs to happen?

A. Family gets into car.
B. They all ride in the car.
C. Car gets there.

Step B could take ten minutes or ten hours; they don't know. They only know that when B is happening, the next thing is C.

It's the same way with Jesus' return. In Matthew 24 he spoke about a future time when he would come back to earth. At his ascension, angels promised that he would return in the

252

same way he left (Acts 1:11). The early church preached about his second coming, and the apostles wrote about it. We have a number of clues about when and how Jesus will return, but there are still many different interpretations.

We long to reach our ultimate destination. Along with the rest of the created order, we wait, groaning, for our final redemption. We want our King to come back and sort out this mess on planet Earth. That's the next thing that needs to happen.

So are we there yet?

EVERY DAY WITH JESUS

Monday: Read part 1. Notice that even though we are not to be deceived by false messiahs, we still must keep watch for the true one.

Tuesday: Read part 2. How is Bible prophecy like a mountain range?

Wednesday: Read part 3. How can you invest your treasure in heaven? We are told to be a cheerful giver. This could be fun!

Thursday: Read part 4. Consider the questions in "In the Mirror."

Friday: What are your talents? How will you invest them?

Saturday: Ask God to show you what you can do for him.

Sunday: Praise God along with David as you read 1 Chronicles 17:20–27.

PART 2

● "Watch out that no one deceives you. . . . No one knows about that day or hour, not even the angels in heaven, nor the Son, but only the Father. . . . Therefore keep watch, because you do not know on what day your Lord will come."

Matthew 24:4, 36, 42

Matthew 24 is a tantalizing collection of prophecies that Jesus made about events in the near future of Israel and in the distant future. The discussion started as Jesus and his disciples left the temple complex and crossed the valley to the Mount of Olives. The temple was still in the midst of a building project, and the huge and beautiful stones being assembled must have impressed the disciples. Jesus predicted that those very stones would be "thrown down." The disciples asked when this would happen, and Jesus began his dissertation on future events.

253

GREEK PEEK

There are three Greek words used for the coming again of Jesus:

parousia: the personal presence. He will come in person.
epiphania (related to epiphany): appearing, like a star, not seen in the day but
  suddenly appearing in the darkness.
apokalupsis: unveiling of one who has been hidden.

There would be "wars and rumors of wars," he said, and natural disasters as well. The faithful would be persecuted, and there would be many false teachers. Through it all, the gospel would go forth, and ultimately the Son of Man would appear in glory. Many of these prophecies came true about forty years after Jesus spoke them, when the Roman army quashed a Jewish revolt. That's when the temple was destroyed. But some of these predictions apparently await a future fulfillment.

Biblical prophecy has been described as a mountain range. You might see a series of peaks that look as if they're very close together, when in fact they're miles apart. Old Testament prophets sometimes made predictions about their current situations that came true then, but later came true in a fuller way in Jesus' ministry—and they might even have pieces that remain to be fulfilled. That's the sort of prediction Jesus was making here.

You may be familiar with various interpretations of what must happen. People do their best to figure out every detail of these hazy prophecies, and they may dazzle you with their theories. But don't be deceived.

Some have tried to pin down the date of Christ's return. This too is futile. Jesus indicated that even he didn't know when the Father would send him back here. Such speculation is just distracting. We have work to do.

Among all the predictions, Jesus told a mini-parable about a servant who was given responsibility to care for the other servants while the master was away. "It will be good for that servant whose master finds him doing so when he returns," Jesus concluded (v. 46). The same is true for us. Let's knock off all the chatter about *when* Jesus will return and get busy doing what he wants us to do *until* he returns.

PART 3

● "Then the man who had received the one talent came. 'Master,' he said, 'I knew that you are a hard man. . . . So I . . . went out and hid your talent in the ground. See, here is what belongs to you.'"

Matthew 25:24–25

So what should we be doing until Jesus returns? *Investing*.

That's the main conclusion we draw from the parable of the talents, which Jesus told during this talk on the Mount of Olives. Three servants received different sums before the master went off on a journey. Two invested their money and doubled their holdings. The third, afraid of losing it, buried the money in the ground.

On his return, the master praised the two moneymakers but scolded the fearful servant. "You should have put my money on deposit with the bankers, so that when I returned I would have received it back with interest" (v. 27).

Note that this parable-teller is the same teacher who blessed the poor and warned against worshiping money. What gives?

Obviously Jesus isn't just talking about money here. There's a larger *principle* involved, so to speak. But let's consider what he has already said about money. He urged his followers to invest their "treasure" in heaven rather than in earthly possessions, and he indicated that one way to do that was to give to the poor. He challenged a rich man to do just that, to liquidate his assets and use them to help the needy. And he told an odd story about a shrewd accountant who got fired from his job but used his lame-duck status to do favors for folks who might give him his next job. The message there: Use worldly wealth for heavenly purposes.

We can see the same idea underlying this parable. We are servants entrusted with some of our heavenly Master's resources. There's no need to play it safe. We should invest wisely but lavishly in the causes that are close to our Master's heart.

Of course, we need to consider *all* our investments—not just money. In Jesus' day, a "talent" was a sum of money. Now it means something quite different. (In fact the word gained its

255

modern meaning *because* of this parable.) For centuries Christians have understood that this story referred to all of the resources God has entrusted to us, especially our gifts and abilities—or "talents." So whatever talent he has given you, don't bury it in the ground. Use it!

PART 4

● "The King will reply, 'I tell you the truth, whatever you did for one of the least of these brothers of mine, you did for me.'"

Matthew 25:40

In one of Shakespeare's comedies, *Measure for Measure*, the king goes off on a voyage, leaving the realm in the charge of his deputy. Sounds like a parable, doesn't it? But in this case, suspecting that the deputy might be disloyal, the king returns to the land in disguise, as a beggar. That way he can find out what his deputy is really doing.

Mistaken identity is a common theatrical device, especially for Shakespeare, but here it made a lot of sense. If the king revealed himself as the king, he would certainly get the royal treatment. But as a beggar, he learns the truth.

In the final parable of his Sermon on the Mount of Olives, Jesus jumped to the end of that drama, when all identities are revealed and everything is set right. The King has returned in glory and assumed his throne, and now he is judging his kingdom. (Jesus depicted the judgment in shepherding terms. The King divides sheep from goats.) And what criteria does he use? "I was hungry and you gave me something to eat, I was thirsty and you gave me something to drink" (v. 35). He says he needed a home, clothing, and health care, and the faithful ones had provided these for him. Even in prison, he received their aid.

Then the King turns to the "goats" and announces their eternal punishment. Why so harsh? Because he had been hungry and thirsty, he had needed all these things, and they refused to help him.

Everyone is confused about this, sheep and goats alike. What was he talking about? They had never seen their King in such need. Then the King explains it all: "Whatever you did for one of the least of these brothers of mine, you did for me" (v. 40).

IN THE MIRROR

If Christ should come today, what would he find us doing? Would he be pleased with our treatment of "the least of these"?

It's very clear that the "King" in the story is Jesus himself. This is the returning Savior, coming in glory, setting things right, punishing the wicked, and rewarding his own faithful flock. And as he reveals his true identity, we realize that he's been near us all along—the panhandler on the corner, the latchkey kid next door, the single mom at church, the guy down the block whose car was just repossessed. They are his brothers and sisters, and we'd better treat them with the honor we owe to Jesus.

No need to get all mystical and say, "Everyone is Jesus," but they might as well be. Jesus cares how we treat all the needy folks who cross our path. We serve him by serving them.

47

IN THE GARDEN

● "My Father, if it is possible, may this cup be taken from me. Yet not as I will, but as you will."

Matthew 26:39

There are few spiritual subjects as misunderstood as the power of prayer. People still have the idea that we can make prayer "work" if we pray the right way or if we pray hard enough. The underlying issue seems to be: How can I get God to do what I want? As we see here in Gethsemane, that is exactly the opposite of the true essence of prayer—not my will but yours be done.

Prayer is a conversation—a meeting of the minds, you might say, but even more than that, a meeting of the wills. We can and should voice our desires—that's exactly what Jesus did in the garden—but we shouldn't stay at that point. God cares about our needs and wants, and he often provides what we ask. He knows our needs better than we do, and—as with Jesus—he often has bigger plans afoot. We can say what we want, but we should also listen to what God wants.

In any case, prayer has no magic formula. Its power comes from God alone. Yes, Scripture indicates that faith leads to answered prayer, but what is faith? It's an openness to the power of God. It's still God's power, not ours.

In the garden Jesus knew that the cup of suffering was at his lips, ready to be tasted. Within the next hours he would be arrested and beaten, crucified and buried. Any of us would quail at the physical pain involved, but Jesus faced something more—the spiritual weight of the world's sin and the resulting separation from his beloved Father. It's understandable that Jesus would ask for a way out, if there were one. Then he prayed as he had taught his disciples to pray, "Your will be done on earth as it is in heaven" (6:10).

Monday: Read part 1 of this chapter. How do you pray? Do you have some magic formula?

Tuesday: Read part 2. Consider this: We know God understands our weak flesh because Jesus lived in the flesh and was tempted as we are.

Wednesday: Read part 3. Does Matthew 26:52 mean we should never go to war?

Thursday: Consider the question in "In the Mirror."

Friday: When you pray, do you try to manipulate God into doing your will, or do you seek to know his will?

Saturday: Pray today that God would give you strength against temptation.

Sunday: Praise God as you read Psalm 141:1–4. He truly hears our prayers.

PART 2

● "Watch and pray so that you will not fall into temptation. The spirit is willing, but the body is weak."

Matthew 26:41

Jesus was sweating blood as he poured out his heart to his Father. In the next grove over, his disciples were dozing. Rousing them, he urged them to keep watch as a guard might patrol the perimeter of Jerusalem from atop the city wall. In fact they might have seen some guards as they looked across the Kidron Valley at the walled city of Jerusalem.

Of course Jesus was talking about the spiritual attack of temptation, something he had already been dealing with as he prayed. In the gospel-based musical *Godspell*, the temptation of Matthew 4 is placed at this moment, in the garden. That makes sense, since the tempter was obviously flinging darts at Jesus that were every bit as fiery as those that were flung three years earlier in the desert. Jesus knew temptation at the beginning and end of his ministry, and he knew it was a constant threat for his disciples as well.

IN THE MIRROR

When are you most
vulnerable to temptation?

What was his prescription? "Watch and pray." Let's think about that. The guard on the city wall can do little by himself to thwart a well-planned attack on the city, but he can sound the alarm. He can mobilize the city's army to beat back the foe. In the same way, we have little power to defeat the tempter on our own, but we can be careful to avoid temptation, to recognize it when it attacks, and to mobilize the power of prayer to combat it. It is always God's power that defeats the enemy, but sometimes we need to call his power into action.

In the garden, this oft-quoted maxim—"The spirit is willing, but the flesh is weak"—seemed to be a gentle nudging. Those sleepy disciples wanted to pray, but they couldn't keep their eyes open, poor guys. But the statement might convey a much deeper truth. The apostle Paul developed the same idea in Romans 7, where he complained, "I have the desire to do what is good, but I cannot carry it out" (v. 18). In the next chapter he continued to explain the struggle between spirit and "flesh." Paul wasn't disparaging everything physical. No. The body can do good or evil. We can put our bodies under the control of God's Spirit, or we can let them follow their own physical desires.

Prayer is like the satellite navigation system on new cars. You can turn it off or ignore it, but then you're likely to get lost. When you pray, you turn to God for guidance. You put his Spirit in charge of your weak flesh. You learn to put aside your own desires in favor of what he wants.

PART 3

● "Put your sword back in its place . . . for all who draw the sword will die by the sword."

Matthew 26:52

A band of soldiers interrupted Jesus' prayer—and the disciples' nap. Judas the betrayer greeted Jesus with a kiss. In the torchlight, Jesus and his disciples might have looked similar, so this was the way Judas pointed out the one the soldiers should arrest. As they dragged Jesus away, Peter grabbed a sword and swung it, cutting off the ear of a servant who accompanied the soldiers. Jesus immediately scolded Peter and healed the servant's ear.

"Those who live by the sword shall die by the sword." Simply put: You get what you ask for. You choose how you will live, and those choices have lasting repercussions. This is not the same as saying you get what you deserve. We certainly don't deserve God's grace, but if we ask for it, we receive it.

JUST WONDERING . . .

How do you think Peter felt in the Garden of Gethsemane? He was probably confused as to what was going on. Jesus had reprimanded him and the others for not staying awake to watch and pray, and now he was told not to fight back. How would you have reacted?

Those who try to solve problems by drawing a sword—fighting over them—will eventually become the problem that someone else solves with a sword. Fighting breeds fighting. There's no happy end to it. And it's especially inappropriate for Jesus' disciples to try to fix things through fighting. As Jesus said after undoing the damage of Peter's sword, he could have launched an armed rebellion if he wished, but that was not the path he chose. He would conquer the world by drinking the cup of suffering.

You might say that this is what happens when you *don't* "watch and pray." The drowsy disciples weren't ready for the crisis, and so they resorted to their animal instincts, the weak way of the flesh. Fight or flight—aren't those what the anthropologists call our natural responses to danger? One drew a sword; the others fled. Peter was tempted to try to fix things in his own way, with a sword—a way that would bring only greater disaster. Had they been praying instead of sleeping, they might have been tuned in to the will of God.

QUOTE TO NOTE

We live in a worried and frightened age, and many of these things are due to no other cause than that men have lost contact with the eternal strength.

William Barclay

48

PETER, TOM, AND MARY

No, Peter, Tom, and Mary are not a trio of folk singers. We're talking about Simon Peter, "Doubting Thomas," and Mary Magdalene, three of the more than five hundred people who saw Jesus at various times after his resurrection.

The surprising thing is that none of them expected to see Jesus. Maybe it really isn't surprising after all. They had seen dead people before, and Jesus was dead. The Roman soldiers had crucified many people, and this crucifixion victim was dead. No doubt about it. The temple guard, in the employ of the High Priest, didn't want to make any mistakes about this Galilean. He was dead, beyond the shadow of a doubt.

And then there was the burial. Joseph of Arimathea and Nicodemus saw that the lifeless body had a decent burial place, and they rolled a huge boulder in front of it just to make sure that no one would desecrate it. The Jewish authorities didn't want anyone to get into that tomb either (or out of it, for that matter), and so the tomb was sealed and they got Pilate's okay to post a guard around it.

So maybe it wasn't surprising at all that none of them expected to see Jesus again.

But then, bright and early on Easter morning, 30 AD, Jesus showed up, not far from the tomb, which was now shockingly wide open.

Maybe you would guess that Jesus' first words would be something like: *I'm back. I've conquered death and hell. You don't need to be afraid of those things anymore.* But his first words were not about himself; instead, they were words of comfort to a weeping woman.

Monday: Read part 1 of this chapter. Would you say you are on a first-name basis with Jesus? As you read his words, is he talking directly to you?

Tuesday: Read part 2. Do you think Thomas was wrong in asking for proof? Jesus seems to be very patient with him.

Wednesday: Read part 3. Consider the question in "In the Mirror."

Thursday: What is your love for Jesus like? Is it a warm affection or a commitment of your entire being?

Friday: The kind of love Jesus wants from Peter carries responsibility with it. He is told to shepherd the flock. How can we do this?

Saturday: There's a Christian song from a generation ago that prays, "You know I love you; help me love you more." Let that be your prayer today.

Sunday: Praise God as you read about love in 1 John 4:7–12.

● "Woman, . . . why are you crying? Who is it you are looking for?"

John 20:15

She had just been saying, "They have taken my Lord away, . . . and I don't know where they have put him" (v. 13). Then she saw this man, whom she thought was a gardener, and this "gardener" asked why she was crying. She still didn't recognize him. Then he spoke her name, "Mary," and that made all the difference.

Common questions: Why are you crying? Who are you looking for? What's the problem? Often we are like Mary, looking for answers in the wrong direction. We fill our time with hollow living to mask our sorrows and our searching. We keep looking at the tomb, through the grave clothes of our lives, and don't turn around to see Jesus. When we turn, our tears of frustration and failure often prevent us from seeing him.

To hear your name called amid the din and drone of human voices—that's a wonderful thing. That will open your eyes as nothing else will. So Jesus keeps calling, softly and tenderly. He's calling your name. Can you hear him?

At this point, it's not necessary to ask Mary if she understands the doctrine of the resurrection. All she needs is a personal relationship with her living Lord.

Christ's last words to Mary in this encounter are: "I am returning to my Father and your Father, to my God and your God." He could have simply said, "I am returning to my Father and my God" (v. 17). But Jesus was assuring her that God was her Father too. When you are related to Jesus, you are related to the Father as well.

PART 2

Mary passed the joyful word along to the disciples in the upper room, where they were still huddled. In fear of the authorities, they had locked themselves in. However, Jesus didn't pay any attention to the "Do Not Disturb" signs. He walked right through the locked doors. Jesus can still show up when he is least expected, sometimes even when he is not wanted.

Thomas wasn't present that Sunday. When the others told him they had seen the Lord, he doubted, earning him his legendary moniker.

A week later, Doubting Thomas was with the other disciples. Once again the doors were locked, and once again the divine Intruder entered with the customary greeting, *Shalom*, peace. Then Jesus invited Thomas to put his finger into the wounds in his hands and place his hand on his side.

Thomas was a doubter no longer. He burst out, "My Lord and my God!" After being a doubter for a week, Thomas gave one of the strongest affirmations of faith that you will find in the New Testament. He affirmed Jesus as God, and Jesus accepted the title.

CHECKOUT COUNTER

Check out Matthew 28:9, 17; and John 20:28 to see how people responded to the risen Christ.

Perhaps we should be thankful that Thomas asked questions. If he hadn't asked for proof, maybe a few more of us would be doubters today.

● **"Because you have seen me, you have believed; blessed are those who have not seen and yet have believed."**

John 20:29

It's the last Beatitude of the Gospels. Here is Jesus, looking down through history and seeing all those who in the centuries to follow would come to believe in him. Millions, even billions, would become believers because of the message of those eleven disciples, hiding in the locked upper room. None of these multitudes had seen the risen Lord with the wounds in his hands and side. But Jesus blesses those who believe, sight unseen.

Accept that blessing. It means he hasn't forgotten you. That should at least bring a smile to your face, if not an outright "Hallelujah!" Jesus himself has blessed you!

PART 3

Next, Jesus told his disciples to get out of that locked room and go up to Galilee. He would meet them there. The disciples didn't argue.

In Galilee, they did what they knew best. They went fishing. Some have criticized these disciples for fishing at this important time, but they had to eat.

The problem was that after a night of fishing, they had caught no fish. Then Jesus appeared on shore and told them to cast their net on the right side of the boat. In the early morning haze, they didn't recognize him, but they did what the voice on shore told them to do. As soon as they did, the net was so full that they couldn't lift it into the boat (John 21:5–6).

"It is the Lord!" shouted John. Wasting no time, Peter jumped into the water and got to shore as quickly as he could.

"Come and have breakfast," Jesus said to all the disciples when they arrived, and then they gathered around the fire he had built and ate fish together. (It was another demonstration of the kind of body that the resurrected Jesus had—and for that matter, that we will have—physical enough to eat fish, spiritual enough to walk through walls.)

After breakfast, Jesus wanted some one-on-one time with Peter. He was the third on the list of reclamation projects: Mary, Thomas, and now Peter.

In talking with Peter, Jesus kept asking the same question over and over again:

● **"Simon son of John, do you truly love me?"**

John 21:16

When Peter answered, "Yes, Lord, you know that I love you," Jesus would say, "Feed my sheep," or words to that effect.

What was Jesus doing? Was it necessary for him to repeat the same question three times?

First of all, Peter had denied Christ three times, so a threefold affirmation made sense. But second, the question wasn't exactly the same each time. The first time Jesus asked the question, he asked, "Do you truly love me more than these?" But did he mean "more than these other disciples love me" or "more than you love these fishing boats"? It could be either one. A few weeks before, Peter had told Jesus that even though other disciples might deny Jesus, he would never do such a thing. (It's always dangerous to compare your level of discipleship with others.)

Of course, Jesus could have been referring to the fishing boats. After all, that's where Jesus knew he would find Peter. It's hard to break away from something we enjoy, something we are good at.

In addition, the word translated "truly love," which Christ used in his first two questions, is the verb form of the Greek word *agape*, which is a commitment of the entire being. Peter responded with the common word for love, *philia*, which conveys warmth and affection. There's nothing wrong with *philia*; it just doesn't have the power of *agape*.

The third time that Jesus asked the question, he used Peter's word.

Our love for Christ is never all that it ought to be either. He calls us to an *agape* love when all we can give him right now is a *philia* love. Yet he accepts as much as we can offer. Weeks earlier, in the upper room, Peter was full of himself, claiming that he, more than any of the disciples, would forsake all to take a stand with Jesus. Now he was humbled, broken, and painfully honest. He truly appreciated Jesus, but that's all he could truthfully say.

IN THE MIRROR

If Jesus asked you, "Do you love me more than these other things in your life?" how would you answer? Think about your love for the Lord.

Despite the limitations of Peter's response, Jesus reinstated him with the challenge "Feed my sheep." Peter was reclaimed.

Despite Mary Magdalene's dark, demon-possessed past, Jesus had reclaimed her and honored her by appearing to her first after his resurrection. Despite Thomas's doubt, Jesus reclaimed him and displayed proofs of his resurrected body. Despite Peter's threefold denial when the going got tough, Jesus reclaimed him and recommissioned him for fruitful service.

So don't give up on Jesus' ability to reclaim. He's pretty good at it.

43

GOING PAST GO

In the game of Monopoly, when you get to the "Go" corner, you usually breathe a sigh of relief—not only because you collect two hundred dollars but also because you have successfully passed the high-rent properties of Boardwalk and Park Place.

For the apostles, the word *go* came up quite often after the resurrection of Jesus, and it was not always accompanied by a sigh of relief.

Shortly after the resurrection, the angels at the tomb told Mary Magdalene and Mary, the wife of Clopas, that Jesus had risen and that he would be going ahead of them into Galilee. Later Jesus appeared to them and repeated the message. They passed the word along to the eleven disciples.

No doubt many of the disciples breathed a sigh of relief to get away from Jerusalem, which was not a pleasant place for followers of Jesus to be on that Passover weekend.

Apparently Jesus directed them to a specific mountain in Galilee. It might have been the mountain where he gave the Sermon on the Mount; we don't know. As the disciples went north into Galilee, they passed the word to other disciples, and probably also to Jesus' brothers. The apostle Paul speaks of Jesus

268

appearing to "more than five hundred" at the same time; this was probably the occasion.

You can imagine the excitement. The Eleven had already seen Jesus. A few of the women had too. But most of the five hundred had not seen the resurrected Lord. Could they believe that the impossible had happened? Could they believe that Jesus had personally appeared to the Eleven and to a few women disciples? What were they expecting to see? Yes, you can imagine the conversation.

Monday: Read part 1 of this chapter. How would you have felt as one of those five hundred? How would you react to seeing the resurrected Lord?

Tuesday: Read part 2. What does it mean to "make disciples"?

Wednesday: Read part 3. For what important events have you had to wait?

Thursday: Read part 4. Where might God be calling you to go?

Friday: Consider the question in "In the Mirror."

Saturday: Ask God to reveal specific things you can do to obey the Scripture in this lesson.

Sunday: Read about Christ's authority in Ephesians 1:18–23. Let your heart be lifted in praise.

Then it happened. Jesus appeared. Matthew writes, "When they saw him, they worshiped him; but some doubted" (28:17). It's perfectly understandable that some of the five hundred doubted. Hadn't the apostle Thomas also doubted when he was first told? This just demonstrates once again that the resurrection was not an anticipated event. A number of Jesus' followers were hesitant at first before coming into full faith and joy.

Then Jesus came closer to them and began to speak:

● **"All authority in heaven and on earth has been given to me."**

Matthew 28:18

Jesus had always claimed unusual authority. After the Sermon on the Mount, listeners were amazed "because he taught as one who had authority." When he healed on the Sabbath day, he assumed the authority to do so as Lord of the Sabbath. The Pharisees wondered how he dared to forgive sins, but he claimed that authority too. So this was not the first time he claimed to have power and authority on earth.

269

But now he was claiming authority in heaven as well.

Can you imagine the reaction of the five hundred now? Jesus of Nazareth, with whom they had chatted during walks on dusty Galilean roads, was King of Kings and Lord of Lords. Unbelievable! But now they believed.

PART 2

● "Therefore go and make disciples of all nations, baptizing them in the name of the Father and of the Son and of the Holy Spirit, and teaching them to obey everything I have commanded you. And surely I am with you always, to the very end of the age."

Matthew 28:19–20

This time the *go* word was even more challenging. For these Galileans, a long trip meant a four-day trek to Jerusalem. Now Jesus was telling them to "go and make disciples of all nations." The word for "nations" is the Greek word *ethne*, from which we get our word *ethnic*. These disciples were told to reach out and make disciples in ethnic groups around the world.

IN THE MIRROR

What's your excuse for not sharing the gospel with your neighbors, fellow workers, or fellow students? Christians today are operating with the same authority and with the same promise as Jesus gave those Galileans.

How are we going to do this? they may have wondered. For that answer, they needed to go back a few spaces, just before they passed Go. If he had all authority in heaven and earth, they could certainly do whatever he wanted. And he was promising to be with them always, so his power would continue to work through them.

During his life on earth Jesus had pretty much limited his ministry to Israel. Now his followers were commissioned to make disciples of all nations. The word for "make disciples" means more than getting someone to raise a hand, join a church, or even participate in a church ritual. It means commitment; it means a partnership in the gospel; it means learning what *go* means.

PART 3

● "I am going to send you what my Father has promised; but stay in the city until you have been clothed with power from on high."

Luke 24:49

● "Do not leave Jerusalem, but wait for the gift my Father promised, which you have heard me speak about."

Acts 1:4

Traveling back to Jerusalem must have been a harrowing journey for the disciples. Jerusalem was where Jesus' enemies were. Yet that's where they needed to be, because the next command Jesus gave was not "Go" but "Stay." This was important enough that Luke repeated it—at the end of his Gospel and at the start of his exciting sequel, the book of Acts. "Do not leave Jerusalem, but wait." In other words, do not pass Go.

Wait for what? The coming of the Holy Spirit. Jesus had promised to send "another Counselor," someone who would guide and teach them as he had. It would happen soon, but they had to wait for his coming.

Then the disciples asked, *Is this when you are going to overthrow the Romans and set up the kingdom of God on earth?* (see Acts 1:6). They wondered if the Holy Spirit would pave the way for the kingdom to come.

It's interesting that this notion was still in their heads. After the feeding of the five thousand, people were ready to crown Jesus king. But now, after Jesus' sacrificial death, you might think the disciples would have a different take on his mission. Apparently they still expected Jesus to lead an armed revolt. He had other ideas.

PART 4

● "It is not for you to know the times or dates the Father has set by his own authority. But you will receive power when the Holy Spirit comes on you; and you will be my

271

witnesses in Jerusalem, and in all Judea and Samaria, and to the ends of the earth."

Acts 1:7–8

The red light had changed to amber and would soon be green. When the Holy Spirit came, it would be *go* time.

Suddenly Jesus was going and gone. After this last instruction, "he was taken up before their very eyes" (v. 9). He ascended into heaven. Then two angels showed up, announcing that Jesus would some day come back "in the same way you have seen him go into heaven" (v. 11).

Now the disciples remembered their instructions: Go, but first wait. They would be worldwide witnesses *when* the Holy Spirit would come. They had no idea what to expect, but they waited and waited. Then about ten days later, there was no doubt about it. They heard the sound of a strong windstorm, and it seemed as if there were tongues of fire on each of them. The Holy Spirit had come, and the fearsome, quarrelsome disciples were changed.

What were those *go* instructions again?

Go where? First, the city of Jerusalem, then the province of Judea (in which Jerusalem was located), then the neighboring province of Samaria (where there were some enemies of the Jews), and then to the ends of the earth. That's a tall order for a few provincial fishermen.

Yet that's what they did. Acts 1:8 serves as an outline for the book of Acts. That's exactly the way Christianity spread, like a pebble thrown in a pond, rippling out from Jerusalem to Judea to Samaria and throughout the world. And within several decades of Christ's commission to his disciples, the gospel had reached the end of the world they knew. A letter ascribed to Justin Martyr in the second century says: "There is not a single race of human beings, barbarians, Greeks, or whatever name you please to call them, nomads or vagrants or herdsmen living in tents, where prayers in the name of Jesus the crucified are not offered up. . . . Through all the members of the body is the soul spread; so are Christians throughout the cities of the world."

By the way, the light is still green. It still says, Go!

QUOTE TO NOTE

What a contrast was this scene in Galilee to the groans in Gethsemane and the gloom of Golgotha.

Charles Haddon Spurgeon

50
OUTSIDE THE BOX

Most of the Bible's red letters, the words of Christ, are found in the four Gospels, the first four books of the New Testament. This is to be expected, of course, because those books tell us of the life of Christ on earth. But outside the box, hidden in the other New Testament books, are several other sayings of Jesus.

The first red letters after Christ's ascension appear in Acts 9. Saul of Tarsus, a bounty hunter for the high priest in Jerusalem, was making terrorist threats against Christians, rounding them up, and hauling them off as prisoners to Jerusalem. Suddenly, when he was on his way to Damascus, 150 miles northeast of Jerusalem, a bright light blinded him. He fell to the ground and heard a voice saying, "Saul, Saul, why do you persecute me?"

"Who are you, Lord?" he asked.

"I am Jesus, whom you are persecuting." Jesus then told Saul, now blinded, to keep on going to Damascus and await further instructions there (see vv. 4–6).

In Damascus Jesus was alerting a Christian named Ananias to meet this bounty hunter in a house on Straight Street. Ananias had heard all about Saul's dirty business, and he wasn't too excited about this idea. But Jesus, knowing the importance of this meeting, spoke again to Ananias:

● "Go! This man is my chosen instrument to carry my name before the Gentiles and their kings and before the people of Israel."

Acts 9:15

As Ananias walked to the house on Straight Street, he must have wondered: *Am I walking into a trap? Was that really the Lord speaking to me? If so, why would he choose me for such an important meeting?*

But just as Saul was to be God's chosen instrument, in this moment Ananias was God's chosen instrument. We never know the fallout from the contacts God arranges for us. We may feel insignificant, and the house on Straight Street may be very ordinary, but if God is arranging the meeting, the appointment is important.

> ### IN THE MIRROR
>
> Do you realize that you are God's chosen instrument, just as Paul was? What might your mission be?

And it certainly was important for Saul, soon to be known as the apostle Paul.

PART 2

Fast-forward sixteen years. As far as we know, Paul had heard no more messages from Jesus. Instead, the Holy Spirit was leading him from city to city. He was pelted with rocks, beaten, imprisoned, and more, but he kept going. In place after place he preached the gospel for a few days or a few weeks and left a few new converts. On this particular journey he'd been jailed in Philippi, run out of town by a mob in Thessalonica, and (when the mob followed him to

> ### EVERY DAY WITH JESUS
>
> **Monday:** Read part 1 of this chapter. Consider the question in "In the Mirror."
> **Tuesday:** Read part 2. How has the Lord encouraged you?
> **Wednesday:** Read part 3. Which do you find more of a blessing: giving or receiving?
> **Thursday:** Read parts 4 and 5. What do the elements of communion mean to you?
> **Friday:** Read part 6. Why do you suppose the Lord did not remove Paul's thorn in the flesh?
> **Saturday:** Pray that you will continue to hear the voice of Christ in your daily life.
> **Sunday:** Read Romans 11:33–36 and bless the Lord.

Berea) forced to flee for his life to Athens. From there, the discouraged apostle went to Corinth, which had a reputation as a wide-open city. But before long another abusive mob threatened him. What should he do?

The following night, in a vision, he heard the voice of Jesus again:

● "Do not be afraid; keep on speaking, do not be silent. For I am with you . . . I have many people in this city."

Acts 18:9–10

It was just the encouragement Paul needed. Obeying the voice of Jesus, he preached there for eighteen months. And in the wild, rugged metropolis of Corinth, a church was built, to which he later wrote two major Epistles.

PART 3

Now five more years have passed, with much of that time spent in Corinth and Ephesus. On his way back to Jerusalem, Paul stops to say good-by to the leaders of the Ephesian church. Finishing his talk, he says, "We must help the weak, remembering the words the Lord Jesus himself said:

● "It is more blessed to give than to receive."

Acts 20:35

When did Jesus say those words? No one knows. When and where did Paul hear them? No one knows. But by this time he had met with the other apostles a few times, and perhaps in private conversation with one of them, he heard this saying of Jesus.

Usually you'll hear these words quoted today when a church offering is about to be collected, but Paul used them to express how we should give of our time and energy to help those who are less fortunate than we are.

PART 4

After saying farewell to the Ephesian church leaders, Paul went to Jerusalem, where, before long, he was arrested and thrown in jail. No surprise there! However, the Roman governor didn't know what to do with him. As a Roman citizen, Paul couldn't be kept in prison without being charged. But if the governor released him, Paul would be killed within hours. Outside, the crowd kept on screaming, "Rid the earth of him! He's not fit to live!" (Acts 22:22).

One night in this dark time, Paul saw the Lord Jesus standing near him and saying:

● "Take courage! As you have testified about me in Jerusalem, so you must also testify in Rome."

Acts 23:11

Once again the word of Jesus gave him the direction he needed. Paul appealed his case to Caesar, and the local Roman governors were happy to put him on a ship to Rome and get rid of the problem. Despite a shipwreck, Paul was confident that he would somehow get to Rome. After all, isn't that what Jesus had promised?

Paul did arrive in Rome, and the local Christians welcomed him. Awaiting trial, he was put under house arrest, but he continued to testify for Christ. His letter to the Philippians, written during this Roman imprisonment, concludes: "All the saints send you greetings, especially those who belong to Caesar's household" (Phil. 4:22).

PART 5

Sayings of Jesus don't pop up very often in the Epistles, but one quotation is very familiar to many because it is repeated in communion services around the world. Jesus said these words in the upper room the night before his crucifixion, and they are recorded in the Gospels with slightly different wording. It's interesting that Paul probably wrote his first letter to the Corinthians before the Gospels were written, so these words of Christ may be the first such words to be written down.

● "This is my body, which is for you; do this in remembrance of me. . . . This cup is the new covenant in my blood; do this, whenever you drink it, in remembrance of me."

1 Corinthians 11:24–25

PART 6

Throughout his missionary service, Paul endured persecution on a routine basis. But one thing bugged him. He called it his thorn in the flesh (see 2 Cor. 12:7). Three times he pleaded with God to remove it, but God didn't. For centuries people have argued about what that thorn in the flesh really was. Paul doesn't say. Paul does say, however, what Jesus told him, which is most important.

● "My grace is sufficient for you, for my power is made perfect in weakness."

2 Corinthians 12:9

Is that an answer to prayer? We might not be satisfied with it, but Paul was. We might want an instant cure or a miraculous deliverance, but Paul thought that Jesus' personal word to him was good enough. The lesson Paul learned was this: "Therefore I will boast all the more gladly about my weaknesses, so that Christ's power may rest on me. . . . For when I am weak, then I am strong" (vv. 9–10).

QUOTE TO NOTE

Your biggest weakness is God's greatest opportunity.

Charles Stanley

51
OPEN THE CURTAINS

Why do people read the book of Revelation? Usually it's because they want answers to questions like: What is the mark of the beast? What are the ten horns and seven heads? When will the millennium come? Are the streets of heaven really paved with gold?

Interesting, isn't it, that the first five words in the book are "The revelation of Jesus Christ," but many readers aren't very interested in what the book reveals about Jesus Christ.

The writer (or transcriber) is John, one of Jesus' closest disciples. The time: probably 95 AD or so, about sixty years after the death and resurrection of Jesus. Peter and Paul had been martyred in the 60s, along with many other believers, in a persecution that Emperor Nero had launched. Now a new emperor, Domitian, was cracking down on Christians, and John was sent into exile on the sixteen-square-mile island of Patmos in the Aegean Sea.

One Sunday John had a vision. It was awesome, indescribable. The person he saw reminded him of someone the prophet Daniel once described (Dan. 10:6): eyes like blazing fire, feet like glowing bronze, voice like cascading water. John fell prostrate.

Then he felt a hand on him, and he heard a voice, a voice he recognized, saying:

● "Do not be afraid. I am the First and the Last. I am the Living One; I was dead, and behold I am alive for ever and ever! And I hold the keys of death and Hades."

Revelation 1:17–18

That voice was familiar to John. He had heard Jesus say those opening words often. "Do not be afraid." On the Mount of Transfiguration, when God's glory covered the place, these were the words of Jesus to his disciples. On storm-tossed Galilee and in the upper room after the resurrection, John had heard those same words. Now John was seeing God's glory again, and once again Jesus was in the middle of it.

In a few words Jesus gives John the assurance that this aging apostle needs: *I'm alive, John. I am a victor over death. I know what you are suffering, John, on this little remote island a long way from home. But you are not alone. I am alive forever and I am with you. The Roman emperor may think he is winning, John. He may hold the keys to the isle of Patmos, but he doesn't hold the keys of death and Hades. I do, and I will be around a lot longer than he will.*

You might excuse John for feeling discouraged. He was probably in his eighties by now. All his fellow disciples had been martyred (except Judas). Now the Roman emperor was demanding to be worshiped as Lord and God, and many Christians were buckling under the pressure, forsaking their faith. John had to wonder whether Christianity would die out when he did.

EVERY DAY WITH JESUS

Monday: Read part 1 of this chapter. Can you imagine seeing Jesus as he was in Daniel 7 and Revelation 1:13–15? This is our friend, yet he appears in awesome glory.

Tuesday: Read part 2 of this chapter and then read Revelation 3:20 again. Try memorizing this verse.

Wednesday: Read part 3. Do you eagerly await the Lord's return?

Thursday: Consider the questions in "In the Mirror."

Friday: Throughout Revelation we see other symbols used to describe various aspects of Jesus' character. See if you can find them. Look in chapters 5, 19, and 21.

Saturday: Pray for those you know who need to let Jesus come into their hearts.

Sunday: Read Revelation 5:11–13 and lift your heart in exaltation.

Of course, in the twenty-first century we don't have all those reasons to get discouraged, but we have others. The words of the awesome Son of God are just as valid for us as they were for John. He is the Living One. He is alive forever and ever, so do not be afraid. He is still in charge.

PART 2

In the second and third chapters of Revelation, the Lord tells John to write short letters to seven churches located in what we now call southwestern Turkey. Each letter follows a pattern, starting with (1) a greeting and (2) a title for the risen Christ, then offering (3) a word of praise (in most cases), (4) some criticism (in most cases), (5) a warning, (6) an exhortation to hear and do, and (7) a promise.

According to many Bible scholars, the last of the seven churches, the church of Laodicea, represents the church of the "last days," the days in which we live.

Whether you agree with their interpretation or not, the letter to that church has a strong message for Christians today. Laodicea, affluent and proud, was an industrial center with banking establishments and a medical school—one of the richest commercial centers in the world. Its people thought they had everything. But the Lord called the church in Laodicea so lukewarm that it nauseated him. No other church got the strong condemnation that Laodicea received. "You are wretched, pitiful, poor, blind and naked" (Rev. 3:17). That's strong language, especially for proud rich folks.

Is there any hope? Oh yes. Jesus gives the invitation:

● "Here I am! I stand at the door and knock. If anyone hears my voice and opens the door, I will come in and eat with him, and he with me."

Revelation 3:20

The classic painting by Holman Hunt (*The Light of the World*) shows Christ outside a door, knocking. Usually we think of this wonderful verse applying to the non-Christian, as the Savior

281

IN THE MIRROR

In Revelation 3:20, first, Jesus is outside wanting to come in. Second, we must open the door. Third, Jesus enters. Consider your own life: What draws you to Jesus? How do you know he wants a deeper relationship with you? What do you do to get the door to your heart open? What difference is there in your life after he enters?

knocks to gain admission to the sinner's heart. But this verse is actually written to the church member, the lukewarm Laodicean, who thinks he already has everything both spiritually and materially. In having such a full life, he has shoved Christ outside.

Here I am! says Jesus. You've enjoyed your church membership, your meetings, and your socials. You're inside, enjoying your church supper, chattering away with your wonderful church friends, and the hubbub is so intense that you can't even hear the knocking on the church door.

Open up, says Jesus. *I want in.*

PART 3

The next section of Revelation deals with the seven seals, the seven trumpets, the seven signs, and the seven bowls. These chapters are loaded with symbolism—and they also stoke the fires of controversy. As you get to the final chapters of Revelation, however, the light shines brighter and brighter. John gets a vision of a new heaven and a new earth, with God wiping away every tear, and he pictures the Holy City, where there will be no night. And he hears Jesus speaking:

- "Behold, I am coming soon! . . . Blessed are those who wash their robes, that they may have the right to the tree of life and may go through the gates into the city. . . . Yes, I am coming soon."

Revelation 22:12, 14, 20

If you become confused with all the beasts and the bowls in the heart of this book, step into the sunshine of the final chapters. The book of Revelation is something like a mystery novel with a complex plot. When the mystery is solved, you say, "Why didn't I realize this all along?" In this case, the solution is the return of Jesus.

Jesus keeps saying that he is coming soon. It's been more than two thousand years. You call that soon? The apostle Peter explains it this way: "With the Lord a day is like a thousand years, and a thousand years are like a day. The Lord is not

> **CROSS REF**
>
> Read more about the glory of the Lord:
> 2 Peter 1:16–18

slow in keeping his promise." But why the delay? Peter says it is because God "is patient . . . not wanting anyone to perish, but everyone to come to repentance" (2 Peter 3:8–9).

Ever since Jesus said, "Yes, I am coming soon," Christians have looked forward to his return with assurance and anticipation. At Christmas a toddler may await the arrival of grandparents. He knows they will come because they have promised to come, and when they come they will be bringing presents. He stands on tiptoe to see out the window; he pushes his nose against the pane. He can hardly wait.

With the same certainty and longing, Christians await the fulfillment of Christ's promise, "Yes, I am coming soon."

PASSION WEEK

PALM SUNDAY

ROCK SONG

● Some of the Pharisees in the crowd said to Jesus, "Teacher, rebuke your disciples!"

"I tell you," he replied, "if they keep quiet, the stones will cry out."

Luke 19:39–40

It was a great day. Jesus rode a donkey's colt into the city of Jerusalem, with fans waving palm branches and draping their cloaks on the road before him. Everybody loves a parade, and this one had cosmic significance. "Hosanna!" the people shouted. "Hosanna to the Son of David!"

The Hebrew word *hosanna* carries a curious double meaning. Literally it means, "Lord, save us!" That's the sort of thing people would cry to a liberating warrior who routed an occupying army. Such moments have happened throughout history. Think of the Allied troops liberating France toward the end of World War II. The captain leads the battalion down the main street of the town, taking firm possession of it, chasing away the previous overlords and setting the citizens free.

"Lord, save us!" It's the cry of a people who know they need saving, shouted out to someone they trust to save them. And so, over the centuries, *hosanna* became a word of praise, akin to *hal-*

lelujah. It's unclear whether the people of Jerusalem knew they were calling out for salvation or if they just thought they were honoring this popular leader with a common salutation. In any case, they were welcoming him, hailing him, praising him.

But some knew Jesus was more than just a pop icon. "Hosanna to the Son of David!" they called. David was the patriarch of the royal dynasty of Judea. For four hundred years after David's time, every ruler of this kingdom was a "son" of David, and even in times of occupation, the prophecies hinted that a new Davidic king would arise—the Messiah.

Of course Jesus had taught daily about God's kingdom, but he had been careful.

Now, though, the crowd was singing, "Blessed is the king who comes in the name of the Lord!" This was the Davidic king riding into the city to take control, not on a warhorse like a Roman general but on a donkey, as prophesied. "See, your king comes to you," the prophet Zechariah had said, "gentle and riding on a donkey" (Zech. 9:9).

The Pharisees urged Jesus to silence the crowd. The people were getting carried away, as the Pharisees saw it; surely Jesus didn't want to start a rebellion. In Matthew's account, the Pharisees call the people who are singing praises "children" (Matt. 21:16). No doubt there were children in the crowd, but perhaps the Pharisees were disparaging Jesus' disciples: *Childish enthusiasm! Surely they don't know what they're saying.*

But Jesus refuses to rein in the praises. This was a majestic moment, and if the Pharisees were too hard-nosed to know it, the stones of the city walls were not. If they succeeded in shutting up the disciples, the stones themselves would raise a ruckus.

At first glance, this seems similar to psalms that mention the trees clapping their hands. All nature joins in praising the Savior of all. But Jesus might have been nodding toward a prophecy in Habakkuk. That prophet berated the proud and greedy leaders of society. "You have plotted the ruin of many peoples, shaming your own house and forfeiting your life. The stones of the wall will cry out, and the beams of the woodwork will echo it" (Hab. 2:10–11).

And it's curious to note that in the midst of his stern rebuke, Habakkuk added a positive contrast. "See, he is puffed up; his desires are not upright—*but the righteous will live by his faith*" (v. 4, emphasis added). This, of course, is the heart of the gospel message, developed by the apostle Paul (see Rom. 1:17) and rooted in Jesus' own teaching. And it's a snapshot of the event on that first Palm Sunday.

The Pharisees had been revealed as arrogant, greedy, and corrupt—puffed up with pride in their own pious traditions. On the other hand, the people were displaying simple faith, calling out for a Savior to save them. These people were the truly righteous, and their faith would bring them life.

MONDAY

HEAVEN SCENT

● "It was intended that she should save this perfume for the day of my burial. You will always have the poor among you, but you will not always have me."

John 12:7–8

Judas had a point. Seriously, you may have heard Judas's argument at a church board meeting or some planning session—and you may have agreed. "Why spend all this money on worship? Wouldn't it be better to give it to the poor?"

It sounds good, compassionate, and practical. But Jesus says no, not necessarily.

The original debate occurred early in the week before Jesus' crucifixion. He was staying at the home of his friends Martha, Mary, and Lazarus in Bethany, a Jerusalem suburb. Jesus had already raised Lazarus from the dead, a miracle that fired up the opposition. Everything was headed for a showdown, and everybody seemed to know it.

So Martha threw a dinner party for Jesus. We don't know who was there besides Martha's family and Jesus' disciples, but we can guess that there was a collection of other friends as well.

Walking those Mideast streets in sandals gave travelers dusty feet, so it was customary for servants to wash the feet of visitors.

Perhaps a good hostess would perform this duty for an esteemed guest. But Mary did something shocking. First she took a pint of expensive perfume and poured it over Jesus' feet, then she loosened her hair and used it to wipe his feet dry.

Imagine being in that room and watching Mary kneel before Jesus. *Oh,* you think, *she's going to wash his feet. For a lady of the house to perform that menial task, well, she must think highly of him.* But then you catch a whiff of the perfume, and you see Mary letting her hair down—something no respectable woman would do in public. Then she uses her hair as a towel—how degrading, how inappropriately sensual! And now the scent of perfume is strong, even overwhelming. This is an outrageous, extravagant act—maybe well meant but certainly uncalled for. You catch a glimpse of Martha's face: *There she goes again, that crazy sister of mine!* How will Jesus respond?

Leave it to Judas Iscariot to bring up the practical objections. Forget about the impropriety of this action—Judas was the treasurer of the disciples, and he cared about the money. This perfume could have been sold for a tidy sum, a year's wages by his calculation. Wouldn't it have been better to use those proceeds to help the poor?

Judas didn't really care about the poor, John says; he just wanted to line his own pockets. But don't let that detract from the fact that his argument is quite compelling. We've heard it often.

How did Jesus answer it? First, he made this a special case. Mary had saved this perfume for a special occasion, and this was it. Without modern embalming processes, corpses were dressed with spices and perfumes before burial. As Jesus approached his death, he saw this as a "pre-embalming."

Then Jesus made a comment that sounds strangely harsh, coming from the Lord of love: "You will always have the poor among you." So there would always be opportunity to honor the Lord by giving to the poor. This was a special time, and Mary gave a special gift.

Yet in his matter-of-factness, Jesus teaches us an important truth. God does not really need our help to feed the poor. He could rain down manna from heaven if he chose to. And thus it is not our job to eradicate poverty. We should use our resources—time and talents, money and perfume—to honor God in whatever way the moment demands. Often that means helping the needy; Scripture makes that clear. But Judas had the idea that money is a savior, and that's a dangerous idea.

Every so often you'll hear of some church, charity, or ministry that gets all wrapped up in money. Oh, they're doing good things with that money, or so it seems, but soon they lose sight of their true purpose, and they start doing whatever it takes to get more money.

Mary understood that Jesus must be at the center of our purpose in life. We feed the poor to honor Jesus. We build cathedrals to worship Jesus. We invest our resources in his name and for his sake. There's only one way our goods do any good: as a gift to Jesus from a grateful heart.

TUESDAY

TRICK QUESTIONS

What gives you the right? That's what the priests and teachers wanted to know.

Jesus had caused a scene in the temple courts, upending tables, sending coins clattering, loosing the sacrificial animals. He had accused the money changers of turning God's house into a robbers' den.

A day or two later, the authorities caught up to him. " 'Tell us by what authority you are doing these things,' they said. 'Who gave you this authority?' " (Luke 20:2).

It was a trap. All along they had been trying to get Jesus to say something revolutionary or blasphemous. Using Roman law or Jewish law, they would find a way to silence this renegade rabbi.

Throughout his ministry, Jesus had chosen his words carefully. He didn't want to give his opponents too much ammunition too soon. Events were now drawing to a climax, but he still remained coy. He answered their trick question with a trick question of his own.

● "I will also ask you a question. Tell me, John's baptism—was it from heaven, or from men?"

Luke 20:3–4

Immediately recognizing the no-win situation, the leaders huddled together and sorted it out. " 'If we say, "From heaven," he will ask, "Why didn't you believe him?" But if we say, "From men," all the people will stone us, because they are persuaded that John was a prophet' " (v. 5).

Clearly, John the Baptist was a man "sent from God" (John 1:6). Well, it had been clear to everyone except these leaders. They had dogged John as they had been dogging Jesus.

Yet John had been enormously popular among the common people. They sensed that a new day was dawning for Israel, that John was a messenger of a coming kingdom. When John stood up against the hated King Herod over a sexual scandal, he eventually paid with his life—and that made him even more of a folk hero. These priests and teachers were supposedly the chief promoters of Israel's righteousness. They had no trouble scolding Jesus for healing people—*healing people!*—on the Sabbath day, but they stayed mum when the king stole his brother's wife. They were political creatures through and through, and on this occasion Jesus used their political savvy to his own advantage.

Jesus' question put these leaders in a bind, and they knew it. Here's the brilliant answer they came up with: *We don't know.* Jesus responded to them:

● "Neither will I tell you by what authority I am doing these things."

Luke 20:8

If you had answered my question, you would have answered your own, Jesus might have been thinking. *If your hearts had been open to John's message, you would have accepted mine.*

Jesus still answers questions with questions. Sometimes that gets frustrating for us. In some dark nights of the soul, we might wonder if it's all true. *Tell me, Lord, if you're really there. Tell me if you really care for me*. We want the heavens to break open and the stars to reconfigure to spell out an answer.

You know, John the Baptist had a dark night like that once. Imprisoned by Herod, he wondered if Jesus was really the Promised One or if he had wasted his life on a lie. When he sent messengers to Jesus with that question, Jesus (once again) refused to give a direct answer. He simply told the messengers to go back and tell John what they were seeing and hearing: people being healed, the truth being preached (Matt. 11:2–6).

We look for answers written in the heavens, but they are scrawled all around us on earth. Look around you. See what God is doing in your church, among your Christian friends, within your own life. What is the power that motivates the miracles you see daily? That should answer your questions about Jesus.

WEDNESDAY

WASH DAY

They say a picture is worth a thousand words. Sometimes an action can be worth even more.

Customarily, a household servant would wash the dusty feet of visitors. It was demeaning work, and certainly none of the disciples would want to take on that servile task. Consider the shock they felt when Jesus grabbed a towel, poured water into a basin, and knelt before them. The Master was doing a servant's work.

Perhaps several others allowed this to happen, but then Jesus came to Peter, who protested. "You, Lord, washing my feet?" He saw the absurdity. Jesus urged him to let it happen; he would understand more later.

But Peter still resisted. It just seemed wrong for him to receive such menial service from the Lord of all. Maybe all the others would let it happen, but Peter had to put his foot down (so to speak). " 'No,' said Peter, 'you shall never wash my feet.' Jesus answered, 'Unless I wash you, you have no part with me'" (John 13:8).

This response takes us to another level. Suddenly they're not just talking about removing road grime. To have a meaningful connection (a "part") with Jesus, Peter had to allow Jesus to "wash" him. The same is true for all of us. We find the cleansing metaphor throughout the New Testament. John writes, "The blood of Jesus . . . purifies us from all sin" (1 John 1:7). Any continuing relationship with Jesus is based on the washing away of our sin.

But there's also an important attitude adjustment we mustn't miss in this story. To continue in his relationship with Jesus, Peter had to let the Master serve him. It went against everything that he believed, but he was required to do so. Why? Because the kingdom that Jesus would rule was an upside-down kingdom. The last would be first and the first last. Leaders would be servants. Jesus said that even he himself "did not come to be served, but to serve, and to give his life as a ransom for many" (Mark 10:45). The entire community of Jesus would be built not on power or authority, not on some merit system or chain of command, but on service and sacrifice. Not only would Jesus kneel to wash the feet of his followers, but he would hang on a cross to cleanse our hearts from sin.

Sometimes people just want a Jesus who lived an exemplary life and said wise things. Like Peter, they seem embarrassed to let him serve them. They never quite claim his sacrifice; nor do they really acknowledge their own need for cleansing. To such people, Jesus is still saying, *Let me serve you; let me wash you. Otherwise you have no part with me.*

As Jesus finished the foot washing, he made the lesson crystal clear.

● "Do you understand what I have done for you?" he asked them. "You call me 'Teacher' and 'Lord,' and rightly so, for that is what I am. Now that I, your Lord and Teacher, have washed your feet, you also should wash one another's feet."

John 13:12–14

The upside-down kingdom has not a chain of command but a chain of service. Those whom Jesus serves turn around and serve others. If our Lord and Master has cleaned our smelly feet, how can we refuse to kneel before others?

MAUNDY THURSDAY

COME AND DINE

Apparently there was some mystery about the location of the Last Supper. Everyone knew Jesus would celebrate the Passover with his disciples, but where? The instructions he gave to two of them could come from a spy novel. "Go into the city and find a man carrying a jar of water. Follow him home, and then say, 'The Teacher needs a room to celebrate the Passover'" (see Mark 14:13–14).

Could it be that Jesus wanted to make sure he could have this feast in peace, before Judas brought the soldiers to arrest him? If so, then he needed to prevent anyone from knowing in advance where he'd keep the Passover meal.

It was an event-filled evening. But the major event came when Jesus picked up the bread and wine and gave them new meaning. Thus the Lord instituted the Lord's Supper, a commemoration that Christians have observed ever since.

The meal was already stuffed with significance, going back to Israel's great exodus from Egypt. It was called Passover because the angel of death, who smote the oppressive Egyptians, "passed over" the Israelite homes with lamb's blood on the doorposts. As the celebration developed, every menu item came to mean something. Bitter herbs represented the torment of slavery. One dip called to mind the clay that the Israelite slaves had used to make bricks. There were four cups of wine, each with a special meaning—the Cup of Sanctification, of Deliverance, of Redemption, and of Thanksgiving. Prayers and blessings were said at certain points of the meal. The youngest child was supposed to ask, "Why is this night different from all other nights?"

We're not sure which cup Jesus took to start his new tradition, but it began with the breaking of the matzo, the unleavened bread.

● "Take and eat; this is my body."

Matthew 26:26

As Jesus cracked the matzo wafer in two, so his own body would be broken. But he wasn't just presenting an object lesson to his disciples; he was inviting them to partake of his brokenness.

Many different churches have different views of the Lord's Supper, but there is one element in common: "Take and eat." The followers of Jesus partake of him. They receive the blessings of his love and the saving effect of his sacrifice. They welcome his cleansing power into their own lives. Christianity was never intended to be a spectator sport. It's a supper, where the faithful are invited to come and dine.

Jesus explained this even further when he lifted the cup.

● "Drink from it, all of you. This is my blood of the covenant, which is poured out for many for the forgiveness of sins."

Matthew 26:27–28

Throughout history, God has made covenants with his people. He agreed to make Abraham the father of many nations, and he essentially signed a contract with the Israelites at Mount Sinai. Sacrifices were part of that agreement. Recognizing their sin, the people would bring bulls or goats or sheep to be killed at the altar. Under the agreement with God, the blood of these animals would be accepted as payment for the trespasses of the people.

Perhaps you've read pirate stories where people make a pact and sign it in blood. Why? Blood means business. Because it involves pain, or even death, blood is serious stuff. You can't take blood-shedding lightly. And so the sacrificial-animal blood testified to the seriousness of the Israelites' sin and their desire to set things right.

But the blood of animals could never actually wash away sin; it was always just a hint of something greater. And through the prophet Jeremiah, God promised to make a new contract offer. "This is the covenant I will make with the house of Israel. . . . I will put my law in their minds and write it on their hearts.

I will be their God, and they will be my people. . . . For I will forgive their wickedness and will remember their sins no more" (Jer. 31:33, 34).

This is what Jesus was talking about as he lifted the cup of Passover wine. *Take this as my blood,* he says. This is the blood that fulfills the contract. This is the blood that truly forgives sins. This is the blood that transforms lives.

GOOD FRIDAY

FAMOUS LAST WORDS

What do people say in their dying breath? From Citizen Kane's "Rosebud" to John Adams wondering if his rival Jefferson was dead yet, such "last words" are interesting trivia for literature and history buffs. But the words of Jesus as he hung on the cross hold a different fascination for Christians. These seven sayings give us insight into his relationship with his Father and the depth of his suffering.

- "Father, forgive them, for they do not know what they are doing."

Luke 23:34

Jesus was led to the hill of crucifixion and nailed to a cross between two thieves. He had already been stripped and beaten, and now he faced the agony of a slow, public death. The Romans had designed crucifixions for maximum pain and humiliation.

You might expect the victims to bark hateful comments at their torturers. But even in death, Jesus displayed a loving, forgiving spirit. As the soldiers gambled over his clothing, Jesus asked his Father to forgive them for this crucifixion.

In our civilized society, we seem to forgive easily. "Pardon me" is said at the drop of a hat, literally, and such pardons are routinely offered for minor offenses. But if you've ever had to deal with a major mistreatment, you know how hard true forgiveness is. The drunk driver who changes your life forever, the ex-spouse who stole your heart and your savings, the best friend who betrayed your confidence—it's tough to forgive people like this. Yet Jesus forgave the people who crucified him.

"They don't know what they're doing," he explained, as if he were a defense attorney pleading with the judge for clemency. Didn't they? In one respect, the Roman soldiers knew exactly how to crucify—they had done it a thousand times. And the Jewish leaders who trumped up the charges against Jesus—they'd been out to get him for years. They were all doing precisely what they intended to do, weren't they?

A few months later, Peter would preach to a crowd in Jerusalem and say, "You killed the author of life. . . . Now, brothers, I know that you acted in ignorance, as did your leaders" (Acts 3:15, 17). Their ignorance was not in what they were doing but in who they were doing it to. Had they taken the time to learn from him, they might have realized who he really was. But as they went about their business, they had no clue.

● "I tell you the truth, today you will be with me in paradise."

Luke 23:43

One of the robbers crucified with Jesus was insulting him, along with some of the passersby. "Aren't you the Christ? Save yourself and us!" It's unlikely that he had any real expectation that this would happen.

The other robber chided the first one: "We are punished justly, for we are getting what our deeds deserve. But this man has done nothing wrong."

Then he said to Jesus, "Remember me when you come into your kingdom" (vv. 39–42). Jesus agreed, promising that they'd meet in paradise. *Paradise* meant "garden" and was sometimes used for Eden and sometimes for a pleasant realm in the afterlife. Jesus was using an image the man would understand. The key phrase here is "with me." *Remember you?* Jesus is saying. *I'm taking you with me!*

● When Jesus saw his mother there, and the disciple whom he loved standing nearby, he said to his mother, "Dear woman, here is your son," and to the disciple, "Here is your mother."

John 19:26–27

The "disciple whom Jesus loved" was John. John apparently "was known to the high priest," so he was allowed to enter the courtyard (18:15). Obviously this connection got John all the way to the foot of the cross, where he witnessed Jesus' death along with several loyal women.

If Mary had borne Jesus when she was a teenager, she was nearly fifty by this time. It's interesting to find Mary in Jerusalem, a four-day journey from her Nazareth home. She must have made this Passover trip with Jesus and his disciples.

Legally, Jesus' death would put Mary in the care of her next oldest son. But Jesus had already stated that the most important family ties were based not on bloodlines but on doing God's will. And so he wants to create a new bond between his faithful mother and his most beloved follower.

● About the ninth hour Jesus cried out in a loud voice, *"Eloi, Eloi, lama sabachthani?"*—which means, "My God, my God, why have you forsaken me?"

Matthew 27:46

Of the many mysteries of the gospel, this might be the most mysterious. It's puzzling enough how God can be three persons in one—Father, Son, and Holy Spirit in a single Tri-unity. And the nature of Jesus himself, fully God and fully man, is equally hard to fathom. But having accepted all of that by faith, we come to this agonizing moment on the cross and we are at a loss to comprehend it.

Oh, we understand the feeling. We've been there. When David originally cried out these words, he was pounding on heaven's door, trying to get some answer from a God who seemed far away. "Why are you so far from saving me, so far from the words of my groaning? O my God, I cry out by day, but you do not answer" (Ps. 22:1–2). From Job to Jeremiah, that's not an uncommon scene.

But there was something far greater going on at Golgotha. The God who seemed far away from Jesus was his own Father and, in a way, his very self. "I and the Father are one," he had said (John 10:30). The apparent forsaking of Jesus was a rending of his identity. Other unfortunate people have faced the agonies of crucifixion and other tortures, yet no one could fully know the spiritual anguish Jesus felt in this moment.

"He himself bore our sins in his body on the tree," Peter wrote (1 Peter 2:24). The forsaking was part of the punishment for our sins. The holy God must judge sin, and he chose to heap our transgressions on the Son and tear himself apart in the process. This was the cup of suffering that Jesus first balked at drinking but then willingly accepted.

● **Later, knowing that all was now completed, and so that the Scripture would be fulfilled, Jesus said, "I am thirsty."**

John 19:28

Composed about a thousand years before Jesus' death, Psalm 22 is a stunning description of the experience of being crucified. No doubt David was referring to some suffering of his own, but the psalm unfolds as if he were right there with Jesus. And we've already heard Jesus use the opening words of that psalm, wondering why God had forsaken him. Here we find Jesus afflicted by something as basic as thirst, and sure enough, that's also in David's account. "My strength is dried up like a potsherd, and my tongue sticks to the roof of my mouth" (v. 15).

Earlier Jesus had rejected a drugged vinegar drink, but now he accepted a sponge of wine vinegar lifted to his lips. John tells us that this too fulfilled Scripture, as Psalm 69:21 says, "They put gall in my food and gave me vinegar for my thirst."

In the early centuries of the church, various cult groups worshiped Jesus as divine but failed to accept that he was fully human. John was especially adamant about portraying Jesus as human, and here's one key example. The crucifixion was certainly a cosmic act that paid our debt before the holy God, but

John doesn't get lost in the spiritual meaning of the moment. He shows a Savior who is human enough to be thirsty.

● **Jesus said, "It is finished." With that, he bowed his head and gave up his spirit.**

John 19:30

Consider a few scenes from everyday life. A young couple has been dating for several months, but then one says to the other, "I can't see you anymore. We're finished." A veteran ballplayer hangs up his spikes after a terrible outing—"I'm finished," he tearfully tells the press. A CEO closes her notebook after a productive brain-storming session with the marketing team and says, "Good work. We're finished here." A college student high-fives his roommate after the graduation ceremonies, shouting, "We're finished!"

Finishing can be happy or sad. You can finish well or fin-ish poorly. There might be a bit of both in Jesus' cry from the cross. The process of crucifixion prolonged agony by using the victim's fight to stay alive. Jesus would have had to pull himself upward to take each breath. This struggle allowed him to say all these things he said from the cross, but at a certain point his strength would give out. The struggle would stop. This was, no doubt, that moment.

But Jesus was well aware of a greater purpose in his life and death. He had been sent, he announced, to give his life as a ransom for many. He would be "lifted up"—on a cross—to draw the whole world in faith to him. He would be buried in the earth like a grain of wheat so that a crop of believers would be raised up.

So this crucifixion was no mere miscarriage of justice, not just a senseless tragedy. It was a mission that had reached its fulfillment. And thus Jesus' exclamation might be understood: "Mission accomplished!"

● **Jesus called out with a loud voice, "Father, into your hands I commit my spirit." When he had said this, he breathed his last.**

Luke 23:46

At this point it was all about breath. Jesus simply lacked the strength to draw any more breath, so he knew his physical struggle was over. He used every last bit of oxygen to shout out a prayer.

There's a bit of wordplay in the Gospel account. His final prayer committed his *spirit* to the Father, and then he *ex-spired*. In Greek, as in other languages, *spirit* means "breath." Of course it also has to do with our soul, our life force, our relationship with God. But it's still interesting to note that Jesus, after struggling to breathe, took a breath that allowed him to call out loudly, committing his breath to the Father (as well as his future existence), and then he stopped breathing.

What if this prayer became ours, not just at death's door, but when we get up in the morning, when we go jogging, when we work and eat and watch TV? "Every breath, Lord, I commit to you. This might be my last breath, or I might have many more breaths coming, but that's up to you, Lord. I realize that every breath is from you, and I want to use every breath for you." This last-breath prayer of Jesus is a quote from Psalm 31:5, which was often voiced by Hebrew children at bedtime—their verison of "Now I lay me down to sleep."

And so Jesus, having forgiven his persecutors, having welcomed a thief, and having provided for his mother, declares his mission accomplished and settles down to sleep. Moments earlier, he had raged in utter pain about being forsaken by his Father, but now he leans quietly into his Father's arms to rest.

SATURDAY

THE SECRET

● As they were coming down the mountain, Jesus instructed them, "Don't tell anyone what you have seen, until the Son of Man has been raised from the dead."

Matthew 17:9

Paul, a young friend of ours, was a great ballplayer, though he didn't look the part. When he connected, he could send a softball into the next county.

One day, playing for the church softball team, he engaged in some trickery. The first pitch floated in, and Paul swung wildly, missing it by a foot. The second swing was also embarrassing. Had he lost his touch while he was away at college? No, he had a plan.

The other team didn't know Paul at all, since he had been away most of the season. All they saw was a scrawny kid struggling to make contact. After each miserable swing, the outfielders moved in about ten feet. But then Paul swung perfectly at the third pitch, sending it well over their heads. He circled the bases, laughing all the way.

Jesus had a plan too. According to appearances, he was a poor rabbi with a motley group of followers. Slowly those disciples realized that he was more than just a man, more than a philosopher or teacher. Peter announced one day that he saw Jesus as the very Son of God, and shortly afterward that identity was confirmed on the Mount of Transfiguration. Jesus appeared in dazzling light, and a voice from heaven said, "This is my Son" (v. 5).

For the disciples, that was stunning stuff, but then Jesus told them not to tell anyone. *It's our secret . . . until I rise from the dead. Let them think of me what they will. Those with ears to hear will know who I am, but others will see me as an embarrassing failure. That's all right. Just wait until I hit that home run, and then you can tell everyone about your glorified, resurrected Lord.*

● When they came together in Galilee, he said to them, "The Son of Man is going to be betrayed into the hands of men. They will kill him, and on the third day he will be raised to life." And the disciples were filled with grief.

Matthew 17:22–23

Doesn't it seem sometimes that the disciples were thick-headed? Why didn't they get it? Jesus clearly told them things that would happen, and then they were utterly shocked when those things happened. Weren't they listening?

Hindsight is 20/20, they say, and we often look back to see warning signs we should have been aware of. Telling the story, a generation later, the disciples might whup themselves on the forehead and say, "Duh! We should have known all along!" So don't be too hard on these guys.

Still, Jesus spoke about his upcoming death and resurrection on several occasions, especially as he approached his final Passover pilgrimage. "When they came together in Galilee" might have been their preparation for this fateful Jerusalem trip. Jesus wanted them to know what they were in for.

Yet it seems that they never even heard the good part. *Betrayed, killed*—words like that made it clear that any hopes of a political takeover would be dashed. As a result, the disciples were "filled with grief." But did they hear about the resurrection? Did they understand it? Or did they assume, as Martha once did, that Jesus was talking about some general resurrection in the afterlife? In any case, they grieved when they could have also rejoiced.

And on that dismal Sabbath, with Jesus' body in the tomb and the disciples scattered about their hiding places, did they remember these words at all? Were they convinced that the party was over, or did they have a spark of hope in the miracle that their Lord of light could pull off?

EASTER SUNDAY

THE LAST LAUGH

Two people are discussing the tragic demise of a loved one, and a stranger joins them. This stranger doesn't seem to know about the death, so they have to explain everything to him.

This would be a tragic scene if it weren't for one important detail. The stranger is, in fact, the "dearly departed" friend. He is actually alive. So now this tragedy turns into a comedy.

We're not viewing some classic Roman stage play here or even watching modern TV. This is the biblical story of the first Easter Sunday, the day when the risen Jesus transformed tragedy into comedy.

We're not sure who these two travelers were. One was named Cleopas, but he isn't mentioned anywhere else in Scripture—except possibly in John 19:25, where Mary "the wife of Clopas" is named as one of the women at the cross. So the companion of Cleopas on the road to Emmaus may have been his wife, Mary. Whoever they were, they had apparently followed Jesus during his ministry, and his death greatly saddened them. "We had hoped that he was the one who was going to redeem Israel," they explained to the stranger (Luke 24:21).

Amazingly the two travelers on the road to Emmaus had *heard* about the resurrection of Jesus, but apparently they didn't buy it. "Some of our women . . . went to the tomb early this morning but didn't find his body. They came and told us that they had seen a vision of angels, who said he was alive. Then some of our companions went to the tomb and found it just as the women had said, but him they did not see" (vv. 22–24).

This jibes with the other resurrection accounts. Women went first and saw angels, but the men didn't believe them. Peter and John went to see for themselves and saw only the empty tomb. It seems that even the empty tomb wasn't enough for the disciples from Emmaus. So Jesus scolded them:

● **"How foolish you are, and how slow of heart to believe all that the prophets have spoken! Did not the Christ have to suffer these things and then enter his glory?"**

Luke 24:25–26

Two things Jesus called them: mindless and slow-hearted. First, they didn't understand the basic facts of the situation. Our story says that "beginning with Moses and all the Prophets, he explained to them what was said in all the Scriptures concerning himself" (v. 27). There was plenty of Old Testament evidence to believe in both the suffering and ultimate glory of the Messiah. Psalm 22 reads like a first-person account of a crucifixion. Isaiah 53 shows the Servant-Messiah suffering for the sins of his people. Yet the Psalms are also packed with references to new life. It's impossible for the Author of life to stay dead.

Not only was Scripture clear, but these disciples on the way to Emmaus also knew about the empty tomb. They had heard the reports of angelic proclamations. The testimony was overwhelming, and *still* they thought their Master was dead. That was "foolish," Jesus said.

But sometimes believing isn't just a matter of the mind. The heart can lead the way. Jesus didn't call these disciples "heartless," but *"slow* of heart." It was the word for someone who's always late, or for a big, heavy boat that takes forever to get across a lake. Sometimes the word was used for the dull, blocky handwriting of a child. *You're taking too long to embrace this idea. The evidence is right in front of you, but your hearts aren't ready for it.*

Even today people respond to Jesus—or fail to respond—in these two ways. Some have mental issues with Jesus as Messiah or with his resurrection. They just don't buy it. These folks need informed Christians to sit down with them and go through the evidence, listening to their objections and trying to explain it on their terms.

But many others are slow of heart. You can present the evidence all day and all night, but they still aren't ready to commit to it. Perhaps they realize that believing in Jesus would change everything for them, and they don't want that to happen yet.

On the road to Emmaus, the disciples still didn't know who this stranger was. Though he had scolded them and instructed them, they were still blind to his true identity. But then they got home and invited him to stay for supper. As he broke the bread, "their eyes were opened and they recognized him, and he disappeared from their sight" (v. 31).

Now they knew. Their dim minds were enlightened and their slow hearts had caught up. They exclaimed to each other, "Were not our hearts burning within us while he talked with us on the road?" (v. 32). Their burning hearts prompted them to get up and go back to Jerusalem. It was a two-hour walk in the evening shadows, but they had to tell the other disciples what had happened.

Other Books by William J. Petersen and Randy Petersen

100 Amazing Answers to Prayer
100 Bible Verses That Changed the World
100 Christian Books That Changed the Century
The One Year Book of Hymns (with Robert K. Brown and Mark R. Norton)
The One Year Book of Psalms

Other Books by William J. Petersen

25 Surprising Marriages
The Christian Traveler's Companion: USA and Canada (with Amy S. Eckert)
The Christian Traveler's Companion: Western Europe (with Amy S. Eckert)
The Discipling of Timothy
Jeremiah: The Prophet Who Wouldn't Quit
Those Curious New Cults

Other Books by Randy Petersen

The 100 Most Important Events in Christian History (with A. Kenneth Curtis and J. Stephen Lang)
The Christian Book of Lists
Giving to the Giver
Stress Test (with Thomas Whiteman)
Your Marriage and the Internet (with Thomas Whiteman)

William J. Petersen served as editorial director of *Christian Life* magazine and *Christian Bookseller* magazine before becoming editor of *Eternity* magazine. A past president of the Evangelical Press Association, he was the first recipient of the Joseph T. Bayly Award for "outstanding service to Christian periodical publishing." He was awarded a doctorate by Eastern College for his contributions to religious journalism. He serves on the editorial board of the Christian Writers Guild and continues to serve as senior acquisitions editor for Fleming H. Revell. He and his wife, Ardythe, are the parents of three grown children and live in Pennsylvania.

Randy Petersen has served as editor of the *Bible Newsletter* and on the staff of *Christian History* magazine. He was content editor of the *Revell Bible Dictionary* and has written a considerable amount of Bible study curricula for youth and adults. He is the author of more than thirty books. He serves on the staff of his Methodist church in New Jersey and also acts, directs, and teaches in local theaters and schools.